The Dialectics of Our America

Post-Contemporary Interventions

Series Editors:

Stanley Fish and Fredric Jameson

The Dialectics of Our America

Genealogy, Cultural Critique, and Literary History

José David Saldívar

Duke University Press

Durham and London 1991

Printed in the United States of America
on acid-free paper ∞
Library of Congress Cataloging-in-Publication Data
appear on the last printed page of this book.

Para Laura Escoto Saldívar

Contents

Acknowledgments

This book took shape during a year at the Stanford Humanities Center (1985–86) and a year at the Stanford Center for Chicano Research (1986–87). Special thanks are due Bliss Carnochan and Renato Rosaldo, directors of the Centers, for the warm and stimulating atmosphere they helped to create. A number of chapters, or parts of chapters, of this book have appeared in previous publications, sometimes in an earlier form: chapter 1, as "The Dialectics of Our America," in *Do the Americas Have a Common Literature?*, ed. Gustavo Pérez Firmat (Durham, N.C.: Duke University Press, 1990): 62–84; chapter 2, as "Ideology and Deconstruction in Macondo," *Latin American Literary Review* 13/25 (January–June, 1985): 29–43; chapter 3, as "The Ideological and the Utopian in Tomás Rivera's *Y no se lo tragó la tierra* and Ron Arias's *The Road to Tamazunchale*," *Crítica* 1/2 (Spring 1985): 100–114; as "Rolando Hinojosa's *Klail City Death Trip*: A Critical Introduction," in *The Rolando Hinojosa Reader: Essays Historical and Critical*, ed. José David Saldívar (Houston: Arte Público Press, 1985): 44–63; and as "The Limits of Cultural Studies," *American Literary History* 2/2 (Summer 1990): 251–66. I am grateful to these editors and publishers for permission to reprint this material. My latest formulations of this project benefited from the editorial advice and encouragement of Fernando Alegría, Sacvan Bercovitch, and the anonymous reviewers solicited by Reynolds Smith of Duke University Press.

I wish to gratefully acknowledge the Special Collections of Green Library, Stanford University, for allowing me to use and quote from the Ernesto Galarza and Arturo Islas manuscript collections. Roberto Trujillo, Curator of the Mexican-American Collections, assisted me in many ways.

This book has been influenced by the Cultural Studies group and the interdisciplinary Chicano faculty studies group, both under the directorship of Renato Rosaldo, at Stanford University. More recently, my colleagues in World Literature and Cultural Studies at the University of California, Santa Cruz, have been a uniquely supportive source of encouragement and will recognize some of our shared concerns. I would like to thank Roberto Crespi, Susan Gillman, Sharon Kinoshita, and Kristin Ross, whose readings of parts of this work have been enormously helpful in clarifying its argument. The book benefited from my similar discussions in 1987 with Houston A. Baker, Jr., at the School of Criticism and Theory, Dartmouth College, and with members of the Latino summer seminar held at Stanford in 1988. For their critical support and searching criticism of an earlier version of this book, I thank Herbert Lindenberger and Sandra Drake. A special debt, reflected everywhere in these pages, is to the late Arturo Islas, my dissertation advisor at Stanford. The book's comparative beginnings were partly formulated in my senior thesis on Borges and Faulkner at Yale University. Conversations with Juan Bruce-Novoa and the late Michael G. Cooke gave me many valuable leads.

Thanks also are due for generous research support from the William Rice Kimball Fellowship, the American Council of Learned Societies, the Ford Foundation Postdoctoral Fellowship for Minorities, and the Academic Senate of the University of California, Santa Cruz.

Countless others have given time, advice, and encouragement during various phases of this project. Gloria Anzaldúa, Héctor Calderón, James Clifford, Terrell Dixon, Marvin Fisher, Albert Gelpi, Rolando Hinojosa, Nicolás Kanellos, Paul Lauter, José E. Limón, Nathaniel Mackey, Steven Mailloux, David Montejano, Cherríe Moraga, Gustavo Pérez Firmat, Mary Louise Pratt, Rosaura Sánchez, Ntozake Shange, and Lois Parkinson Zamora are only the most memorable names. I want to especially acknowledge Ramón Saldívar and Sonia Saldívar-Hull for their solidarity and their generosity.

Reynolds Smith of Duke University Press provided valuable advice, and Robert Mirandon did more than usual as copy editor. Laura Escoto Saldívar and David X. Saldívar know that this book would not exist without their love and support. Their encouragement has been indispensable.

J. D. S.
Santa Cruz, California

Preface

This book proposes to use insights derived from the ongoing debates in American literary history about the shortcomings of traditional methods of analysis—on the one hand, the narrow textuality of Anglo-American New Criticism, and on the other, the naiveté of the old historicism as context—in order to shed new light on a sequence of relatively unknown Cuban, Afro-Caribbean, African American, and Chicano texts. More specifically, I attempt to continue that new line of comparative American studies extending from Roberto Fernández Retamar to such recent commentators as Vera Kutzinski, Lois Parkinson Zamora, and Gustavo Pérez Firmat.[1] *The Dialectics of Our America* thus charts an array of oppositional critical and creative processes that aim to articulate a new, transgeographical conception of American culture—one more responsive to the hemisphere's geographical ties and political crosscurrents than to narrow national ideologies.

I began pondering the knotty issues of pan-American literary history when I was invited to participate in a new comparative American project, *Do the Americas Have a Common Literature?*, under the editorial direction of Pérez Firmat. My thoughts, which initially took shape as selected dialogical readings of Caribbean, Latin American, African American, and Chicano texts by José Martí, Roberto Fernández Retamar, Gabriel García Márquez, Rolando Hinojosa, and Ntozake Shange derive their focus from one central question Pérez Firmat asked his contributors: Do the Americas have a common critical heritage? If we take Pérez Firmat's question seriously, we find that it involves a rigorous reassessment of all kinds of familiar literary and cultural categories and conventions. Traditionally, American literary criticism has treated the literatures of the Americas as "New World" literature, examining it in relation to its "Old World"—essentially European—counterpart. This book redirects the Eurocentric focus of earlier scholarship in American Studies and identifies a distinctive postcolonial, pan-American consciousness.

The title of this book, *The Dialectics of Our America*, points to José Martí's modest formula in "Nuestra América"—"Our America"

(1891), which above and beyond race, language, and secondary circumstances embraced the hemisphere's diverse communities "from the [Río Bravo] to the Patagonia" and which are distinct from what he called "European America." It also calls attention to a widespread discomfort about the restrictions inherent in the privileged term "America." Although America does apply to the whole hemisphere, the term, as Sacvan Bercovitch argues, has been used in the United States to refer exclusively to itself as an "over-arching synthesis, *e pluribus unum*."[2] And, finally, the term refers to our distinctive *mestizo* American culture—a culture of hybrid Americans, ethnic and cultural descendants of aborigines, Africans, and Europeans. My aim, therefore, is less in "canon-busting" than in exploring and exploiting the possibility of canon expansion, for my study offers a challenging perspective on what constitutes not only the canon of American literature (as it is usually understood in the Anglocentric model prevalent in our normal curricula) but the notion of America itself.

Although I have mentioned the principal authors in my comparative project, a further word on the book's makeup may be in order. *The Dialectics of Our America* is divided into three parts: Metahistory and Dependency, Magical Narratives, and Caliban and Resistance Cultures. My motivations have several facets.

Part I, "Metahistory and Dependency," analyzes how José Martí, Roberto Fernández Retamar, Gabriel García Márquez, and Rolando Hinojosa incorporate, examine, and transform the common history of dependency in the Americas. This section uses the exciting work of "world system theory," namely, that of Immanuel Wallerstein.[3] What distinguishes world system theory from other economic theories of development is the way it sees underdevelopment of the Americas as a direct result of contact with capitalism. In so doing, it understands dependency in terms of a global capitalist system where different modes of production define the degrees of dependency. In other words, the first three narratives that I examine often dramatize how surplus value is produced in the economic and Border zones of the periphery and is appropriated at the center. Additionally, this section attempts to show that many pan-American texts are orchestrations of multivocal, crosscultural exchanges occurring in politically charged situations.

Chapter 1, "The Dialectics of Our America," traces the existence of what the Cuban poets and revolutionaries José Martí and Roberto

Fernández Retamar see as two distinct Americas: "Nuestra América" and "European America." Beginning with Martí's cultural critique of North American monopoly capitalism in the 1880s, I move through several debates between North American and Latin American intellectuals. Chapter 1 further traces the genealogy of more recent oppositional writers and intellectuals such as Fernández Retamar and García Márquez. The genealogical work of these three writers has established itself as a powerful alternative to the dominant forms of "knowledge production" in the Americas, and thus my brief history describes the emergent political debates and cultural conversations between Our America and "the America which is not ours."

Chapter 2, "Squeezed by the Banana Company," looks at the early nonmimetic narrative modes of García Márquez's *Leafstorm* (1955), "Big Mama's Funeral" (1962), and *One Hundred Years of Solitude* (1967). Grounded in the political and historical formations of Our America, the dislocations in García Márquez's magical narratives are mediated equally through the apparatuses of various kinds of dependencies in Macondo, colonial and postcolonial, and underwritten by feudal survivals and nationalisms. The power of his magical narratives lies in his ability to create themes in which different modes of production, social formations, and ways of ethnographic and historical representation overlap in Macondo as the ground for conflict, contradiction, and change. Additionally, this chapter reconstructs from García Márquez's cultural work as a novelist and intellectual associated with the Cuban-Marxist Casa de las Américas organizations an image and function of the writer that many Anglocentric writers and intellectuals have lost—the writer who combines the traditional intellectual's commitment to language and image with the organic intellectual's commitment to politics and revolution.

Chapter 3, "Chicano Border Narratives as Cultural Critique," explores how Rolando Hinojosa's nine published narratives form an ongoing chronicle in the tradition of García Márquez's narratives about Macondo. Hinojosa's mythical territory, Belken County, Texas, like Macondo, is situated in a society whose traditional organization is being transformed by world market changes. Only by situating Hinojosa's chronicle, the *Klail City Death Trip* series, in relation to the historical conflicts that erupted in the Texas-Mexican Border zones and in the cultural conversations and debates among

Walter Prescott Webb, Américo Paredes, and Tomás Rivera can we grasp the social meanings of Hinojosa's avant-garde, textual innovations.

The book thus continues to focus on the relationship between global history and local knowledge by examining Hinojosa's reconstruction of two hundred years of U.S. and Mexican Border history. Chapter 3 consciously crosses the methodological borders between Marxist and postmodernist criticism by showing how Hinojosa's particularisms in south Texas offer no escape from world system interconnections, for local metanarratives never tell the whole story. In this and other chapters, we see that both local and global metanarratives are relevant to a comparative study of the literatures of the Americas. Each kind of narrative undermines the other's claims to tell the "whole" story. Perhaps we are condemned to oscillate between two metanarratives—one of totalization and the other of emergence.

Hinojosa gives us two distinct worlds in his dialogical narrative: a Mexican ranch society and an Anglo-American farm society. He dramatizes the domination of farming over ranching and the consequent emergence of a striking segregation of the races. What is crucial in my reading of the "traffic" between the local and global in south Texas is the view that the white supremacist farm society did not peacefully implant itself. Rather, as is shown in Américo Paredes's *"With His Pistol in His Hand": A Border Ballad and Its Hero* (1958), it was a violent intervention. (Against the American grain, Paredes's crosscultural book offers ideological analysis and literary criticism or, given the broad historical range of his study from 1749 to the late 1950s, discursive analysis and broad critical-cultural study of the kind we associate with Antonio Gramsci and Raymond Williams.) In its most dramatic form, then, Hinojosa's Chicano narrative, following in the oppositional cultural tradition established by Paredes, shows us how the conflict between the old ranch society and the new farm society expressed itself in the armed rebellion of Chicanos and their thorough suppression by the Texas Rangers. White supremacy, for Paredes, Rivera, and Hinojosa, is thus a variable and open-ended process, the result of what historian George Fredrickson called "long term historically conditioned tendencies" that led to rigorous, self-conscious race domination.[4]

In these first three chapters, we are continually forced to recollect the political content of the terms "history" and the "novel." Not surprisingly, this demonstration depends on the dialogue of cultural and institutional history informed by and emerging from literary analysis. Such a reading, Myra Jehlen points out, is not merely background for a writer's individual production. Instead, "if we take literature's link to history seriously, we will have to admit that it renders literature contingent, like history itself."[5]

In Part II ("Magical Narratives"), this concern with metahistory—the rewriting of the history of the Americas in the novel—is merged with magic realism by examining two double-voiced ethnic American writers who have turned south to such Caribbean and Latin American magic realist writers as Alejo Carpentier and García Márquez to transform their visions of history and tradition in the United States. This analysis, however, does not simply describe these cultural conversations in isolation; rather, it locates their intersecting institutional dialogues in 1960s, 1970s, and 1980s Havana, the alternative political and artistic capital of the Americas, where an international group of literary judges selected Latin America's premier literary prize—the Casa de las Américas Award. (García Márquez, Hinojosa, and Ntozake Shange, among others, in the thirty-year history of the prize either judged, won, or participated in its three-week annual celebration.) Hence, this constructing of oppositional versions of history for many ethnic American writers relates to a desire to challenge the narrow Anglocentric concept of "tradition" and the linear view of history on which it is predicated.

As an example of this challenge, chapter 4, "The Real and the Marvelous in Charleston, South Carolina," investigates how Shange's *Sassafrass, Cypress & Indigo* (1982) is anchored in an Afro-Caribbean and African American world that is folkloric, mythical, and magical. Incorporating the African heritage of the slave world, she, like García Márquez, produces *lo real maravilloso*—a poetic transfiguration of the object world itself—in Charleston, where most of the novel is set. In the process of producing this poetic two-toned transfiguration, she reawakens the sense of radical difference within her African American society; moreover, she revives the sense that it is not really necessary to live in a solitary, postmodernist world and that people can live otherwise. What is most compelling and powerful in *Sassafrass, Cypress & Indigo* is the author's dramatization of both older, precapitalist forms of society, and newer, as yet unimagined collective forms, which she believes it is our task to create.

"The Hybridity of Culture" (chapter 5) continues to focus on magic realism by studying Arturo Islas's *The Rain God: A Desert Tale* (1984). A novel about the postcolonial world of migration, Islas's book is also about the magical, transforming powers of Amerindian mythology, dreams, and family history. Because the novel was turned down by more than twenty New York publishers (eventually, it was published by a small press in northern California), this chapter also addresses the issue of why the novel, written by a Chicano, seemed deficient to the East Coast publishing conglomerate and its aesthetic system. Since many of the mainline editors who define what counts as culture refused to see Islas's hybrid narrative as his attempt to negotiate the two terrains of American Western literature and the Latin American *nueva narrativa,* this chapter analyzes how our cultural texts are written, produced, marketed, read, evaluated, and censored in post-contemporary U.S. culture.

Part III, "Caliban and Resistance Cultures," provides another example of how literary and critical texts become a part of the cultural debates and historical conflicts of the Americas. This final section leans heavily on Cuban-Marxist insights into American cultures and Third World identity by Fernández Retamar, one of the leading theoreticians in Latin America today, editor of the journal *Casa de las Américas,* and a professor of philology at the University of Havana. In 1900, José Enrique Rodó argued that the Latin American intellectual's model in relation to Europe and North America could be Shakespeare's Ariel. Some seventy years later, Fernández Retamar recast the model as Caliban. His conception of "Caliban"—the negative of the master-slave relationship—as the new protagonist in American literatures in the broad sense is by now well accepted.[6] This chapter attempts to explore the ways in which Caliban as an ideology of Self helps explain several pan-American experimental narratives by some postcolonial Caribbean, Chicano/Chicana, and African American writers. In its most general intention, Fernández Retamar's *Caliban* involves a total shift in perspective—in opposition and resistance to ruling culture in the Americas—for no longer do we see history and the canon from the viewpoint of that familiar protagonist Prospero, but rather we can rethink our history and culture from the viewpoint of the Other, Caliban. The better to theorize the role of pan-American intellectuals and writers in a postcolonial world, George Lamming's *The Pleasures of Exile* (1960), Aimé Césaire's *A Tempest* (1969), Fernández

Retamar's *Caliban* (1971), Ernesto Galarza's *Barrio Boy* (1971), Richard Rodriguez's *Hunger of Memory* (1982), Cherríe Moraga's *Loving in the War Years* (1983), and Houston Baker, Jr.'s *Modernism and the Harlem Renaissance* (1987) are seen to be written, considered, and experienced by Caliban (Shakespeare's anagram for cannibal), who desires either to participate in the historical process of hegemony or to resist its domination.

The Dialectics of Our America has been enriched by the recent postcolonial decenterings of "theory" by such Borderland intellectuals as Guillermo Gómez-Peña, Gloria Anzaldúa, Renato Rosaldo, and the writers discussed in this book, who move theories in and out of discrepant contexts. While the Cuban-Marxist work of Fernández Retamar is indispensable for analyzing theory in terms of location and the dialectics of difference, it needs modification when extended to our global Borderland context. His supremely mutable polemics of marginality and centrality, of the same and the other, cannot entirely account for the hybrid appropriations and resistances that characterize the travel of theories and theorists who migrate between places in our "First" World and "Third" World. If Fernández Retamar revised and updated such essays as "Our America and the West" and "Caliban Revisited," he would no doubt grapple with the migrations of intellectuals whose condition is not that of exile, but of hybridity and betweenness.[7] His work in the 1990s, along with that of many postcolonial intellectuals, sees his productions as inescapably political, always "written for" alliances in our global Borderlands.

I

Metahistory and Dependency

1 The Dialectics of Our America

> In the absence of a pope, what are we to do about the problem of the canon in rewriting American literary history?
> —Werner Sollors, *Beyond Ethnicity*

In light of developments within the American literary historical community, Werner Sollors's rhetorical question about the American canon provides us with an appropriate frame of reference. Indeed, the new "ideological" school of American literary history led by Sacvan Bercovitch and Myra Jehlen, among others, has in many ways underlined and strengthened the need to study our literary and historical past.[1]

Thus, the new American literary historians have directed their attention to new writers, addressed themselves to new problems, and, above all, sharpened their methodological tools. For example, Bercovitch in *Reconstructing American Literary History* (1986) has argued for what he calls a "dialogic mode of analysis." More precisely, his history of American literature resembles Bakhtin's description of the novelistic form: it is often marked by a clashing plurality of discourses, fragments, and a polyethnic system of American codes in what he sees as our age of "dissensus."[2] Other Americanists, among them Paul Lauter, Juan Bruce-Novoa, Jane Tompkins, and Houston A. Baker, Jr., have centered their "dialectics of validation" on aspects of American literature such as race, class, gender, and difference that had received little attention; such scholars have given a new impulse to the study of subjects ranging from the reevaluation of what constitutes a "classical" American text to the role of a distinctly slave "vernacular" in American discourse in general and in African American literature in particular.[3] The theoretical boundaries within which American literary history and interpretation unfold have been redefined in the theoretical works of Fredric Jameson, Frank Lentricchia, Hayden White, and Edward Said. Each has questioned the premises on which the concepts of American hermeneutics, alterity, history, and historiography rest.[4]

Within the ideological framework of these varied tendencies I would like to add two oppositional voices to our new literary history—namely, the Cuban poets and revolutionaries José Martí and Roberto Fernández Retamar.

What lies behind this chapter is a growing awareness of the extremely narrow confines and conservative practices of literary study as it is now performed in the academy, and, with that, a growing conviction about the social and political implications of this exclusionary practice. As a literary theoretician outside the mainstream, educated in a segregated farm society in south Texas, I have been particularly sensitive to the absence of writers from Our America. In my view, the greatest shortcoming of the work being done on the American canon is not its lack of theoretical rigor, but its parochial vision. Literary historians (even the newer ones) and critics working on the reconstruction of American literary history characteristically know little in depth about the history, symbologies, cultures, and discourses of the Americas. One value of focusing on comparative cultural studies is that it permits us to escape from the provincial, limiting tacit assumptions that result from perpetual immersion in studying a single culture or literature.

The Dialectics of Our America proposes a new American literary, cultural, and critical cosmopolitanism that fully questions as much as it acknowledges the Other, thereby serving as a more adequate and chastening form of self-knowledge. This new critical cosmopolitanism neither reduces the Americas to some homogeneous Other of the West, nor does it fashionably celebrate the rich pluralism of the hemisphere. Rather, by mapping out the common situation shared by different cultures, it allows their differences to be measured against each other as well as against the (North) American grain.

I

During the past generation the new cultural history of America has been fractured into various professional shards: social history, ethnic history, women's history, African American history, and Chicano history. No longer is American history conceived exclusively as the story of Anglo-Saxon men from the first settlements in the Chesapeake Bay area in 1607 to the present. Looking at American history "from the bottom up," this revisionist scholarship has shattered the traditional consensus.[5] But there has not been enough major revisionist scholarship. Moreover, a stark fragmentation of American intellectual history has plagued some of our revisionist historians, and the literary history of the Americas must be made whole again. Efforts to achieve this wholeness have been begun in the genealogical texts of Martí and Fernández Retamar who in their oppositional discourses attempted to unify the history of the Americas. By looking at the Americas as a hemisphere and by analyzing the real and rhetorical, often hostile, battles between the United States and what Martí called "Nuestra América"—"Our America"—it is possible to perceive what the literatures of the Americas have in common. After the U.S. codes of fetishization—of transforming the realities of dependency, conquest, and military intervention into rhetoric about freedom, virtue, and an "Alliance for Progress"—have been negated, Martí's "Nuestra América" (1891) and Fernández Retamar's *Caliban* (1971), "Nuestra América y Occidente" (1976), and "Algunos usos de civilización y barbarie" (1977) are texts on which to base an illuminating indigenous American cultural studies critique.

Let me emphasize my goals in reconstructing pan-American literary history: first, to place the leading oppositional intellectual figures from Our America within a limited genealogy of their discursive and nondiscursive practices; second, to show how responsive to their historical situations of hegemony and hostility they have been.

As Jean Franco explains in *An Introduction to Spanish American Literature* (1969):

> Only Martí significantly enriched and transformed the [Spanish literary tradition] on which he drew. He saw art neither as propaganda tools nor as play but as the expression which was communicable because universal. Yet this genuinely original poet and thinker had no followers and it was to be some time before his own optimistic statement [in "Nuestra América"] that "el libro importado ha sido vencido en América por el hombre natural" ["the imported book has been vanquished in America by natural man"] was truly applicable to the literature of the continent.[6]

Enrico Mario Santí suggests, moreover, that because Martí never collected his prose works in book form, the "piecemeal, fragmented, and foreign publication of the first edition of Martí's collected works between 1900 and 1933 constitute both a cause and effect of this initial vacuum."[7]

As the United States underwent the transition from "competitive" capitalism to "monopoly" capitalism in the 1880s, Martí grew more critical about the bourgeois way of life there. In "The Modernity of Martí," Fernández Retamar argues that Martí "identified and denounced the characteristics of what we now recognize as the beginnings of the last stage of capitalism: the rise of the monopolies ("The monopoly, says Martí, sits like an implacable giant at the door of the poor"), and the fusion of banking capital with industrial in a financial oligarchy ("those iniquitous consortia of capital").[8] In "Nuestra América" and in his newspaper analyses of the United States, Martí constructed a powerful cultural critique of capitalism and Anglocentrism.

From 1881 until just before his death in 1895 (he died battling the Spanish empire in Cuba), Martí rarely left the United States. As one scholar put it, "In the U.S., Martí became a politician, a chronicler of North American history, and a man of action."[9] Although as chronicler he wrote on a variety of North American topics (for instance, Grant's Tomb, Whitman as the great poet of the Americas, Emerson as philosopher) as well as on subjects such as Darwin and Marx, he emerges in "Nuestra América" as a firm anti-imperialist who wrote about the emergent empire: "I know the monster; I have lived in its entrails."[10]

Emerson's "The American Scholar" (1837) established the grounds for a popular national American literature: "Each age must write its own books; or rather, each generation for the next succeeding. The books of an older period will not fit this."[11] Martí's "Nuestra América" similarly provided a base for a national Latin American literature capable of incorporating both the Spanish and First American experiences in the New World. In "Nuestra América" and "Madre América," as elsewhere, his view of the American hemisphere is cast in a Manichaean struggle. He proposed in *La Nación:*

> On the one hand, there is in [the Americas] a nation proclaiming its right by proper investiture, because of geographical morality, to rule the continent, and it announces . . . that everything in North America must be its, and that this imperial right must be acknowledged from the Isthmus all the way south. On the other hand, there are the nations of diverse origins and purposes . . . [Nuestra América.][12]

Any revisionist literary history of the Americas would have to contend with Martí's conviction of a profound gap between "Our

America" and the other America, which is not ours. "Nuestra América" in particular can provide the central oppositional codes on which to base a dialectical view of the American continent and of the Americas' many literatures.

"Nuestra América" marks the beginning of a new epoch of resistance to empire in the Americas. As a specific intellectual in Foucault's sense, Martí stands between two ways of thinking: the last representative of a nineteenth-century romantic idealism and the first forerunner of a Latin American socialist ideology of continental solidarity. Cuban Foreign Minister Raúl Roa, speaking to the United Nations in May 1968, emphasized: "At the level of international relations, the fundamental antagonism of our epoch is expressed in the struggle between imperialism and the peoples of the underdeveloped world."[13] Martí is one of the first cultural critics from Our America bold enough to document to the rest of the hemisphere what he saw as emerging U.S. ideas, languages, and reality of empire. (Parenthetically, the Nicaraguan "modernista" poet Rubén Darío would join Martí in attacking Teddy Roosevelt's "Big Stick" policy in his 1903 poem "To Roosevelt.") Martí prophetically stated in "Nuestra América":

> Our America is running another risk that does not come from itself but from the difference in origins, methods, and interests between the two halves of the continent, and the time is near at hand when an enterprising and vigorous people who scorn or ignore Our America will even so approach it and demand a close relationship. And since strong nations, self-made by law and shotgun, love strong nations, and them alone; since the time of madness and ambition—from which North America may be freed by the predominance of the purest elements in its blood, or on which it may be launched by its vindictive and sordid masses, its tradition of expansion, or the ambitions of some powerful leader—is not so near at hand, even to the most timorous eye, that there is no time for the test of discreet and unwavering pride that could confront and dissuade it; since its good name as a republic in the eyes of the world's perceptive nations puts upon North America a restraint that cannot be taken away by childish provocations or pompous arrogance or parricidal discords among Our American nations—the pressing need of Our America is to show itself as it is, one in spirit and intent, swift conqueror of a suffocating past, stained only by the enriching blood drawn from the hands that struggle to clear away ruins, and from the scars left upon us by our masters.

> The scorn of our formidable neighbor who does not know us is Our America's greatest danger. And since the day of the visit is near, it is imperative that our neighbor know us, and soon, so that it will not scorn us.[14]

Stylistically, the passage is typical of Martí's rhetorical grace, power, and lexical play: the balanced schemes of repetition, especially anaphora; the willingness to use alliteration to present harsh judgments; the amused, delicate use of understatement ("an enterprising and vigorous people . . . will demand a close relationship"); the tropical cadence of apostrophe; and the active use of a binary methodology. Its content, however, is a striking description of "the development of underdevelopment" in Latin America, for Martí's primary concern in the passage is the reality of relentless expansion by the North Americans. No Cuban has surpassed Martí in his lucid denunciation of American empire. No writer has been more graceful and clear than Martí in describing the negative way of life in the United States.

By 1882 Martí became convinced that the United States had given up its rhetoric of freedom and dignity. In New York he witnessed the huge influx of European immigrants bringing with them "their wounds [and] their moral ulcers." Describing the miserable life of the underclass there, he wrote: "He who can observe the deplorable life of today's wretched workingman and woman in the cold latitudes without feeling his soul wrenched with pity, is not only barely insensitive, but commits a criminal act" (*Obras Completas* 32:168). He also observed, with pen in hand, the rise of blatant forms of white dominance over nonwhite populations in the urban metropole—blacks, Chinese, and the First Americans (Amerindians) were characteristically discriminated against by a white supremacist ideology.[15] So it came as no surprise to Latin American readers of "North American Scenes" when, in 1886, he wrote of the prototypical North American character: "[Achieving a] fortune is the only object of life. . . . Men, despite all appearances, are tied together here only by interests, by the cordial hatreds that exist between those who are bargaining for the same prize. . . . It is urgent to feed the lamp of light and reduce the beast."[16]

Thus, to fully understand Martí's call for Latin American cultural autonomy, nationalism, and self-determination in "Nuestra América," it is essential to note his emergent sociopolitical radicalization in the United States. At the same time, his antiimperialism stemmed from a close reading of U.S. "manifest destiny" doctrine.[17] His allegory of reading the imperial designs of North American foreign policy became a warning to Our America to prepare itself to withstand relentless expansion. From 1881 to 1889, then, he clearly perceived that U.S. foreign policy and industry would need both a cheap source of raw materials and a world market for their surplus goods. Our America, he predicted, was ripe for both: "The descendants of the pilgrim's father had their celebrations. What a difference though! Now they are no longer humble, nor tread the snow of Cape Cod with workers' boots. Instead they now lace up their military boots aggressively and they see on one side Canada and on the other Mexico."[18] What Martí dramatizes for us in his voluminous essays, letters, and journalistic pieces (collected in seventeen volumes by Cuban publishers) is an alienated Cuban, exiled in the ghettos of New York, one of the first Latin American intellectuals of his time audacious enough to confront U.S. imperial history, its imperial ethic, and its imperial psychology. Imperialism, he suggests, penetrated the very fabric of North American culture and infected its imagination. The U.S. metropole, once and for all, would now enjoy and exploit a structural advantage over the Latin American "periphery." He reads the grammar of imperialism and dramatizes how U.S. domination of the weaker economies in Our America (and its political and social superstructure) were to ensure the extraction of economic rewards—what André Gunder Frank calls the "development of underdevelopment."[19]

As a handbook describing the codes of imperialism, "Nuestra América" not only analyzes the overdetermined causes of "Yankee" domination, but points out strategies to resist it. He believed that the first step for governing "our republics" is a thorough knowledge of the diverse elements that make up the Americas as a continent, for "the able governor in Our America is not the one who knows how to govern the Germans or the French; he must know the elements that compose his own country; and how to bring them together, using methods and institutions originating within the country. . . ." (p. 86). Second, he contended that Our America must refrain from rewriting its narratives of government according to paradigms not their own—with laws, constitutions, discourses, and systems taken from totally different cultural contexts: "A decree by Hamilton does not halt the plainsman's horse" (p. 86). Leaders from

Our America would have to account for the popular indigenous elements within each culture and recognize their inherent value.

In rejecting the "monumentalist" European university for the American, Martí, like many of today's cultural studies critics, believed that one of the principal sites of contention was to be the university: "The European university must yield to the American university. The history of America, from the Incas to the present, must be taught letter perfect, even if the Argonauts of Greece [are] never taught. Our own Greece is preferable to the Greece which is not ours" (p. 88). What is at stake in Martí's view of the university are competing political and intellectual visions. What should count as knowledge and critical thought in the education of our hemisphere's future generations? How can we prepare students to enter the multicultural world of the future? In negating European and North American colonial and neocolonial rule (the imposition of European institutional, nondiscursive practices over American), "Nuestra América" also anticipates Caliban's revolutionary overturning of Prospero's disciplinary techniques of mind control, repression, and anxiety in January 1959—namely, in the Cuban Revolution.

For all its rhetorical significance, its expressive emphasis, its tropic melodic variety, and its delicate use of repetition and balance, the real power behind Martí's discourse is not merely in its grammatical play, but in its historical challenge to U.S. domination. Against the Eurocentric reading of American history and the canon ("Our own Greece is preferable to the Greece which is not ours") "Nuestra América," like "The American Scholar," privileges an indigenous American cultural studies practice. For Martí, political discourse and what he called *versos sencillos* (simple verses) had to be written "*en mi propia sangre*" ("in my own blood"), not in "*tinta de académicos*" ("academic ink"). What is significant for our new American literary history, then, is the lessons he teaches. He warns us that two distinct peoples, set poles apart by language and psychology, inhabit the same hemisphere. His America spoke mainly in Spanish, worshiped non-Protestant gods, and struggled against the political and economic realities of U.S. empire.[20]

It would be an understatement to say that Martí has profoundly influenced the course of Cuban-Marxist oppositional thinking in the twentieth century. Although one Marxist-Leninist critic, Juan Marinello, has chastised Martí for being a romantic idealist, most

Cuban-Marxists (including Fidel Castro) acknowledge their revolutionary ties to Marti's political, aesthetic, and social philosophy.[21] Others, like Fernández Retamar, have had to insist that they are not rewriting Martí as a Marxist revolutionary, which he was not. In his numerous studies of Martí, Fernández Retamar illuminates the ties between his oppositional criticism of North American culture and the Cuban-Marxist ideology of resisting U.S. empire as a way of life. What is essential in Fernández Retamar's interpretation of Martí's work can be summarized in this way: Martí took the first necessary step toward ending Cuba's peripheral status by advocating the solidarity of all indigenous peoples of Our America. By April 1960, Che Guevara was able to state about Cuba, with biting irony and self-mockery: "Sometimes we even thought it was rather pompous to refer to Cuba as if it were the center of the universe. Nonetheless, it was true or almost true. If someone doubted the revolution's importance he should read the newspaper. . . . Man, we're strong and dangerous. We have poisoned the American environment and threatened the sweet democracy of Trujillo and Somoza. . . . Oh it is so great and comfortable to belong to such a strong world power as dangerous as Cuba."[22] Only after the Cuban Revolution did U.S. "institutional practices" begin to invest aggressively in "Latin American Studies." According to Roberto González Echevarría, "the financing of literary journals had a crucial bearing on the creation [and reception] of the new Latin American literature of the sixties."[23] I would add that it certainly had an ideological bearing on how an "idealist" literary aesthetic was imported into American universities, for the importing of typically colonial writers such as Jorge Luis Borges rendered Latin American radicalism safe for the so-called Free World.

II

> What is our history, what is our culture, if not the history and culture of Caliban?
> —Roberto Fernández Retamar, *Caliban*

This section, dealing with Foucauldian motifs of power, genealogy, and history, originates in my attempts elsewhere to write a brief history of the profound influence of the new Latin American narrative on postmodernist, ethnic American literatures.[24] In the process of writing it became clear that the discourses of these new pan-American writers were themselves historically situated acts that can be understood only as events within larger networks of discursive and nondiscursive practices in the American hemisphere at the height of what Ernest Mandel calls "late capitalism."[25] It became apparent, moreover, that there was no way to grasp the past and present social and cultural role of this new narrative except by seeing it as situated within an intense quarrel between North American domination and a new (Cuban) Latin American Marxist resistance to U.S. empire.

In the limited genealogy that follows, Fernández Retamar becomes central to an oppositional American literary history precisely because his work makes clear that Latin American *nueva narrativa,* literary history, and intellectual power are specifically situated historical practices enacted within a set of hostile relations in the American hemisphere. Focusing on the tensions between "Nuestra América" and "el Occidente," then, permits us to look at American cultures anew. My main concern is with the role of the committed artists and critical intellectuals associated with Fernández Retamar's literary organization, journal, and cultural center—Casa de las Américas. Fernández Retamar has produced perhaps the most powerful model of oppositional critical practice in Our America since Martí. In large part, his project results from his organic relationship to Castro and Guevara's practice of a new Latin American Marxism, which, in turn, explains his passionate desire for solidarity and social change in the Americas as a continent.

Fernández Retamar is an oppositional figure who has learned many of the lessons of Martí's, Guevara's, and Castro's anti-imperialist efforts. An erudite critic, he is known for his meticulous efforts to dismantle the impact of Eurocentrism (with its implied theory of world history) on pan-American societies. But, as González Echevarría states, "To read him is to discover not the bilious ideologue that some imagine, but a searching, groping essayist with an academic bent, who is far from being a doctrinaire Marxist-Leninist."[26] My own view is that he is important to the history of modern criticism, to the new American literary history, and to comparative cultural studies precisely because in his numerous books and essays the question of the writer-intellectual in a post-colonial context emerges as the central issue in post-contemporary critical practice in the Americas. His writings are intimately engaged with the problematics of Latin American history—how it has had to serve the economic, political, and cultural "barbarism" of the West. In this regard, he is dialectically overturning Marx and Engels's use of the term "barbarism" in *The Communist Manifesto* (1848): "Just as [the bourgeoisie] has made the country dependent on towns, so it has made barbarian and semi-barbarian countries dependent on civilized ones, nations of peasants on nations of bourgeois."[27] On the other hand, he is subverting Domingo Faustino Sarmiento's idealist vision of an epic struggle between "civilization" and "barbarism" in Argentina. In his highly influential *Facundo Quiroga: Civilization and Barbarism* (1845), Sarmiento equated all that was wrong with the marginalized and the periphery—the gauchos and the pampas.[28] Again, I think González Echevarría is correct when he writes that "though there is a progressive loss of specificity with respect to literature [in his essays in *Casa de las Américas*] one finds a greater ideological and methodological coherence" (p. 74). It is precisely this "ideological" coherence in Fernández Retamar's work that I would like to examine.

Like Edward Said's oppositional criticism in *Orientalism,* Fernández Retamar negates in *Caliban* (which preceded Said's work by seven years) what he sees as an insidious "Prosperean" and "Occidental" ruling culture of anxiety and mind control in Our America.[29] Put more forcefully, he deconstructs these hierarchical terms, empties them, and reveals their hegemonic function to oppress those excluded from their domains, or to exclude those who are other. Defined in this light, Fernández Retamar's deconstruction is the inversion of hierarchies and systems, the overthrow of entrenched authority in the West, and the reversal of the subjugated "concepts" in the hierarchies.

In "Nuestra América y Occidente," Fernández Retamar suggests that we should recatalog the organizing "Discovery of America" in our historical textbooks in terms of what, in fact, it really was: "El Desastre." He says:

> A lo largo de la historia, hay numerosos casos de encuentro de dos comunidades y sojuzgamiente de una por otro. El hecho ha solido llamarse de muy diversas maneras: a menudo, recibe el nombre de invasión o migración o establecimiento. Pero la llegada de lo paleocidentales a estas tierra, llegada que podria llevar distintos

> nombres (por ejemplo, El Desastre), ha sido reiterdamente llamada descubrimiento, *"El Descubrimiento."* Tal denominación, por si sola, implica una completa falsifación, un Cubrimiento de la historia verdadera.
>
> (The encounter of two communities, and the subjection of one by the other, has been known throughout history by many names: invasion, migration, or foundation. But the arrival of the paleo-Western European on these shores, an event that could have been variously designated (e.g., The Disaster), has been repeatedly referred to as a discovery, *The Discovery.* Such a name, per se, is a complete falsification of history, a covering up of true history.)[30]

From the beginning of European versions of history in Our America, he continues, "Los hombres, las culturas de estas tierras, pasan así a ser cosificados, dejan de ser sujetos de la historia para ser 'descubiertos' por el Hombre, como el paisaje, la flora y la fauna" ("Thus are the people and cultures of these lands reified—ceasing to be subjects of history. Rather, they are "discovered," like landscape, flora and fauna, by Man" [p. 359]. In other words, he shows us how Western culture depersonalizes the First American as subject, and, in the process, falsifies Our American historical experience. Like E. L. Doctorow's reading of metahistory in "False Documents" (1983), Fernández Retamar examines how history is explicitly connected with "the power of the regime" and self-interest.[31] His criticism recognizes the political materiality of culture. He does not merely turn "Our American culture" into a literary myth, but as a Cuban-Marxist he describes how culture is related to the idea of hegemony.[32] For him, "Western culture" is both a literary sign and a social structure and concept that must be negated.

Fernández Retamar's Cuban experiences of colonialism and dependency account for his negative attitude toward what he sees in Our Amcrica as a fairly monolithic "Occidental" culture. As is clear from his many references to Fanon, Césaire, and Lamming in his *Casa de las Américas* essays, he has been influenced by their "studies of resistance" and their multiple meditations on the problem of critical cosmopolitanism, or, of the possible relationships to be established between an uneven global system and a socialist collective project. In his autobiographical "pamphlet," *Caliban*, his description of the colonial domination of Western culture in Our America is scandalous, powerful, and moving:

> The white population of the United States (diverse, but of common European origin) exterminated the aboriginal population and thrust the black people aside, thereby affording itself homogeneity in spite of diversity, and offering a coherent model which its Nazi disciples attempted to apply even to other European conglomerates—an unforgivable sin that led some members of the bourgeoisie to stigmatize in Hitler what they applauded as a healthy diversion in Westerns and Tarzan films. Those movies proposed to the world—and even to those of us who are kin to the communities under attack and who rejoiced in their evocation of their own extermination—the monstrous racial criteria which has accompanied the United States from its beginnings to the genocide in Indochina.[33]

Given Fernández Retamar's strong sense of Western culture's oppression (it is even dramatized for him in Westerns and Tarzan films he saw as a boy), it is not surprising to find him, like Martí, advocating an "alliance" pan-American politics: all Americans, he claimed, including "el indio autoctono" and "el negro indigena importado" were engaged in a hostile struggle between "Nuestra América" and "el Occidente." Broadly conceived, his discourse is about the role of Third World American intellectuals and writers in a postcolonial world—how in their work in and on culture they choose either to involve themselves in or avoid the political work of social change and cultural critique. As he suggests in *Caliban*, intellectuals (Ariels) have a choice to make: either they can side with Prospero (the Occidental metropole) and help fortify ruling culture and hegemony or they can side with Caliban, "our symbol," and help resist, limit, and alter domination in the Americas.[34]

Since my primary concern is less with Fernández Retamar's literary theory and more with his intellectual leadership in the Casa de las Américas' literary organizations and cultural center, his work as editor and publisher is especially relevant, particularly for understanding how the new narratives and poetics produced by some Latin American and ethnic North American writers are inscribed within the discourses and institutions based in Havana.

In literature, film, and politics, Havana has become an alternative capital of the Americas, an alternate possibility of some sense of a new, pan-American postcolonial identity. Each year for the past thirty, writers, professors, and intellectuals from across the Americas are invited to Havana to judge the Casa de las Américas Award, what Steve Hellman, a recent judge of the prize, called "the Cuban Pulitzer."[35] Since its inception in 1960, the award has been judged by such brilliant writers as Alejo Carpentier, Julio Cortázar, Carlos Fuentes, Allen Ginsberg, Gabriel García Márquez, and Edward Kamu Brathwaite and has been presented to outstanding writers who include Roque Dalton (El Salvador), Austin Clarke (Barbados), Reina María Rodriguez (Cuba), Rigoberta Menchú (Guatemala), and the Chicano novelist Rolando Hinojosa (United States).

Perhaps for our purposes the most significant cultural conversation between Havana and the United States occurred in 1976 when Hinojosa was awarded the prestigious prize for *Klail City y sus alrededores* [*Klail City and Its Environs*], a chronicle of U.S. and Mexican Border hostility. Hinojosa's Chicano novel immediately became an international success. Almost overnight, Hinojosa's ethnopoetic American subject, his mythical county, Belken, and Klail City in particular, became required reading not only for intellectuals in Our America, but also for leftist intellectuals in Germany (both formerly East and West), Spain, France, Italy, and England.[36]

Klail City y sus alrededores was praised by Carlos Onetti (Uruguay), Domingo Miliani (Venezuela), Lisandro Otero (Cuba), and Lincoln Silva (Paraguay) for its postmodernist dialectical forms and content, its artistic use of the revolutionary avant-garde form—the collage—for its folkloric Texas-Mexican motifs (such as the *décimia* and the *corrido*), and for its multiplicity of sociopoetic dialogues. No longer could Chicano narrative be seen by U.S. literary critics as an anomalous North American discourse—a product of a marginalized tradition. Instead, through Hinojosa's novel that narrative had joined the lofty tradition of the *nueva narrativa* exemplified by the works of García Márquez, Fuentes, Guillermo Cabrera Infante, and Isabel Allende.

Why is this moment significant in radically altering the course of American literary history? Because of Fernández Retamar's leadership in helping to include Chicano narratives within the Latin American *nueva narrativa* in general and the Cuban-Marxist literary canon in particular, American literary history no longer can be written by separating the ethnic groups (even Yankees and WASPS, according to Werner Sollors, are ethnic!) that produced such literatures. The dominant assumption is that North American writers have little in common except their so-called national "ethnic roots." As Sollors tells us in *Beyond Ethnicity*: "The published results of this procedure are the readers and compendiums made up of random essays on groups of ethnic writers who have little in common . . . ; meanwhile, obvious and important literary and cultural connections are obfuscated."[37] I propose, instead, that we take the Casa de las Américas' cultural conversations between Havana and the United States as a possible model for both a broader, oppositional American literary history and a new comparative cultural studies project. If we are to map out this new American literature, we would start by examining what the new narratives by García Márquez (who helped found *Prensa Latina* in Havana after the revolution in 1959), Fuentes (who initially supported the Cuban Revolution by completing his novel about the Mexican Revolution, *La muerte de Artemio Cruz*, at the home of Alejo Carpentier in Havana in May 1960), Julio Cortázar, and Allende have in common with ethnic North American works produced by such U.S. writers as Rolando Hinojosa and Ntozake Shange whose radical ethnopoetics have been dialectically validated by the Casa de las Américas. To be sure, all of these pan-American writers are rewriting American history from a subversive, "Calibanic" typology, in opposition to the U.S. ruling "center."[38]

It would seem that as Sollors has suggested, if anything, our new American literary history "ought to *increase* our understanding of the cultural interplays and contacts among writers of different [national] backgrounds, the cultural mergers and secessions that took place in [the] America[s], all of which can be accomplished only if the categorization of writers as members of [national] ethnic groups is understood to be a very partial, temporal, and insufficient characterization at best" (p. 15). Recast in this way, American literatures can be understood only as part of the larger debates and confrontations between "Our America" and the "other America, which is not ours." Whether they know it or not, writers, teachers, critics, and literary historians participate in this rhetorical war of positions. At least since 1960, Cuban-Marxist intellectuals have known this to be the case. Fernández Retamar, in particular, has tried to develop a new terminology that goes beyond a North American and Latin American "idealist" criticism, for Casa de las Américas was born in the very struggle between American imperialism and Latin American Marxism.

To understand how far his editorial leadership in Casa has evolved, let us consider one more dialogue in June 1981 in Havana:

namely, El primer Encuentro de Teatristas Latino-Americanos y del Caribe, sponsored by Casa de las Américas. In her "Diario Nicaragüense" (1982), Shange tells us how American playwrights from Colombia, Mexico, Brazil, El Salvador, New York, and San Jose, California—including the U.S. writers Ronnie Davis of the Amigos del Teatro de los Estados Unidos, Miriam Colon of the Puerto Rican Traveling Theater, and Adrian Vargas of the Teatro de la Gente—talked of theater, "palabras y balas. Poesia & dying," and how they performed their "teatros" in Cuban factories at 2 A.M.[39]

It should not be surprising that one of Casa's most sought-after African American writers is Ntozake Shange. She is singled out by the Cubans, perhaps because she best reflects a new African consciousness in the Americas: "I write in English, French, & Spanish," she tells us, "cuz my consciousness' mingle all New World African experiences."[40] What is especially attractive to Cuban audiences of her work is that in her "choreopoems" and new narratives she reveals in subaltern pan-American images and conceits the inner nature of white supremacy, sexism, and exploitation in the colonized Americas. Her African American discourse thus mediates a powerful contact between at least four cultures: African, English, Spanish, and French. This cultural mediation is illustrated spatially and graphically in "Bocas: A Daughter's Geography," where Shange dramatizes an alternative map of the world and a strong critique of patriarchy:

> i have a daughter/mozambique
> i have a son/angola
> our twins
> salvador & johannesburg/cannot speak
> but we fight the same old men/in the world. . . .
>
> i have a daughter/la habana
> i have a son/guyana
> our twins
> santiago & brixton/cannot speak
> the same language
> yet we fight the same old men.[41]

What is powerful and moving in Shange's feminist ethnopoetics is her vision of cultural critique. As in most of her work, she envisions a new sort of geographical space altogether in which new kinds of social and sexual relations, denied by the older classical

American literatures, might flourish. Her geography is thus always sociopoetic, and in her discourse places act as "ciphers" for alternative visions of social existence in the Americas. Russell A. Berman suggests in a different context: "Geographical designations, even the apparently most objective, are never neutral. Names, distances, and directions not only locate points but establish conceptualizations of power relations. The nomenclature of space functions as political medium."[42] From this point of view, Shange's "Bocas: A Daughter's Geography" allegorizes the persistence of an antithetical geographical space in the New World. Her archaeology of Our America uncovers many layers of New World identity opposed to the Occidental tradition that constantly tries to project its structures outward, creating and re-creating its North-South dichotomy to render the South as "Other" and victim.

Hence, when we investigate the literary history of the Americas and analyze "New World" group formation in transgeographical terms, we will be better served by Martí's oppositional cultural studies vocabulary in "Nuestra América" and Fernández Retamar's negative, dialectical, Calibanic typology of the self than by the separatist, formalist baggage contained in idealist readings from both North America and Latin America. Further, reconstructing the history of Casa de las Américas will negate North American parochial versions of literary history, and it will subvert traditional models of contemporary Latin American literary history as well, as is illustrated in the institutional history of *nueva narrativa.* Traditional histories of the "new writing" in Latin America usually recount the genealogy of fiction from Borges to García Márquez and Cabrera Infante, but fail to adequately explain why those narratives came to dominate.[43] For example, Emir Rodríguez Monegal skillfully shows that, although Latin American poetry (as practiced by Pablo Neruda, Octavio Paz, and César Vallejo) was the leading force during the avant-garde in Latin America, the new narrative produced in the 1940s by Borges and in the early 1950s by Carpentier soon rose to international prominence. According to Rodríguez Monegal, it was the new fiction "that projected Latin American literature onto the global stage."[44]

When a group of European and U.S. publishers awarded the first Formentor Prize *ex aequo* to Samuel Beckett and Jorge Luis Borges in 1961 (Rodríguez Monegal's symbolic starting date for the rise of the *nueva narrativa* in Latin America), Our American literature was finally given its rightful place. Borges's *Ficciones* (1941) was immediately translated into various languages, and, according to Rodríguez Monegal, "aroused general interest" in the totality of new Latin American fiction that Borges "so brilliantly represented" (p. 686, *Borzoi Anthology* [*BAL*]). Traditional accounts of the new narrative thus give a prominent place to Borges's *ficciones*. (As an aside, let me remind readers that John Barth, among many others, has dedicated enthusiastic essays to Borges's work.)[45] Because of Borges, Rodríguez Monegal concludes that "the new Latin American novel was no longer the exclusive provenance of specialists but was recognized and discussed all over the world" (p. 687, *BAL*).

Rodríguez Monegal's analysis, however, does not grant Casa de las Américas a proper role in determining the final political shape and influence of the new narrative. His "idealist" reading of Latin American literary history must be supplemented with a reading in terms of an oppositional, rhetorical, hermeneutic model; in this reading, textual facts, are, in Steven Mailloux's words, "never prior to or independent of the hermeneutic activity of readers and critics."[46] Against this incomplete view, I submit an alternative reading in terms of a wider historical set of topics, arguments, tropes, and ideologies that determine how discourses are established as meaningful—that is, through socially symbolic, rhetorical exchanges between "Our America" and "the other America, which is not ours." As Mailloux contends, we "should provide histories of how particular theoretical and critical discourses have evolved" (p. 629).

If anything, this model is part of a Calibanic practice, an intervention in cultural politics, just as the emerging new narratives by Cortázar, García Márquez, Fuentes, and Allende, among others, in Latin America, and by Hinojosa, Shange, and Margaret Randall in the United States are part of a global social and cultural struggle that reached its zenith at the end of the 1950s: the ascendancy of the American typology of Caliban, the negative of the master-slave relationship, over its bourgeois white supremacist counterpart, Prospero. What Castro and Che Guevara initiated in their negation of Prospero (and in the process subverting the U.S. Empire that began asserting its seignorial rights in Our America in 1823 with the Monroe Doctrine, prohibiting "outside" intervention in the "American" hemisphere) was completed at the discursive level by García Márquez and his pan-American heirs. In the words of Robert

Coover, the *nueva narrativa* from Latin America "was [thus] for a moment the region's headiest and most dangerous export."[47]

III

The interpretation of our reality through patterns not our own serves only to make us ever more unknown, ever less free, ever more solitary.
—Gabriel García Márquez, "The Solitude of Latin America"

Of the many nonfiction writings that, in preliminary ways, articulate and decenter the historical and cultural conflicts between Our America and the West, one has been particularly influential; García Márquez's "The Solitude of Latin America." His 1982 Nobel Prize address was among the first to begin resisting Reagan's, Bush's, and NATO's cold war mapping of the world.

This "cold war" of positions in the Americas is precisely the one that García Márquez chose to attack. He wanted his address "to be a political speech presented as literature."[48] Contesting NATO's hostile views of socialist Latin America, he asserted:

> Latin America neither wants, nor has any reason, to be a pawn without a will of its own; nor is it merely wishful thinking that its quest for independence and originality should become a Western aspiration. . . .
>
> Why is the originality so readily granted us in literature so mistrustfully denied us in our different attempts at social change? Why think that the social justice sought by progressive Europeans for their own countries cannot be a goal for Latin America, with different methods and for dissimilar conditions? No: the unmeasurable violence and pain of our history are the result of age-old inequities and untold bitterness, and not a conspiracy plotted 3,000 leagues from our homes. But so many European leaders and thinkers have thought so, with the childishness of old-timers who have forgotten the fruitful excesses of their youths as if it were impossible to live at the mercy of the two great masters of the world. This, my friends, is the very scale of our solitude.[49]

Almost as if to deconstruct his earlier negative dialectical hermeneutic in *One Hundred Years of Solitude* [1967], where "races condemned to one hundred years of solitude did not have a second opportunity on earth,"[50] here he presents a more positive position: his "utopian" side of the hermeneutic dialectic. He tells us that it is not too late to create a "new and leveling utopia of life where no one can decide the form of another person's death" (p. 17). As any reader of his fiction knows, this utopian view is much more optimistic than any yet depicted in his literature. His Nobel Prize address offers, in fact, a profound affirmation of the essentially humanistic imagination in Latin American socialism: "In spite of this, to oppression, plundering and abandonment, we respond with life. Neither floods nor plagues nor famine nor cataclysm nor even the eternal wars throughout centuries and centuries have managed to reduce the tenacious advantage of life over death" (p. 17).

Although he begins his speech playfully by referring to the magical and exaggerated visions inspired by the "discovery" of the New World (El Dorado, the fountain of eternal youth, the indigenous giant of Patagonia described by a sailor on Magellan's voyage, who when shown a mirror for the first time "lost his sense, overwhelmed by his fear of his own image)," he ends his address by describing a Frankfurt School, Marxist ideology of hope, a vision, where "races condemned to one hundred years of solitude will have at last and forever a second opportunity on earth" (p. 17).

By presenting this limited institutional genealogy of American discourse from Martí and Fernández Retamar to García Márquez, Hinojosa, and Shange, we can begin to identify areas of agreement and confluence and lay the groundwork for finding historical, ideological, and cultural simultaneity in the imaginative writing of the Americas.

2 "Squeezed By the Banana Company" Dependency and Ideology in Macondo

> Underdevelopment is total, integral in [Latin America;] it affects every part of our lives. The problems of our societies are mainly political. And the commitment of a writer is with the reality of all society, not just a small part of it. If not, he is as bad as the politicians who disregard a large part of our reality. That is why authors, painters, writers in Latin America get politically involved. I am surprised by the little resonance authors have in the U.S. and in Europe. Politics is made there only by the politicians.
> —Gabriel García Márquez, *New York Times*, December 5, 1982

> Shaken by the invisible breath of destruction, [Macondo] too is on the eve of a silent and final collapse. All of Macondo has been like that ever since it was squeezed by the banana company.
> —Gabriel García Márquez, from *Leafstorm*

Among the Latin American novelists of the past thirty years, one stands out among his celebrated peers as the most significant in contemporary pan-American and world letters, one who—judging from conversations among African American, Chinese-American, and Chicano writers—has most shaped the course of U.S. minority discourses in the 1970s and 1980s: Gabriel García Márquez.[1] We find in this 1982 Nobel Prize-winning writer from Aracataca, Colombia, on the Caribbean coast, the essential course of the new narrative from Our America. The achievement of García Márquez and his pan-American heirs, viewed individually or collectively, indicates that to an appreciable degree the writing of fiction in Our America has retained its autonomy, like U.S. Southern literature, by making its subject the very loss of its subject.[2]

Although not the whole of his achievement, García Márquez's work is singularly marked by the creation and peopling of a mythical pueblo in the district of La Magdalena, Colombia, called Macondo. The task of creating this mythic world (which has its real counterpart in Colombia) has occupied him from 1955 to the present. The major portion of his task has been accomplished during the past decades when he published *Leafstorm* (1955), *No One Writes to the Colonel* (1961), *The Evil Hour* (1962), *Big Mama's Funeral* (1962), *One Hundred Years of Solitude* (1967), *The Story of a Shipwrecked Sailor* (1970), *Innocent Eréndira and Other Stories* (1972), *The Autumn of the Patriarch* (1975), *Chronicle of a Death Foretold* (1981), *Clandestine in Chile: The Adventures of Miguel Littín* (1987), and *Love in the Time of Cholera* (1988). In 1990 he published *The General in His Labyrinth,* which reverses his attempts to transform the ordinary into the mythical, for in this controversial novel he takes on the saintly image of the Great Liberator, Simón Bolívar, by rendering this mythical hero as a man of ordinary and even crude attributes.

Put in more hemispheric and historical terms, García Márquez, like Hawthorne and Faulkner in the United States, and Neruda in Latin America, set out to create a native American tradition, in his case by creating in the 1950s and 1960s a whole pueblo, its people, myth, and (meta)history, and proceeded to do so on the aesthetic grounds prepared by Cervantes, Kafka, Borges, and Faulkner.[3] Fernando Alegría, for instance, in *Nueva historia de la novela hispanoamericana* (1986) recalls Neruda comparing García Márquez with Cervantes, and Yevgeny Yevtushenko saying that he is the "best contemporary writer."[4]

From the start, García Márquez produced intense fiction—the greatest when he wrote explicitly about his native Caribbean soil. There is no doubt that, at its best, his early fictions about Macondo created something new in American cosmopolitan literatures—nothing like Macondo appears in world literature. At his best, he dramatized the single most agonizing experience of his region in Colombia: the crisis and long aftermath of the development of underdevelopment in Macondo. The formal and thematic explorations in which his finest early work engaged were preparations for things to follow, culminating in his mature work about the rise and fall of Macondo, *One Hundred Years of Solitude.*

Additionally, his activity as an intellectual associated with the Casa de las Américas literary organizations and other cultural groups based in Havana demands to be mentioned, and this is his role as occasionally judging the annual Casa de las Américas prize in literature and his more recent work with the Foundation for the New Latin American Film, where, since its founding in 1985, just outside Havana, he has served as the organization's president. Each year he migrates from Mexico City to Havana, where he spends six weeks at the foundation, teaching workshops on screenplay writing to students from across the Americas, including the United States.

From his cultural work as a novelist and screenplay writer we can reconstruct a certain image and function of the writer/intellectual that many U.S. Anglocentric intellectuals have lost. Like Roberto Fernández Retamar, García Márquez offers us two kinds of identification: as novelist/screenplay writer (most recently he composed a series of six films, "Amores Difíciles" ["Dangerous Loves"], to raise money for the Havana film school) who combines the traditional intellectual's commitment to language and image; and as an organic intellectual whose commitment to politics and to revolution is equally absolute. In other words, in sharp contradistinction to the dominant Anglocentric tradition of narration and (post)modernism, for García Márquez and for many writers associated with the Casa de las Américas literary and cultural organizations there is no inconsistency between aesthetics and politics in this new, alternate Our American tradition. With characteristic generosity, García Márquez allows this alternate possibility to be dramatized by the revolutionary thinker of another, related, but distinct historical tradition in the Americas, that of Simón Bolívar: "all of [my work with the film foundation] forms part of a bigger idea I have, which is the total integration of the Americas, as Bolívar saw it."[5] But what García Márquez's own cultural work in literature and film can mean is a narrative art and aesthetics fulfilled by the Cuban Revolution.

We may now ask ourselves whether it is any longer appropriate to consider García Márquez as merely another canonical writer, who, after all, has won the Nobel Prize, has been well-received in the U.S./British literary circles, and, in the much-cited words of Aijaz Ahmad, "delight[s] . . . readers brought up on modernism and postmodernism."[6] What García Márquez demands is a rather different call for situation specificity, a positioning that always remains concrete and reflexive. His cultural work grows out of a socialist context—in the Americas in general, and in revolutionary Cuba in particular—where the word "Cuba" has a scandalous power that refuses to be absorbed by First World and Third World literary criticisms.

The methodology of this chapter, which often depends on reconstructing a context for García Márquez's fiction out of this transgeographical American historical experience, and which depends on more explicit treatments of his political ideas about dependency in Latin America, may strike some readers as unwarranted or simply wrong. The predominant mode in Anglocentric readings of his work, especially *One Hundred Years of Solitude*, has been formalistic. Many complex institutional factors are involved in this tendency. But one would be that many scholars and critics trained to read texts within the Anglocentric tradition have yet to learn to think dialectically, or see a need for a new literary and cultural internationalism that always involves risks and calls into question national borders of every sort. My own position is that García Márquez has not discouraged readers from speaking critically about questions of political conflict in his work, from seeing his work as a sustained critique of bourgeois ideology, or from thinking about his narratives as forming part of a "bigger idea"—the total integration of the Americas as Bolívar and Martí saw it.[7]

The Dialectics of Underdevelopment

In *Leafstorm*, his first novel, García Márquez begins to lyrically describe the real relations between the culture of the dominant "metropolis" and that of its underdeveloped "satellite"—Macondo.[8] In other words, his initial fiction about Macondo is largely based on the political idea that the Latin American pueblo is intimately and structurally linked to the dominant Western nations. In the author's more mature renderings of this paradigm of dependency, Macondo's ties to the world economic system stem from a number of major events. *One Hundred Years of Solitude*, for example, fantastically renders Macondo as having participated within an earlier mercantilist phase of world dependency, where its markets and geography, like the rest of the New World, were dominated by the colonizing powers of Spain, England, and Holland. As in most of García Márquez's work, this political idea is stated subtly and idiosyncratically, with a whiff of *lo real maravilloso americano*. Thus, early in the novel when the patriarch José Arcadio Buendía tries to leave Macondo, he has to cut his way through a magical jungle of bleeding lilies and golden salamanders. And instead of finding a way out of Macondo's solitary wilderness, he comes across the hull of a Spanish colonial ship anchored in the pan-American wilderness:

> Before them, surrounded by ferns and palm trees, white and powdery in the silent morning light, was an enormous Spanish galleon. Tilted slightly to the starboard, it had hanging from its intact masts the dirty rags of its sails in the midst of its rigging, which was adorned with orchids. The hull, covered with an armor of petrified barnacles and soft moss, was firmly fastened into a surface of stones.[9]

In all of García Márquez's fiction, history is the base for the tropic stylistics of magic realism. "Every single line," the author tells us, "in *One Hundred Years of Solitude,* in all my books[,] has a starting point in reality. I provide a magnifying glass so readers can understand reality better."[10]

As the Buendía family's personal history is narrated into the nineteenth century, one can readily see the emerging bourgeois class, empowered by the colonial forces, begin to displace the founding families. This sort of battle between the classes in which neither conservative nor liberal political parties can wholly defeat the emergent bourgeois state is admirably dramatized as a tragicomic, mock-epic alternation of civil wars. At the end of the novel, Macondo is even depicted as undergoing a third stage of development whereby multinational corporations develop satellite industries, like the Banana Company, in the underdeveloped Americas by using and abusing cheap labor.

In *Leafstorm* this latter stage of dependency begins the history of Macondo and its people. Elements appear that recur in nearly all of García Márquez's fictions about Macondo: a doomed town in the tropics, intimately related to the North American metropolis; bitter historical feuds between conservatives and liberals; and the foreign outsider hated by local townspeople.

Leafstorm (*"La hojarasca,"* in Spanish, also suggests waste, rubbish, and dregs) concentrates on three characters, who are contemplating the circumstances leading to the town's downfall, and a vegetarian doctor who eats grass—his medical practice, the author suggests, has been displaced by the Banana Company's medical staff. Essentially, the narrative focuses on a grandfather—a retired colonel—his daughter, Isabel, and her son, a ten-year-old boy, who are attending the funeral of the doctor, who years earlier refused to attend the wounded after a political battle.

Like Faulkner's *As I Lay Dying* (1930), a modernist tale about the intimate entanglement of love and grief, *Leafstorm* is a heroic story of the colonel's attempts to bury the doctor in the face of local hostility and government corruption. Technically, *Leafstorm* experiments radically with narrative points of view, though in García Márquez's relatively inexperienced hands his spiraling narrative occasionally gets out of control.[11]

Although the dialectic between developed and underdeveloped zones in the world economic system is not one of the novel's central preoccupations, it is brilliantly and metaphorically foregrounded:

> Suddenly, as if a whirlwind had set down roots in the center of the town, the banana company arrived, pursued by the leaf storm. . . . The whirlwind was implacable. It contaminated everything with its swirling crowd smell. . . . In less than a year it sowed over the town the rubble of many catastrophes that had come before it, scattering its mixed cargo of rubbish in the streets (p. 1).

Almost overnight, buildings spring up, foreigners appear and just as quickly disappear. Macondo's modernization is appalling: "Arriving there, mingled with the human leaf storm, dragged along by its impetuous force, came the dregs of warehouses, hospitals, amusement parlors, electric plants . . ." (p. 1). Modernization victimizes the masses, concentrates property in a few hands, and develops an administratively centralized nation-state with its uniform code of laws to enforce the system.

Macondo's downfall, its history of underdevelopment, from García Márquez's Our American point of view, is caused not because local industries have not had the chance to blossom, but precisely because Macondo has been forced by the Banana Company to become part of the global economic system, a satellite within the world system. This idea of dependency is straightforwardly stated: "The leaf storm had brought everything and it had taken everything away" (p. 89). His foremost achievement, as John Updike has said in the *New Yorker,* was to articulate "his remembered Caribbean backwater with a certain urbanity" and to render convincingly "the stagnation and poverty" of Macondo.[12] *Leafstorm* already thematizes one dimension of Our American experience of dependency, where Macondo is "on the eve of a silent and final collapse . . . squeezed by the banana company" (p. 89). In *One Hundred Years of Solitude* everything in Macondo perishes.

Leafstorm, it can be argued, anticipates many of García Márquez's political themes and re-creates a number of historical moments of dependency that reappear in his later work. In particular, this early history anticipates the central idea of his new narratives: the reification of the present relates to the "catastrophes" of the past. Rhetorically, *Leafstorm* also anticipates his narrative stylistics—its gratuitous contortions, its Faulknerian mix of pathos and ridicule (for example, a local priest reads from the Bristol Almanac instead of the Bible, and the word is as acceptable as the pronouncement of any other prophet in Macondo). However, as one reads his early rhetoric, there can be no doubt that, at its best, it is an aggrieved torpor, or, in Updike's more poetic words, a "music of obsessive circling."[13]

The Liquidation of "Big Mama's" Official Culture

If *Leafstorm* foregrounds García Márquez's dialectical new narrative in relation to the historical conflicts that erupted in Colombia, "Big Mama's Funeral," a mythical tall tale set in Macondo, spells out his beginning critique of authority, power, and "official culture" in the Latin American *pueblo.* Because the tale poses a special problem with which traditional modes of literary criticism have never dealt successfully—the author's juxtaposition of mythic and legalistic discourse—this section also comments on his skill in mediating these discourses to subvert the authority of official culture in Macondo.[14] In this way, "Big Mama's Funeral" shows us how power is exercised at the micro level of society. Who is served by the discourse—Big Mama?, the state?, or both. Put succinctly, the "incorporation of power" is allegorized; overblown and fat, Big Mama, Nicanor, Father Isabel, and the President of Colombia embody the will to power in Our American pueblo.

A hyperbolic story told in two parts (preceded by a folktale-like introduction, where the narrator parodies the role of an unofficial ethnographer, in opposition to the "official" professional historians of his region), it is the author's first sustained deconstruction of ruling class and official culture in Macondo. A local ruling-class family on the verge of losing its power and leadership is emblematized in the hulking figure of Big Mama: "When she sat on her balcony in the cool afternoon air, with all the weight of her belly and authority squeezed into her old rattan rocker, she seemed, in truth, infinitely rich and powerful, the richest and most powerful matron in the world."[15]

Ever since her father's death, when María del Rosario Castañeda y Montero (Big Mama) turned twenty-two, the local matron-tyrant has ruthlessly ruled over the town and its people—what she sees as her personal kingdom. Like many Third World dictators, she dictates social harmony by using and abusing the electoral process: "For many years Big Mama had guaranteed the social peace and political harmony of her empire, by virtue of the three trunks full of forged electoral certificates which formed part of her secret estate" (p. 194).

In this story, García Márquez destroys the official regime of truth in Macondo—Big Mama's abuse of legal documents. Like Mikhail M. Bakhtin, he divides society into those who constitute the power establishment and control people's lives, and those who are subject to this control but do not participate in the decisions of power.[16] Although Big Mama throughout her first seventy years in power allows the townspeople to celebrate her birthdays, which are "the most prolonged and tumultuous carnivals within memory," her own "special guests" and "legitimate members" of Macondo's ruling-class families set themselves off from the changing, open, unstable popular culture of the carnival by celebrating in a closed, refined, and elitist way: they "danced to the beat of the old pianola with the rolls most in style" (p. 188).

Big Mama's power represents official culture and bourgeois cultural capital in the Americas. In her "two-story mansion" she is the center of civilization. "During this century," García Márquez writes, Big Mama "had been Macondo's center of gravity, as had her brothers, her parents, and the parents of her parents in the past, in a dominance which covered two centuries" (p. 186). Because this story about Macondo constitutes a baring of Colombia's and Latin America's deepest ills—authoritarianism and the suppression of subordinate classes through judicial discursive practices—it is important to examine the author's undermining of Big Mama's hegemonic culture and power. He does this by setting his tall tale in a present that dramatizes the steady dissolution of Big Mama's personal empire. In the second half of the story, even Big Mama's corpse dissolves before the reader's eyes: "her body filled with bubbles in the harsh Macondo September" (p. 195).

Like Faulkner's comic-grotesque narratives, although without

Faulkner's southern conservatism, García Márquez wryly examines the spectacle of a ruling civilization, uprooted and dying. The first half concentrates on the matron's last breathing hours. She spends most of her time "put[ting] the affairs of her soul in order" and meticulously preparing to "put her worldly affairs in order" (p. 185). As in his best work, he describes his ruling-class members' power and authority through his well-known tropes of hyperbole—thus, in a jesting manner, inverting established values and order. Big Mama's nephew, Nicanor, for example, who uses strong-armed tactics and a ".38 caliber long-barreled revolver" to keep the subordinate classes repressed, is depicted as "gigantic and savage." And later, the local priest, Father Anthony Isabel, is characterized as being so fat that "ten men had been needed to take him up to Big Mama's bedroom" (p. 185).

Almost literally, then, Nicanor, Father Isabel, and Big Mama, with "monumental buttocks," incorporate power in Macondo. However, Big Mama, "from the depths of her enormous body,"[17] as Roberto González Echevarría puts it, enumerates power magically: "No one knew the origin, or the limits or the real value of her estate, but everyone was used to believing that Big Mama was the owner of the waters, running and still, of rain and drought, and of the district's roads, telegraph poles, leap years, and heat waves, and that she had furthermore a hereditary right over life and property" (p. 186).

Clearly, "Big Mama's Funeral" is García Márquez's carnivalesque allegory concerning the relationship between the culture of Macondo's dominant and subordinate classes. On a certain level, it is also a metacommentary, as González Echevarría suggests, on the Latin American narrative of the *tierra.*[18] In other words, his analysis of authority and official culture is both a parody and critique of the traditional flat characters and commonplaces represented in the narrative of the *tierra*. Hence, Macondo is described as run-down, its elite townspeople bovine, and their customs and superstitions preposterous.

What is significant for our purposes, however, is his hilarious mimicking of the rhetoric of the notarial arts—the documents of power Big Mama loves to dictate. By coarsely describing her lower body stratum, and by exaggerating her material and spiritual estate, he explodes, in a jesting manner, the central scene in his tall tale where she dictates her last will and testament:

> Big Mama raised herself up on her monumental buttocks, and in a domineering and sincere voice . . . dictated to the notary this list of her invisible estate: the wealth of the subsoil, the territorial waters, the colors of the flag, national sovereignty, the traditional parties, the rights of man, civil rights, the nation's leadership, the right of appeal, Congressional hearings, letters of recommendation. . . . (p. 192)

In an irreverent and critical way, he dramatizes Big Mama's absolute control over Macondo and its townspeople, much the same as he will later delight in representing his symbolic Father, the old General, in *The Autumn of the Patriarch.*

Because the notary public attests to the state legitimacy of Big Mama's enumeration in her discourse, and thus certifies the document's "truthfulness," the story gives us in brief form García Márquez's explanation of how official power is constructed and manipulated in Macondo. Although Big Mama is certainly a simulacrum, she, unlike the symbolic Father in *The Autumn of the Patriarch*, is not an eternal myth—she dies enumerating her power, cut off hilariously by a belch: "She didn't manage to finish [dictating to the notary]. The laborious enumeration cut off her last breath. Drowning in the pandemonium of abstract formulas which for two centuries had constituted the moral justification of the family's power, Big Mama emitted a loud belch and expired" (p. 192).

In the second half of the story, the narrator cloaks himself with the borrowed authority of ethnographic and folkloristic discourse. He even mimics the professional rhetoric of the ethnographer to pay homage to the grandeur of the symbolic, archetypal Mother. He describes in detail how the entire world mourns Big Mama's death, how the President of Colombia attends the funeral, and how even the Holy Father arrives from the Vatican and hands out hard Italian candies to the town's subordinate classes. Although her royal status is officially recognized around the globe, at the more local, familial level, her heirs sack the matron's decaying mansion, thus illustrating the essential greed of Macondo's ruling-class families: "No one noticed that the nephews, grandchildren, servants and protégés of Big Mama closed the door as soon as the body was taken out, and dismantled the door, pulled the nails out of the planks, and dug up the foundations to divide up the house" (pp. 199–200). At the end, our parodic ethnographer-narrator hints at Macondo's future apocalyptic demise by stating that "tomorrow, Wednesday, the garbage men will come and sweep up the garbage from her funeral, forever and ever" (p. 200).

Yet a question remains. Why does García Márquez use the opposed discourses of myth (legend, the folktale) and the notarial arts (the legal document) to represent the interrelationships between the ruling-class and subordinate-class culture in Macondo? On the surface, "Big Mama's Funeral" is simply a tall talc signifying how the diverse social classes mourn an archetypal matron's death. Below the surface, however, he gives us through his parodic ethnographic narrator (a native talking back) a striking metacommentary.[19] In a coarse narrative representing the voice of the subordinate classes, he discloses how the legendary matriarch literally and figuratively incorporated an oppressive authoritarianism.

Thus, in his best work, legalistic, scientific, and ethnographic discursive practices are employed irreverently to undermine their conventionality. Legalistic rhetoric is the mediating discourse par excellence, precisely because of the historical place it occupies in the New World. It seems self-evident, that García Márquez is commenting historically on the use and abuse of notarial discourses by the hegemonic Spanish crown to gain control over, dominate, and eradicate the First Americans in the New World. In other words, our history and fiction in the New World, as González Echevarría suggests, were created within the language of the laws.[20]

"Big Mama's Funeral" gives voice to García Márquez's initial attempts to represent the open, egalitarian culture of Macondo's subordinate classes. In briefly suggesting this carnivalization, the author likewise celebrates the jesting inversion of all ruling-class values and established order in Big Mama's oppressive empire. By keeping this disparity in mind, his pan-American fiction becomes comprehensible. Its comic and exaggerated quality is directly linked to the carnival themes of popular culture and to subordinate-class reality. Indeed, this carnivalization of Our American culture, it seems to me, is what makes García Márquez's new narratives so popular with North American ethnic writers such as Toni Morrison, Rolando Hinojosa, Arturo Islas, and Ntozake Shange. As the author has said: "Reality is also the myths of the common people, their legends; they are their everyday life and they affect their triumph and failures. I realized that reality isn't just the police that kills people, but also everything that forms part of the life of the common people."[21]

A circular, reciprocal, not merely dichotomous relationship between the cultures and classes therefore interweaves in García Márquez's allegorical new narratives. His major contribution to pan-American letters in the 1950s and 1960s can be summarized: he assumes civilization's forms of the documents that have been endowed with truth-bearing power at specific moments in history. At the same time, he mimics these discourses from a subordinate-class perspective to radically undermine the documents' conventionality. Using authorial tactics that poststructuralists and cultural studies critics would recognize as their own, he shows how truth-bearing documents are themselves disguised narratives. In the end, his exaggerated tales always warn readers not to be deceived by the narratives' claims to truth and omnitemporality.

Ideology and Negation in *One Hundred Years of Solitude*

All that exists deserves to perish.
—Karl Marx, *The Eighteenth Brumaire of Louis Bonaparte*

It is now a commonplace in post-contemporary Latin American literary studies to find a historical and ideological framework in García Márquez's books. He often describes his own act of reading *One Hundred Years of Solitude* in terms of the text's real frame of reference—Colombian history—saying that

> it would be difficult for the reader to understand the thirty-two civil wars of Colonel Aureliano Buendía, the baseness of the fights waged between conservatives and liberals, fights that served little purpose, because the country today would still need the same vindication that liberals demanded a hundred years ago, you see, and the three thousand dead men of the plaza of Macondo that no one remembers having fallen dead by the soldiers' machine guns, none of this means anything to whoever ignores or has not lived the history of Colombia.[22]

It is not my purpose to explore the complete historical frame of reference in *One Hundred Years of Solitude*, for such studies have been done well by several scholars.[23] Rather, my aim is to relate García Márquez's ideological and aesthetic perspectives in that novel to a radical deconstructive reading of institutions in the text, a critical interpretation that may illuminate his rewriting of Colombia's history from an ideological point of view. Put more precisely, new perspectives concerning his use of Colombian history might be gained by rereading the novel's famous Banana Company episode where the issues of Macondo's history, dependency, and deconstruction are more clearly dramatized. The Banana Company episode is one of the most self-conscious and significant ideological moments in recent pan-American literary history. In it, he alludes to the controlling principles that regulate not only his sociopoetic novel, but the genre of pan-American, metahistorical narration itself.

García Márquez is not a traditional Marxist writer, nor is *One Hundred Years of Solitude* an orthodox Marxist text. This does not mean, however, that the novel has no radical implications and uses. It is precisely here that his philosophical, metafictional, popular cultural perspective of the fiction-making process, and his ideological reading of dependency in the Americas are most clearly aligned, for in the novel we explore both a (post)modernist and popular text.

In *One Hundred Years of Solitude* we can sense the emergence and full blossoming of what will be (post)modernism, the boom epoch in the literary Americas (*lo real maravilloso* and the "total" novel), but also, still juxtaposed with it, of what will be termed popular or mass culture, the commercialized discourse of a *telenovela* (soap opera) and mass media society. This dual development is most dramatically registered by what many readers have felt as a tangible "break" in mid-narrative, a qualitative shift of intensity as we move from the master codes of myth—the founding and settling of Macondo by the patriarch and his quest for knowledge and desire—to the slower-paced trajectory of mock-epic—the biography of the Colonel—and to the wonderful parody of the Buendía family's nineteenth-century soirées round Pietro Crespi's pianola. This middle section, roughly unnumbered chapters four through sixteen, is a virtual paradigm of mock-epic and a model of the subgenre into which twentieth-century mass culture of the Americas will be articulated—the television soap opera.

Briefly, in this section we get not only the "Europeanization" of Macondo (symbolized by Pietro Crespi's pianola) and Macondo's revolutionary period (Colonel Aureliano Buendía's thirty-two civil wars), but we find the words, deeds, and intimate relationships of the Buendía family.[24] In the soap opera passions that involve Amaranta, Rebecca, and Pietro Crespi, who is always in the Buendía house, there is the classic imitation of the nineteenth-century bourgeois novel, along with the (post)modernist *telenovela* cameo description and conservative Hispanic etiquette. The Buendía family, of course, owes its existence and continuance in Macondo to Úrsula Buendía, the sun around whom the family orbits. She alone constructs ideology in the family, namely, a coherent set of values, representations, and cultural beliefs, and she alone condemns or condones Macondo's morals and ethics.[25] And, finally, we must not forget that Úrsula keeps the entire family financially sound with her enterprises. By paying for and redesigning the house, she provides a powerful antipatriarchal focus. As García Márquez has said: "Úrsula is a prototype of that kind . . . of woman."[26]

The novel not only oscillates between two narrative conventions, but two cultural spaces, that of high or ruling culture, and that of subordinate culture. Schematically, its form is a deconstruction of the older realisms and magic realisms from which emerge both postmodernism and two reconstructed literary and cultural structures, dialectically interrelated and mediated: the institution of high literature and what the founders of the Frankfurt School, Horkheimer and Adorno, called the "culture industry," that is, the apparatuses for the production of popular or mass culture.[27]

The coexistence of these distinct but as yet imperfectly differentiated cultural spaces in García Márquez's fiction marks his production of the novel as a unique occasion for analysis of broadly defined cultural and more narrowly defined literary forms. It also offers an occasion to begin what Fredric Jameson articulates in *The Political Unconscious* as an ideological and formal "metacommentary" that reevaluates conflicting interpretations of a given text's reception.[28] The book's dialectical text has produced a bewildering variety of competing and incommensurate interpretive options. Implicitly, we have already touched on mythic, epic, and formalist analyses of *lo real maravilloso.* Alongside these strategies, we can distinguish other readings and rewritings in which the text is seen as articulating universal archetypes.[29] There is the Borgesian reading that raises the issues of time and space;[30] the Freudian, in which the incest taboo is central to the Buendía family;[31] the ethical, where García Márquez "constructs a literary space in which freedom and dialogue become possible" in Latin America;[32] the phenomenological, in which the text is an intersubjective experience, seeking to establish the deepest ties between symbolic language and self-understanding;[33] and, perhaps most formidable, the generic mythoi reading of the novel as either a "satire" in which the author attempts to "demythologize a national history so that everyone may return to a tabula rasa and find better fictions"[34] or as a "rare comedy" that nonetheless "ends in apocalypse."[35] Joan Didion in her nonfiction work, *Salvador*, has observed that spending time in war-torn El Salvador had made her see García Márquez in a new light—as a "social realist."[36]

The competing claims and conflicts of these interpretations constitute a compelling constellation of leitmotifs. Further, a dialectical reading of the novel subsumes these competing interpretations.

Ideology and Aesthetics in Macondo

As each successive story of Colombia unfolded from García Márquez's fictions, he wrote to friends to insist on the geopolitical and ideological new realism of his works.[37] Years later, in "The Solitude of Latin America," he made this insight into Latin America's "outsized reality" explicit: "Poets and beggars, musicians and prophets, warriors and scoundrels, all creatures of that unbridled reality, we have had to ask but little of imagination, for our crucial problem has been a lack of conventional means to render our lives believable. This, my friends, is the crux of our solitude."[38] Yet he constantly returns in numerous interviews and essays to his central concern for de(con)struction and subversion in art. For example, during his famous conversation with Mario Vargas Llosa, he says, "I know of no good literature that serves to praise established values. I have always found in good literature the tendency to destroy the established, the accepted, and to contribute to the creation of new societies, in the end, to better the lives of men."[39] All "good" literature challenges the ideological assumptions of its time, he asserts. In addition, he believes that a writer's aesthetic preoccupation reflects of what we may call the productive ideology of the text.

Like many of his Latin American and ethnic North American contemporaries, García Márquez feels deeply committed to both literature and social change. All art, he says, springs from an ideological conception of the world, for there is no such thing as a work of art entirely devoid of ideological content:

> when I sit down to write a book it is because I am interested in telling a good story. One that will appeal. I also have an ideological position and if it is firm, if the writer is sincere at the moment of telling his story, be it Red Riding Hood or one of guerrillas, to cite the two extremes, if the writer, I repeat, has a firm ideological position, this position will nurture his tale and it is from this moment on that the story can have the subversive forces of which I speak. I do not think it is deliberate, but it is inevitable.[40]

As he suggests, ideology and storytelling are allied: the writer's ideology nurtures the tale. The duty of the engaged storyteller, then, is to tell a good story. Further, in his estimation a "good" story mediates the aesthetic, political, and subversive force of content in the narrative itself. His preoccupation with storytelling and subversive ideology, the de(con)struction of established values and authority, as a means to better the lives of all men and women defines the negative dialectical force of *One Hundred Years of Solitude*.

From García Márquez's Our American perspective, the central theme of the novel, solitude, is metaphorically allied with the Marxian idea of alienation and to a biblical alienation from meaning. Briefly stated, alienation for Marx describes the way the workers' labor and the product of their work become estranged and take on a life apart from them. In other words, as modern society runs its course, "the worker becomes the poorer the more wealth he produces and the more his production increases in power and extent. The worker becomes a cheaper commodity the more commodities he produces. Hand in hand with the exploitation (Verwertung) of the objective world goes the depreciation of the human world."[41]

Solitude, in the context of this principle, assumes numerous forms in García Márquez's novel. In Macondo, as in the real world, members of the Buendía clan become the slaves of things and events.[42] Throughout the novel, the author uses the powerful metaphors of ice and mirrors to represent the world in which individuals are caged within a glassy, frozen solitude. We also see the Buendía world—the world of their production (sexual and material)—reflected back to them, but insubstantially. Furthermore, *One Hundred Years of Solitude* dramatizes what the author describes as an alienation from meaning, for to interpret the novel "as meaning 'no one will ever understand us' is correct," he tells us. "Everyone is afraid of solitude. . . ."[43] Indeed, the text, figuratively and literally, strains with signification, yet we are never really confident that what it is saying can be reduced to more than a descriptive statement of meaning. In this regard, *One Hundred Years of Solitude* follows the paradigmatic structure of the Bible, what William Blake called "the great code of art." Like the biblical text itself, García Márquez's heterogeneous narrative is always both revealing and concealing; hence, we can say that we experience a sudden "alienation from meaning" in the text.[44]

To be sure, the Marxian and biblical influences on García Márquez's novel are not merely master codes and archetypes, as many astute readers have suggested. But Marx and the Bible play a decisive role that reminds us how precarious our grasp of the Real is, and how we must constantly probe the world and its disguised narratives. Further, Marx and the Bible give the novel its great themes: history, paternity, disobedient children, cities, prophecy, paradise, fall, apocalypse, and solitude.

Structurally, *One Hundred Years of Solitude* embodies a dialectic of biblical and Marxian paradigms. Generally, it is modeled on the biblical movement from Genesis and Eden through Apocalypse by means of prophecy and "world-historical" events.[45] When we begin reading, the fully developed world of Macondo is utopian and precapitalistic: "The world was so recent that many things lacked names, and in order to indicate them it was necessary to point" (p. 11). After José Arcadio Buendía, the patriarch, kills his neighbor and symbolic brother, Prudencio Aguilar, a mirroring of the first murder in the Bible, the founders of a New World civilization stop in Macondo because Buendía, like Cain, the founder of cities, has dreamed of a great pueblo:

> One morning, after almost two years of crossing, they became the first mortals to see the western slopes of the mountain range. . . . One night, after several months of lost wandering through the swamps . . . they camped on the banks of a stony river whose waters were like a torrent of frozen glass. . . . José Arcadio Buendía dreamed that night [that] right there a noisy city with houses having mirror walls rose up. He asked what city it was and they answered him with a name he had never heard, that had no meaning at all, but that had a supernatural echo in his dream: Macondo. (pp. 31–32)

In this passage Buendía prophesies Macondo's apocalyptic future: it is a city of ice, or rather mirrors, where repetitions of solitude and violence multiply, and the successiveness of history stops. As with Sophocles' Oedipus, Buendía already knows, even as he does not know, what is to come. Throughout the rest of the novel, the author dramatizes Macondo's history in the violent nineteenth and twentieth centuries with events prophesied before they occur: plagues, a deluge, and final apocalyptic wind reminiscent of Alejo Carpentier's "green wind" in *The Kingdom of This World* that destroys Haiti.[46]

Mediated within the general biblical structures of *One Hundred Years of Solitude,* García Márquez also represents several world historical events and Third World American histories: that of European and Western science, from Greek magnets to Portuguese navigational equipment; that of sea routes and flying carpets; that of gold, ice, and bananas; and that of the New World, its dependency and underdevelopment by Spanish colonialism, Western mercantilism and capitalism, and North American Empire as ways of life. In their founding of Macondo, José Arcadio Buendía and his clan repeat the founding of the New World. Colonel Aureliano Buendía takes us through Colombia's nineteenth-century civil wars, and José Arcadio Segundo leads us through Macondo's dependency, banana boom, and the twentieth-century massacre of banana workers.

One Hundred Years of Solitude thus dramatizes a Marxian and biblical history of men and women in Macondo. It is plotted first as an ascent, as the Buendía family gains greater control of nature and their resources through a development of Melquíades's Western science and esoteric technology; and second, as descent, as the Buendía family grows more alienated from each other as well as from their fellow villagers. This mediation of paradigms allows García Márquez to dramatize the family's entire history as heading toward a crisis in which the clan can come into its kingdom on earth or destroy itself. The novel, in brief, is a metaphor for dependency, alienation, history, and negative hermeneutics in Latin America. Nothing in García Márquez's metahistory is set down with malice. Throughout the text, he gives voice to the silent, profound discourses of solitude. Solitude, to be sure, takes on a variety of overdetermined meanings in the text; however, solitude is closely related to the Marxian political idea of anti-solidarity in the community. According to the novelist, solitude "comes from the lack of solidarity in Macondo, the solitude which results when everyone is acting for himself."[47] In other words, the novel dramatizes solitude as a *negation* of solidarity.

The Banana Company Episode: Metahistory, Dependency, and Deconstruction

> When the trumpets had sounded and all
> was in readiness on the face of the earth,
> Jehovah divided his universe:
> Coca-Cola Inc., Anaconda,
> Ford Motors and similar concerns:
> the United Fruit Company Incorporated
> reserved for itself the most succulent
> morsel of all, the midsection
> and coasts of my country
> the sweet waist of America. . . .
> —Pablo Neruda, from "La United Fruit Co.," *Canto general*

As we read García Márquez's Banana Company episode in *One Hundred Years of Solitude,* it becomes clear that the author's critique of the development of underdevelopment, or dependency, in Macondo is in the radical tradition of Pablo Neruda's blistering attack on the U.S.-based United Fruit Company in his encyclopedic, epic-like poem about the Americas—*Canto general.* The ideological link between Neruda's and García Márquez's work, to my knowledge, never has been pointed out sufficiently; yet their attack on late capitalism and multinational corporations in Latin America has a common denominator.

Sprawling over fifteen sections and three hundred poems, Neruda's *Canto general* is in the poet's own words "a vast landscape" of the Americas. Melquíades's erudite, modernist manuscript, "One Hundred Years of Solitude," written in coded poetry, it can be argued, is also encyclopedic, what Enrico Mario Santí, using Northrop Frye's ideas on literary form and referring to *Canto general,* calls "an extensive literary pattern clustering a series of related episodes around a central theme."[48] Further, García Márquez's novel, like Neruda's poem, exposes a historical pattern of social injustice—a utopian beginning in Macondo that is negated by repeated foreign invasions and corrupt politics. Briefly stated, the Banana Company episode, properly read, is a socially symbolic act in the Latin American Marxist tradition of cultural critique that Neruda made famous. Whereas Neruda's irreverent poem is a mock-narrative, unmasking the myths—"the comic opera"—promulgated by multinational corporations in Latin America, García Márquez's Banana Company episode is an unrelenting deconstruction of the United Fruit Company's powerful "regime of truth" in Colombia's La Magdalena region.

The elements of form and substance, high culture and mass culture, ideology and aesthetics interpenetrate *One Hundred Years of Solitude*. According to the author, an appropriate form and language had to be used to communicate a world in which "todo es posible, todo es real" ("everything is possible, everything is real").[49] The novel is a subversive text because it dialectically dramatizes the profound alienation, dependency, repression, and falsification that have characterized Colombia's historical development in relation to advanced capitalism, while at the same time it posits what Kumkum Sangari accurately describes as "the politics of the possible."[50]

In his novel, deconstruction is not an abstract, formalist issue, but a concrete dialectical project that begins with García Márquez breaking down the traditional genres of myth, epic, romance, comedy, satire, and tragedy. An ideological and a deconstructive discourse in the novel work on each other in his attempt to develop a new social (ideological) and tropological (deconstructive) form of analysis in the Americas.

In a brilliant chapter in *Marxism and Deconstruction*, Michael Ryan maintains that Jacques Derrida's deconstruction of logocentric philosophy "deconstructs the self-evident nature [of philosophy] by showing that it is constructed, a product of numerous histories, institutions, and processes of inscription which cannot be transcended. . . ."[51] Ryan's suggestive reading is important to our reading of the Banana Company episode for these reasons. First, implicit in the episode is the proposition that historical events are not produced by concatenated events. Instead, the author suggests, history is a multifaceted, multi-rooted matter whose truth cannot be fully plotted or easily resolved. In this sense the historical event is presented like a text that can be deciphered and deconstructed. What García Márquez represents, then, is how discourse is *constructed*. Second, if we accept that the historical world is produced, as García Márquez demonstrates, as a process of differentiation in which specific events are subsumed by larger structures and sequences, then we must acknowledge that the production of historical discursive practice is necessarily institutional and rhetorical, that is, ideologically constructed. Deconstruction is García Márquez's positive way here of placing limits on ideological language. If the past is represented as a series of texts, it is by definition a series of ideological fictions.

The Banana Company episode is based on an incident in which workers on strike from a local plantation were shot by government soldiers at the Ciénaga railway station in December 1928,[52] when García Márquez was almost a year old. As Lucila Inés Menes recounts, many strikes occurred, but this one, the most serious, was bloodily suppressed.[53]

The workers demanded a raise in wages, a regular wage in lieu of payment on the basis of piecework, abolition of company stores, and the construction of hospitals in the zone. Under radical socialist leadership, they also had much to say about American imperialism in Latin America—specifically, the entrance of the United Fruit Company in Colombia in 1889. They saw the Boston-based company for what it patently was: an imperialistic force in their local economy. In analyzing their "enclave economy" whereby foreign investment capital originates outside the country, García Márquez dramatizes how the company's value was increased by the exploitation of local labor forces that transform nature and produce goods sold in foreign markets.

To resist this exploitation, the workers went on strike. However, the company's business manager refused to consider laborers who worked only part-time as his employees, and their demands were rejected. When workers tried to sabotage the cutting and transporting of bananas, troops were sent in. On December 6 at 1:30 A.M. General Carlos Cortes Vargas had his famous Decree Number 4 read by his secretary, ordering the strikers to disperse. An investigator of the massacre, Jorge Elicer Gaítan, has written that before the terror was over, government soldiers "en esa misma noche movieron numerosas cadáveres en camiones y los arrojaron al mar y a un zanjon previamente abierto. . . ." ("on that same night moved numerous cadavers in buses hurling some of them into the sea and others into an open ditch. . . .").[54] The government count of murdered workers was officially thirteen, but Menes is on target when she says, "Nunca se sabra exactamente el número de muertes ocurridas en este trágico acontecimiento" ("One will never know exactly the number of deaths which occurred in that tragic event").[55]

This section of the novel, in which García Márquez presents a structural breakdown and an interpretive analysis of the real historical event from a radical point of view, is perhaps the most significant ideological event in Third World American narratives. He dramatizes the company's exploitation of the workers and clearly takes their point of view in describing their plight: "The protests of the workers this time were based on the lack of sanitary facilities in their living quarters, the non-existence of medical services, and terrible working conditions" (p. 278). The workers in the novel, moreover, are not paid in real money but in script that will buy the Virginia ham sold in company commissaries. Whether or not they are suffering from cold, constipation, or malaria, the workers are given pills the color of copper sulfate that the children in the village collect and use for bingo markers.

Through his accumulation of such details, García Márquez attacks the authority established by foreign investors, lawyers, local government officials, and conservative historians who relate the "official" version. Although José Arcadio Segundo leads the workers in drawing up their list of demands for improvement of conditions, the Banana Company is helped by the lecherous and "mournful" lawyers whose "sleight of hand," rhetorical fabrications, and manipulations of legal discourse, truth and falsity, justice and injustice prove that the demands are not only inaccurate but also that they "lacked all validity for the simple reason that the banana company did not have, never had had, and never would have any workers in its service because they were hired on a temporary basis . . . and by a decision of the court it was established and set down in a solemn decree that the workers did not exist" (p. 280). The conscious parodying of legalistic rhetoric and thinking point clearly to one of the underlying issues from a radical, deconstructive perspective: at what level and by whom are authority and truth initiated in Macondo? By the lawyers? The Court? The Colombian government? Or by language itself? Obviously, García Márquez is proposing here, as he previously did in "Big Mama's Funeral," that all discourses including institutional decrees (false documents) are rhetorical constructs, the rhetorical nature of which have been forgotten by convention and habitual use.

To break out of their solitude, the workers are forced to call for a strike. *Huelga* and the politics of the *huelga* arrive in Macondo. Fruit begins to rot on the trees, and idle workers spill over into the town. What follows is seen primarily through Arcadio Segundo's eyes. His view of the massacre of workers, women and children among them, will later be juxtaposed with the government's, the army's, and even the regime's historical textbook version of the massacre. First, we are told:

> He went out into the streets and saw them. There were three regiments whose march in time to a galley drum made the earth tremble. Their snorting filled the glow of the noon with a pestilential vapor. They were short, stocky and brute-like. They perspired with the sweat of a horse and had a smell of suntanned hide. . . . (p. 281)

Through the simplicity and humor of his prose, García Márquez's descriptions of the army as "brutes" and perspiring animals capture us where political rhetoric never could.

The massacre of banana workers is cast by García Márquez in the order of two opposing states: dream and reality. A dreamlike "gigantic whirlwind" is related to the real firing of machine guns. By providing "a magnifying glass" to the surreal events of Ciénaga, he produces *lo real maravilloso.*

When Arcadio Segundo regains consciousness, the nightmarish dream vision continues in a more pronounced and harrowing way. At this point he realizes:

> Several hours must have passed since the massacre because the corpses had the same temperature as a plaster in autumn and the same consistency of petrified foam that it had, and those who had put [the corpses] in the car had had time to pile them up in the same way in which they transported bananas. Trying to flee from this nightmare, José Arcadio Segundo dragged himself from one car to another . . . he saw corpses, women corpses, child corpses who would be thrown into the sea like rejected bananas (p. 284).

When Arcadio Segundo finally escapes from this death train, his special kind of solitude begins to reveal itself; no one believes what has happened. Not even his brother, Aureliano Segundo:

> He did not believe the version of the banana massacre or the trip of the train loaded with corpses traveling toward the sea either. The

> night before he had read an extraordinary proclamation to the nation which said that the workers had left the station and had returned home in peaceful groups. The proclamation also stated that the union leaders, with great patriotic spirit, had reduced their demands to two points: a reform of medical services and the building of latrines in the living quarters (p. 287).

A week later, the "official version" of the regime is repeated in Macondo through every system of communication:

> there were no dead, the satisfied workers had gone back to their families, and the banana company was suspending all activity until the rain stopped . . . the military denied it even to the relatives of the victims who crowded the commandant's office in search of news. "You must have been dreaming" the officer insisted. Nothing has happened in Macondo, nothing will ever happen. This is a happy town (p. 287).

We are left with two diametrically opposed versions: either it was a nightmarish dream that did not happen, or it was a tragedy deliberately covered up by the government, newspapers, and history books. García Márquez's response is to reveal how the massacre was made into a false document. In other words, he negates the "official" version. The aim of deconstruction in the novel, then, is to show the limits of historical discourse. He demolishes the government's and the textbooks' version by showing how historical, governmental, and discursive practices of the news media are constructed. Like the textbook that denies that Macondo ever had a banana plantation, much less a massacre, all texts, according to García Márquez, are written to deceive their readers. Colombia's past in official textbooks is as much an ideological fiction as is his own metahistory of Colombia in the novel. The critical difference between these two kinds of documents of civilization is that he is self-conscious about his fiction; his narrative reveals the deceiving intentions of all texts and how they should be read. The novel's final pages therefore show us how Macondo can exist only in the pages of the book that depicts it. In the end, the city of mirrors is a metaphor for a country of mirrors, mirages, and speaking fictions.

This point is made on the novel's last page. Macondo is a book, and when the book ends, so does Macondo. Throughout its history, the Buendía family has been indebted to Melquíades, the all-knowing Old World gypsy. Before he actually dies for the second time, Melquíades writes the entire history of the family in an incomprehensible code. The manuscript is left to the last of the Buendía line, Aureliano Babilonia, who discovers that it is written in Sanskrit. Yet even when he learns Sanskrit and translates the text, he finds it is written in another incomprehensible code. He finally masters the code, and what he reads is described in these words:

> It was the history of the family, written by Melquíades, down to the most trivial details, one hundred years ahead of time. He had written it in Sanskrit, which was his mother's tongue, and he had encoded the even lines in the private cipher of the Emperor Augustus and the odd ones in Lacedaemonian military code. The final protection . . . was based on the fact that Melquíades had not put events in the order of man's conventional time, but had concentrated a century of daily episodes in such a way that they coexisted in one instant of time. (pp. 381–82)

As the passage suggests, the effect of Melquíades's modernist text is not unlike Joyce's ambition in *Finnegans Wake* to construct all of humankind's life on earth, or Proust's monumental achievement in *A la récherche du temps perdu* to construct an altar where all dualities meet.

On the last page, Aureliano Babilonia reads of the "biblical hurricane" that finally destroys Macondo, and as he reads, the hurricane itself begins to assail him:

> Macondo was already a fearful whirlwind of dust and rubble being spun about the wrath of the biblical hurricane when Aureliano skipped eleven pages so as not to lose time with facts he knew only too well, and he began to decipher the instant he was living, deciphering it as he lived, prophesying himself in the act of deciphering the last pages of the parchments, as if he were looking into a speaking mirror. Then he skipped again to anticipate the predictions and ascertain the date and circumstance of his own death. Before reaching the final line, however, he had already understood that he would never leave the room, for it was foretold that the city of mirrors (or mirages) would be wiped out by the wind and exiled from the memory of men at the precise moment when Aureliano Babilonia would finish deciphering the parchments, and that everything written on them was unrepeatable since time immemorial and forever more, because races condemned to one hundred years of solitude did not have a second opportunity on earth. (p. 383)

Aureliano Babilonia is thus trapped in a magic room in which time stops forever. The final Buendía, he is condemned to a solitude forever lost in a world of mirrors, of mirages: a book.[56] Like Borges's extended metaphor (the book) in "Las ruinas circulares," where he suggests that we are projections of the imaginations of others (like the magician in the story who dreams a son, only to find out that he, himself, had been dreamed by someone else), Aureliano Babilonia discovers that he, too, is a figure (a trope) who has been dreamed by another.[57]

To summarize, García Márquez's early writing about Macondo—from *Leafstorm* to *One Hundred Years of Solitude*—is, as Sangari notes, his direct attempt to fulfill an emergent society's needs for self-description and radical assessment, to dismantle the master narratives of the West, and to displace traditional categories by which the "core" construes other American cultures in its own image or as "periphery" (see note 53). Whereas different modes of production, social formations, and ways of representation are dramatized in the author's emblematic figure of Big Mama, García Márquez criticizes the Western metanarratives of progress and modernization in *One Hundred Years of Solitude,* asserting within Melquíades's modernist text an indigenous hybrid realm of possibility in characters such as the two-hundred-year-old Francisco El Hombre, whose songs "told in great detail the things that had happened in the towns along his route, from Manaure to the edge of the swamp, so that if anyone had a message to send or an event to make public, he would pay him two cents to include it in his repertory" (p. 52). In these songs, García Márquez thematizes a mode of existence prior to the advent of capitalism and bourgeois society. And in *One Hundred Years of Solitude,* Francisco El Hombre's songs coincide with the function of songs in Paredes's, Rivera's, and Hinojosa's *corridos* and Shange's blues as the unwritten text of history and culture. In so doing, García Márquez implants in post-contemporary pan-American narratives a dialectic of historical transition where individual genealogy evokes the history of economic expropriation from core to periphery, and borderlands to metropolis.

3 Chicano Border Narratives as Cultural Critique

"Culture" is always relational, *between* subjects in relations of power. . . . Culture is contested, temporal, and emergent.
—James Clifford, *Writing Culture*

Roberto Fernández Retamar's Cuban-Marxist cultural critique of U.S. Empire as a way of life in the Americas and his moving deconstruction of the impact of Eurocentrism on Our American societies in *Caliban* and "Our America and the West" for some time have had a secure place in postcolonial critical scholarship in the Americas.[1] Likewise, García Márquez's allegorization of dependency in Macondo has become validated in Western literature courses. This is not true of the texts that form the basis of this chapter and the two following chapters: *"With His Pistol in His Hand": A Border Ballad and Its Hero,* by Américo Paredes; *Y no se lo tragó la tierra/And the Earth Did Not Part,* by Tomás Rivera; the *Klail City Death Trip* series, by Rolando Hinojosa; and *Borderlands/La Frontera: The New Mestiza* by Gloria Anzaldúa (chapter 3); *Sassafrass, Cypress & Indigo,* by Ntozake Shange (chapter 4); and *The Rain God,* by Arturo Islas (chapter 5).

Because these ethnic texts by Chicano/a writers and by an African American feminist writer appealed in the Americas to an oppositional audience in general, and to U.S. minority and feminist readers in particular, because some of these narratives were written in Spanish, or written in an African American vernacular, because all were written in response to white supremacy in the Southern and Southwestern United States, they have been excluded from the U.S. literary canon. This chapter makes the same kinds of arguments as the previous ones on Martí, Fernández Retamar, and García Márquez for taking U.S. minority discourses seriously as cultural critiques. As suggested in chapter 1, there are profound institutional continuities among Fernández Retamar, García Márquez, Hinojosa, and Shange. The chief continuity is their participation within the Casa de las Américas literary and cultural organizations in Havana. Put differently, in varying degrees all of these texts are engaged in the ongoing conversation of American cultures.

Let me be clear on this point. In *The Philosophy of Literary Form,* Kenneth Burke described this ongoing conversation:

> Imagine that you enter a parlor. You come late. When you arrive, others have long preceded you, and they are engaged in a heated discussion[,] too heated for them to pause and tell you exactly what it is about. . . . You listen for a while, until you decide that you have caught the tenor of the argument; then you put in your oar. Someone answers; you answer him; another comes to your defense; another aligns himself against you, to either the embarrassment or gratification of your opponent, depending upon the quality of your ally's assistance. However, the discussion is interminable. The hour grows late, you must depart. And you do depart, with the discussion still vigorously in progress.[2]

Burke depicts the cultural conversation as a series of rhetorical exchanges, with people asserting, questioning, answering, defending, attacking, and sometimes changing their arguments. It is an unending conversation that also contains rhetorical battles and skirmishes, rhetorical allies and enemies, and struggles for persuasive power. But so that we do not become too entangled, with pistols in hand, he supplies a nice twist: he places the verbal contests in a genteel parlor setting.

This ironic description of rhetorical politics will prove useful for framing our analysis of contemporary Chicano/a and African American narratives. At the outset it should be emphasized that literature's relationship to ideology, institutional practices, and cultural critique is complex. But as Steven Mailloux suggests in his study of Mark Twain's *Huckleberry Finn,* a text

> can be a topic in the cultural conversation, or it can be a participant who is motivated by and has effects on the conversation. As a participant, a literary text can take up the ideological rhetoric of its historical moment—the rhetoric of political speeches, newspaper editorials, book reviews, scholarly treatises, and so forth—and place it on a fictional stage. Readers thus become spectators at a rhetorical performance.[3]

With these critics' ideas in mind, we can turn to some of the staged arguments in contemporary Chicano Border narratives. In south Texas between 1958 and 1991, there has been a unique Chicano intellectual and cultural studies response to the white supremacist texts of the 1930s and 1940s by the eminent historian

Walter Prescott Webb and his followers. For many of south Texas' "organic intellectuals" it may be argued that their crosscultural scholarly outpouring in ethnography, history, historiography, and literature has been marked by a feeling for the concrete and specific, a familiarity with regional struggle, a sense of community and wholeness, and a sense of the tragic.[4] These Chicano/a intellectuals and writers from south Texas, like U.S. writers in the Southern Renaissance, engaged in an attempt to come to terms with the inherited values of a Chicano tradition in Nuevo Santander, but also with a certain way of perceiving and dealing with the past, what Nietzsche called "monumental historical consciousness."[5] Increasingly since 1958, the white supremacist tradition of Webb and his heirs has been progressively demystified and negated by Paredes, Rivera, Hinojosa, and Anzaldúa.

Ideological Rhetoric in Texas

> Ask the Apache the why of his going,/Ask the Comanche, he's not knowing,/Question the Mexican thief and marauder/Why his respect for the great Texas Ranger/Question them all, these beaten-back strangers,/White-lipped they'll tremble and whisper, "The Rangers."
> —Albert Edmund Trombly, "Texas Rangers"

> Then said Gregorio Cortez, With his pistol in his hand, Ah, so many mounted Rangers/Just to take one Mexican.
> —"El *corrido* de Gregorio Cortez"

Américo Paredes's *"With His Pistol in His Hand": A Border Ballad and Its Hero* appeared in 1958 in the midst of a long, heated quarrel over what Webb, among others, had to say about Mexicans in the United States. By the end of the nineteenth century, the ideological rhetoric of white supremacy dominated Southern and Southwestern politics and eventually became institutionalized in state discourses, laws, and narratives regulating relations of whites with nonwhites, especially blacks and Chicanos. In the twentieth century Webb was one of the leading spokespersons of his period's institutionalized racism. As one of his close friends, Necah Furman, said: Webb "subconsciously . . . had the Alamo-Texas Ranger chauvinistic myth deeply engraved."[6] In *The Texas Rangers: A Century of Frontier Defense* (1935), for example, Webb characterized Mexicans in this way: "Without disparagement, there is a cruel streak in the Mexican nature, or so the history would lead us to believe. This cruelty may be a heritage from the Spanish of the Inquisition; it may, and doubtless should, be attributed partly to the Indian blood."[7]

Although Webb had proposed the integration of blacks into the Texas State Historical Association, he, like other native white supremacists in Texas, had a profound prejudice against Mexicans on both sides of the border. Quotations such as the one above illustrate his regional stereotyping of Mexicans. To understand the cultural conversation in Texas more fully, then, it is important to examine his institutional study of the Texas Rangers.

When in 1918 Webb joined the history department's faculty at the University of Texas at Austin, he began scholarly research on the institution of the Texas Rangers, which culminated in his M.A. thesis. In 1935 he published his history with Houghton Mifflin. Almost overnight, in the words of one writer, his book became "acknowledged as the definitive study of this frontier law enforcement agency."[8] With a Southern white supremacist orientation, he traced the Rangers' changing functions from the heroic roles they played in frontier and Border communities in the 1830s to their institutional reorganization in 1935, when a Chicano state representative, J. T. Canales, from Brownsville, led an investigation of their abuse of power as "peace officers."[9]

Although Webb's "objective" and "disinterested" institutional history was filled, in the author's own words, "with deadening facts," *The Texas Rangers* soon became a best-seller. His description of the Rangers as "very quiet, deliberate gentle person[s]" (p. ix) became so popular that Paramount Pictures purchased the film rights for $11,000, a fee that undoubtedly made Professor Webb's depression days at the university easier to bear. *The Texas Rangers,* ninety-five minutes in length, was directed by King Vidor, who also had directed such favorites as *Billy the Kid.* Fred MacMurray, Jack Oakie, Lloyd Nolan, and Elena Martinez were the stars. Not surprisingly, the movie was made in association with the state's centennial celebration. A mediocre sequel, *The Texas Rangers Ride Again,* was released in 1941 with John Howard and Ellen Drew. The 1936 original was then remade as *Streets of Laredo* in 1949, with William Holden, Macdonald Carey, and William Bendix in starring roles.

Unfortunately, the racial strife that existed between Chicanos and Texas Rangers on both sides of the U.S./Mexican Border was characteristically absent in both Webb's and Hollywood's dashing portrayals of the lawmen. To understand the underside of the history of the Texas Rangers in more detail, we need to examine the cultural studies of Paredes, Rivera, Hinojosa, and Anzaldúa as socially symbolic responses to Webb.

Criticism in the Borderlands: The Cultural Work of Paredes, Rivera, Hinojosa, and Anzaldúa

Into this rhetorical battle and institutional cultural conversation on the Rangers at the University of Texas at Austin came the oppositional voice of Américo Paredes, a Chicano from south Texas, the son of a revolutionary father who "rode a raid or two with Catarino Garza."[10] By the 1930s Paredes was a superb singer of *corridos* (ballads of Border conflict) and an accomplished composer and guitarist. He had even performed with Chelo Silva, the well-known Texas-Mexican vocalist. During World War II he wrote for *Stars and Stripes*, the U.S. Army's daily newspaper. After the war, he returned to Texas, where he entered the university at Austin—Webb's home turf. According to José E. Limón, one of Paredes's students, "By taking course overloads and summer school, [Paredes] compressed two years of college work into one and took his B.A. in 1951 with highest honors. . . . Then, for Américo Paredes anyway, it was quite simply a matter of five years for a master's degree and a Ph.D. in English. . . ."[11] In 1957 Paredes joined the university's English department, and by the end of that year the University of Texas Press accepted his doctoral dissertation for publication. It would have been controversial enough if Paredes's *"With His Pistol in His Hand"* had been written by an Anglo-American Northerner, but a book written in the Southwest by a Chicano, taking on Webb and the Rangers in polemical argument was almost unthinkable.

Paredes begins his narrative of Gregorio Cortez, a Border vaquero of the early 1900s who resisted legal justice, fought the Texas Rangers, and became a folk hero to the Chicano community, by presenting a lengthy chapter on Border culture—Nuevo Santander—and on the aesthetics of south Texas. In the words of Teresa

McKenna, Paredes "gives an encompassing view of an area which geographically, as well as politically and culturally, stands as figure and metaphor for the transition between nations and the complex of connections which continue to exist for all Mexicans whether border residents or not."[12] Moreover, Paredes begins by offering, in profuse detail, a critique of Southern white supremacist ideology. He claims that "the English speaking Texan . . . disappoints us in a folkloric sense. He produces no balladry. His contribution to the literature of the border conflict is a set of attitudes and beliefs about the Mexican which form a legend of their own and are the complement to the *corrido,* the Border-Mexican ballad of border conflict."[13]

Paredes then analyzes the "set of attitudes and beliefs about the Mexican which form a legend" and perpetuate the stereotype of Mexicans as "cruel," "cowardly," "inferior," "passive," "mongrel," and "treacherous." This ideological definition allows Texan Anglos to justify their abridgment of Chicano liberties. According to Paredes, however, this invidious, crude, and humiliating view of the Mexican is found not in folktales of the people of Texas, but in publications of nonfolk origin: "It is in print—in newspapers, magazines, and books" (p. 16).

By choosing to analyze a Border ballad of resistance, Paredes critiqued Webb's romanticized and ideological reading of Texas Rangers. For to investigate the *corrido*'s rhetoric, according to Paredes, is to unfold its complicated critique of white supremacy as ideological performance. And by staging rhetorical exchanges and debates with Webb—in his story of Gregorio Cortez—Paredes maneuvered his audience to cooperate in this narrative performance. His debate with Webb begins in the following way: "In more recent years, it has often been the writer of history textbooks and the author of scholarly works who have lent their prestige to the legend [about Mexicans]" (p. 17). He counters Webb's proposition ("there is a cruel streak in the Mexican nature . . .") by noting, ironically, that "one wonders what [Webb's] opinion might have been when he was in a less scholarly mood and not looking at the Mexican from the objective point of view of the historian" (p. 17). The irony is that what Paredes playfully denies about Webb's "objective point of view" as historian, Webb affirmed in action and deeds.

Not surprisingly, the ideological drama of Paredes's *"With His Pistol in His Hand"* relies for much of its persuasive success on the author's irreverent sense of humor and irony. As he says of the voluminous writings about the Texas Rangers, "If all the books written about the Rangers were put on top of the other, the resulting pile would be almost as tall as some of the tales they contain" (p. 23).

The historical and biographical information contained in the first part of *"With His Pistol in His Hand"* is meant as a tonic for those readers, like Paredes himself, for whom Webb's and Hollywood's portrayal of the Rangers had for so long been anything but "objective": "The shoot-first and ask questions later method of the Rangers," he writes, "has been romanticized into something dashing and daring, in technicolor, on a wide screen, and with Gary Cooper in the title role" (p. 28). After discussing the history of Nuevo Santander, the aesthetics of the Border, the *corrido,* and its folkways—Paredes turns to rhetorical analysis. Part II concentrates on the many versions of the *corrido* of Border conflict and on a close reading of the *corrido* proper. He establishes these crucial points about the Border ballad's ideological form: (1) the *corrido* is a multifaceted discourse, with reflexive, narrative, and rhetorical-propositional elements; (2) *corridos* as social texts tend to be historical, personal, and inscrutable; and (3) *corridos* make assertions that derive from the collective outlook and experience of the Mexican ballad community on the Border.[14] Finally, as a composer, guitarist, and singer, he sees the *corrido* as a performance-oriented genre sung mostly by men, but occasionally by women.

But Paredes was no mere formalist. He interpreted the *corrido* as a literary form of resistance to the encroachment of Anglo-Americans, arguing that the *corrido,* as a socially symbolic act, usually recounts the exploits of a hero who surpasses all odds to prevail with dignity, grace, and courage against those in power. Specifically, in "El corrido de Gregorio Cortez," he examines how the hero, who was falsely accused of horse stealing and murdering Sheriff Morris, outran and outsmarted a wild posse of Rangers over half the state of Texas. In overturning the passive view of the Chicano, Paredes recounts how common Mexicans defended their Border communities and families through confrontations with the Anglo-American ruling class and their agents—the Texas Rangers. As asserted by the *corrido* (which I often heard as a young boy in Brownsville), Cortez was exemplary of those who defended their rights "con la pistola en la mano."

Paredes's *"With His Pistol in His Hand"* thus is the first sophisticated Chicano narrative to begin to overturn established authority in Texas and the Southwest. He shows how the *corrido* itself broke down white supremacist hierarchies: the "gentle," brave men of Texas, the Rangers, were, in fact, cowardly and foolish ("All the rangers of the county/Were flying, they rode so hard." . . . "But trying to catch Cortez/Was like following a star";)[15] a "macho" Major Sheriff screams out to Cortez "as if he was going to cry"; the inferior slave, Cortez, turns out to be superior to his Texas Anglo masters: "Then said Gregorio Cortez, With his pistol in his hand,/ Ah, so many mounted Rangers/Just to take one Mexican." This overturning of hierarchies functions, Paredes argued, to dismantle the opposition on which much of the white supremacy of Webb and others was based.

It is not surprising, then, that Chicano cultural critics and literary historians often mention the momentous impact Paredes's work had on Chicano literature. Renato Rosaldo writes, "Ahead of its time, [it] embodied a sophisticated conception of culture where conflict, domination, and resistance, rather than coherence and consensus, were the central subjects of analysis."[16] Similarly, Ramón Saldívar in "The Form of Texas-Mexican Fiction" asserts that "with impeccable scholarship and imaginative subtlety, Dr. Paredes' study . . . may be said to have invented the very possibility of a narrative community, a complete and legitimate Texas-Mexican *persona,* whose life of struggle and discord was worthy of being told."[17] Finally, Tomás Rivera and Rolando Hinojosa have acknowledged the influence that Paredes's narrative of resistance had on their own emergent literary production.[18] To be sure, however, Rivera's, Hinojosa's, and Anzaldúa's rhetorical performances in their narratives were just as subversive of racist, white supremacist ideology as Paredes's more explicit attacks.

The Rhetoric of Ideology and Utopia in South Texas

> Utopia is an ideological critique of ideology.
> —Louis Marin

Tomás Rivera's Quinto Sol prize-winning *Y no se lo tragó la tierra*—misread in its early years[19]—is one of the Southwest's richest dialectical novels. Rivera's fiction delves deeply into the life of a young, anonymous migrant worker by analyzing his growth and maturity within the cyclical frame of a year. *Tierra* not only studies the protagonist's rites of passage, but shows how his solitary, chaotic life fits together within a class pattern of solidarity among other migrant farmworkers. This collective class pattern, in turn, has its own utopian patterns because Rivera's performed ideology of the text is not an uncritical picture of a U.S. social and economic world, but a reality apprehended in terms of a large cultural and political conversation during the 1940s and 1950s in south Texas. The work's aesthetic qualities, moreover, are achieved through a cultural conversation with the Latin American new narrative—specifically, the strategies rendered in Mexican novelist and short story writer Juan Rulfo's *El llano en llamas*.

Among semiotic forces, the most significant in Rivera's *Tierra* are its negation of a fixed, coherent narrative sequence and the structural breakdown of conventional cause-and-effect. His new narrative, like Rulfo's text, offers a disordered and fragmented story line but succeeds in creating a view of the Chicano migrant world from the protagonist's consciousness.

Rivera's rendering of the migrant farmworker's stark social and economic conditions is profoundly accurate. The novel's atmosphere is full of shocks, tragedies, and political and social repressions. Unfulfilled passions and desires, fear and chaos, stand out as tangible phenomena. The migrant farmworkers who live and die on the agricultural fields of south Texas, and on the long, lonely roads of Midwestern America, are treated as nameless individuals whose lives are filled with suffering, misery, and anguish. Collectively, however, these migrant farmworkers, like their honorable and dignified ancestors celebrated in the *corridos* of the Southwest Borderlands, struggle against injustice, hardship, and physical and psychological abuse. Beyond the anonymous protagonist's fragmented inner world lurks an unspeakable world of violence and suffering: murder, child abuse, labor exploitation, guilt, and grief. Nevertheless, the protagonist, like his fellow farmworkers, lives on and struggles. In addition, Rivera's contribution to American cultural conversation stems from his depiction of a dawning sense of Chicano farmworkers' solidarity with other members of their race and class. Class consciousness in *Tierra* expresses the utopian unity of a collectivity.[20]

To understand Rivera's bold cultural conversation and grasp his striking folkloric and postmodernist representation of the Chicano farmworker's character, one must comprehend the novel's dual purpose as part of a social documentation of rural America in the 1940s and 1950s and as a heterogeneous, multidimensional Chicano novel. In its entirety, as Rivera tells us, the novel is an expression and commentary on the Chicano farmworker's struggle.

Tierra thus registers and apprehends an emerging consciousness of political resistance that came into being during the late 1960s and early 1970s in the United States. Rivera not only was responding to a white supremacist view of Chicano farmworkers who were treated "worse than slaves," but was dipping his own argumentative oar into the debate that Paredes had started in 1958. In a real way, Rivera entered the parlor of American literature and aligned himself with Paredes. In a famous interview with Juan Bruce-Novoa, he clearly spelled out his relationship with Paredes:

> I was hungry to find something by a Chicano or a Mexican-American. ["*With His Pistol in His Hand*"] fascinated me because, one, it proved it was possible for a Chicano to publish; two, it was about a Chicano, Gregorio Cortez, and his deeds. And the ballads, the *corridos* too. I grew up with the *corridos* de Texas. That book indicated to me that it was possible to talk about a Chicano as a complete character. . . . More importantly, [Paredes's book] indicated to me a whole imaginative possibility for us to explore.[21]

It can be argued that Rivera's migrant farmworkers, like Paredes's characters, are simple, honorable men and women who will defend their families, homes, and communities with grace and courage. Likewise, on a metahistorical level, after reading Paredes's narrative, Rivera came to see himself clearly as a potential documenter of Chicano social history: "I felt that I had to document the migrant worker para siempre (forever), para que no se olvidara ese espíritu tan fuerte de resistir y continuar (so that their very strong will to resist and endure under the worst of conditions would not be forgotten) because they were worse than slaves" (pp. 150–51).

Other windows for Rivera's development as an artist opened. During 1968–69, when *Tierra* was written, Chicano political activity was at its peak. According to the Chicano historian Ricardo Romo, as a result of protests among students, antiwar demonstrations, and the development of La Raza Unida Party, the Chicano Movement was born.[22] With considerable success, Romo stresses, the

Chicano Movement attempted to instill ethnic pride and point out inequities in the judicial system; it was these developments that gave rise to a new political consciousness. Gutíerrez's La Raza Unida Party in Crystal City for the first time in Texas history began to appropriate political power from what until then had been a politically dominant Anglo minority.[23] Many members of this new political party were migrant farmworkers; indeed, Rivera's family itself had been part of this migratory cycle (Bruce-Novoa, pp. 139–41). *Tierra* took up the ideological rhetoric of the moment and dramatized the farmworkers' world for all to see. Indeed, its rhetoric fought for American history's remembering these forgotten and undocumented workers' social struggle. Thus, for the first time, readers became spectators of the vivid shocks and fragmentation that Chicano migrant farmworkers experienced in late capitalism in rural America.

In *Tierra,* Rivera's anonymous protagonist initially is unable to decide whether he wakes or dreams, whether his own voice is present or absent. In other words, this migrant child is unable to distinguish between the realms of consciousness and unconsciousness: "oía que alguien le llamaba por su nombre pero cuando volteaba la cabeza a ver quien le llamaba, daba vuelta entera y así quedaba mismo" ("He would hear someone call him by name. He would turn around to see who was calling, always making a complete turn, always ending in the same position and facing the same way").[24] From the first chapter, then, the protagonist is caught in a vicious cycle of subjectivity from which he desperately wants to escape. In the book's early parts, the protagonist has little or no contact with the outside world, with other migrant farmworkers, for he is figuratively trapped in the prison house of self. Not until he enters the fresh air of the outside world in the last section of the novel, "Debajo De La Casa," does he emerge into the collective and utopian world of the human community, for he now desires to see "a toda esa gente junta. Y luego si tuviera unos brazos bien grandes los podría abrazar a todos" ("all those people together. And if I had long enough arms, I could embrace them all at the same time") [p. 125].

From the novel's first section, its events create psychological urgency since we realize that the protagonist has no clear sense of his identity and does not perceive himself as free to create one.[25] Further, he is always thinking or attempting to think dialectically:

"Se dio cuenta de que siempre pensaba y de allí no podia salir" (He discovered that he was always thinking that he was thinking, and he couldn't stop this") [p. 1]. That is, as Fredric Jameson said in *Marxism and Form,* dialectical thinking is "thought about thought, thought to the second power which at the same time remains aware of its own intellectual operations in the very act of thinking."[26] Such self-consciousness is the very subject the novel dramatizes. Indeed, "El año perdido" expresses the beginning of consciousness and the inability to articulate it; the novel also shows why dialectical thinking is both indispensable and almost impossible. In broad terms, we should regard Rivera's new narrative as a text about the development of political and dialectical thinking, where the reader reconstructs, critically analyzes, and reorganizes the past.

In "La noche estaba plateaba," "Y no se lo tragó la tierra," and "Cuando lleguemos," Rivera's ideological arguments are most discernible. In "La noche estaba plateaba," for example, the protagonist begins to break down his mother's passive and ideological strategies of containment in Catholicism with its binary oppositions of good and evil, God and Devil. At midnight the boy walks into the woods to summon the Devil. He searches for the Devil because he has been immersed in Mexican and Chicano folkloric tales: "Lo del diablo le había fascinado desde cuando no se acordaba" ("The thought of the Devil had fascinated him ever since he could remember") [p. 40]. Like many young people with Catholic backgrounds, the boy simply desires to know whether or not the Devil, and by extension God, exists, for "si no hay diablo no hay. . . . No, más vale no decirlo" ("And if there is no Devil, then there is. . . . No, I'd better not say it") [p. 42]. The boy calls out for the Devil, but the Devil never appears. If there is no Devil, then it follows for the boy that there is no God.

This deconstruction, more logical than political in Rivera's new narrative, is followed by another cultural critique in "y no se lo tragó la tierra." The chapter begins in the midst of a hot south Texas day in an agricultural field. Suffocating humidity hangs in the air as a small group of migrant farmworkers weed a crop. Working in these horrible, dehumanizing conditions, the boy's father had suffered a heatstroke the previous day. Beginning with an account of this event, the boy recalls the events that will lead him to curse the supreme authority in his culture—God. Next he tells us how he yelled at his mother, for all his brothers and sisters to hear: "Qué se gana, mama con andar . . . [clamando por la misericodia de Dios?] . . . si Dios no se acuerda de uno. . . . N'ombre a Dios le importa nada de uno. . . . Dígame usted por que? Por qué nosotros nomás enterrados en la tierra como animales sin ningunas esperanzas de nada?" ("What do you gain by doing that, mother . . . [clamoring for the mercy of God?]. . . . God doesn't give a damn about us poor people. . . . Tell me why should we always be tied to the dirt, half-buried in the earth like animals without hope of any kind?" [p. 50]. From this picture of the reality of conditions in the fields, the boy has to face the tragic reality of his younger brother's heatstroke: "Por qué a papa y luego a mi hermanito? . . . Por qué?" (Why my father, and now my little brother?" [p. 54].

Instructed by his parents never to curse God, lest he be swallowed up by the earth, he violates a Catholic taboo: "Entonces le entro coraje de nuevo y se desahogó maldiciendo a Dios" ("Then anger swelled up in him again and he unleashed it by cursing God") [p. 54]. Although the boy imagines that the earth is opening to "devour" him by this subversive act, once and for all he breaks free from his mother's Catholic ideology. And just as he had experienced a joyous serenity in "La noche plateaba," here he feels "una paz que nunca habia sentido antes" ("a peace he had never experienced before") [p. 54]. In short, by liberating himself from the idealism of Catholicism, he is able to continue on his lonely road of reconstructing a holistic sense of self and group identity.[27] As such, Rivera's *Tierra* dramatizes the symptoms of the protagonist's experience in consumer capitalism. Only in the emergence of a postindividualistic social world, only in the reconstruction of the collective and the utopian, can one begin to achieve a new consciousness, Rivera's protagonist finds. Only through a new and original form of collective social life in the human community can one overcome the self's isolation so that an individual consciousness can be lived.

Although Rivera's novel contains many moments of hopelessness, and he often rhetorically dramatizes the anguish, fear, and chaos of the existential Chicano subject, the overriding history he recounts is less tragic than hopeful. This occurs because he sees a future made out of the stark working conditions of the past, an ideological order of solidarity and liberation reasserted in such brief chapters as "Cuando lleguemos." Here, he focuses on everyday events, that is, on the scene of all social struggle in human lives.

"Cuando lleguemos" dramatizes the journey of more than forty workers traveling on the back of a truck on a seemingly endless journey from south Texas to Minnesota. Often going an entire day without rest, the workers survive with an indomitable will to endure. One night, somewhere near Des Moines, the truck breaks down. The workers must wait until repairs can be made. As in most of the novel, Rivera gives us stream-of-consciousness monologues that contain the thoughts of about ten men. Each nameless individual voices a variety of thoughts, especially frustration and suffering. Although one of them reflects on the profound beauty and stillness of the stars before dawn ("De aquí se ven a toda madre las estrellas"), the majority express the futility of their lives: "Cuando lleguemos, cuando lleguemos, ya, la mera verdad estoy cansado de llegar" ("When we arrive, when we arrive, at this point, I'm tired of always arriving") [p. 114]. In the end, what keeps them struggling is the faint hope implied in the repeated phrase "cuando lleguemos." "Cuando lleguemos" ["When we arrive"] can be said to represent the utopian surplus of the workers' unfulfilled dreams and desires. The chapter and phrase is the novel's motif. Rivera's concept of hope is a concrete utopia, grounded in immanently developing tendencies working from the present toward something better. There is always a solid, underlying hope that the workers will someday arrive in the full light of equal opportunity, employment, and desegregation. As one of them says, "Yo creo que siempre lo mejor es tener esperanzas" ("I suppose it is always best to have hope") [p. 94].

Writing Border Culture and History: The Poetics and Politics of Hinojosa's *Klail City Death Trip* Series

I write about Belken County and its people . . . who knows them as well as I do?
—Rolando Hinojosa, from *Chicano Authors*, by Juan Bruce-Novoa

Paredes and Rivera saw their own narratives not only as texts that embody enduring themes but as attempts to change the social order in Texas and the Southwest. With Rolando Hinojosa's *Klail City Death Trip* series, Chicano narratives begin to speak an "internationalist" cultural language. From his wonderful blending of history and myth in the style of Faulkner and García Márquez in

Estampas del Valle to his postmodernist detective novel, *Partners in Crime,* Hinojosa's emergent historical novel about south Texas is itself a *mestizaje,* a cross-breeding, of traditional and nontraditional North American and Latin American literary and cultural traditions. When in 1976 *Klail City y sus alrededores,* Hinojosa's second novel was awarded the Casa de las Américas' prize for the novel, contemporary Chicano narratives in general and Hinojosa's narratives in particular became serious objects of literary study among the Left in the Americas and Europe.

Two years after its initial publication in Havana, *Klail City y sus alrededores* was translated into German by Yolanda Julia Broyles, and *Klail City und Umgebung* was disseminated and read throughout the Eastern European bloc.[28] Suhrkamp Verlag, the Federal Republic of Germany's premier publisher, then adopted Broyles's translation for publication in the West. According to Broyles, "the publisher's only problem was whether to market the work as part of the Latin American program or part of the United States literature program" (p. 109). Hinojosa's new narrative dramatizes Chicano literature's profound intertextual and crosscultural footing in both U.S. and Latin American literatures. Indeed, the new narrative, as Broyles rightly suggests, "is a prime example of the type of Chicano literature which is *sin fronteras* [without borders]. It is born at the spiritual, political and economic intersection of the Anglo and Mexican worlds" (p. 109).

In 1973, with the publication of *Estampas del Valle y Otras Obras* [*Sketches of the Valley and Other Works*], the first of nine volumes about Klail City and its environs, Hinojosa offers us another powerful example of the way the Chicano Border culture thinks about itself, articulating and redefining the cultural conversations that shape a particular historical moment. His series tells us, in a fragmentary, decentered manner, much about the complex story of change and race relations in south Texas. As the author has said, "The books are a telescopic view tracing a 200 year history."[29]

The past, Karl Marx wrote, "weighs like a nightmare on the brain of the living."[30] The history of race relations in south Texas between "fuereño" white supremacists and native Chicanos seems a striking illustration of this dictum. A rigid and political dichotomy between white Texas Anglo farmers and Chicano ranchers, an ideology of racist xenophobia, a dependent labor force with limited economic opportunities—these and other patterns seem always to survive. As George L. Robertson suggested in a letter to his sister, Texas Anglos characteristically loathed the native peoples of the Rio Grande Valley:

> I am getting tired of the Rio Grande and the greasers, of all the contemptable, despecable [*sic*] people on the Earth, the greasers in my estimation are the lowest, meaner than the Comanche. They are ugly, thieving, rascally in every way and to be educated only makes a greaser the grander rascal. I think the whole nation ought to be peoned rich and poor, they would make the best plantation hands in the world. They fear and respect authority and are a great deal moore [*sic*] humble and less intelligent than our negroes.[31]

Robertson's white supremacist position was not an anomalous Texan ideology of unbridled racist hostility toward Chicanos. Moreover, in light of the long tradition of armed resistance by Chicanos recorded in numerous Border *corridos,* Robertson's reading of the Texas-Mexican's "fear" and "respect" for authority was not historically accurate. His remarks, however, represent the way white male settlers thought about Chicanos. But what caused this invidious racism?

According to the historian Arnoldo De León, "Americans moving to the west . . . had much more in mind than settling the land and creating prosperous communities. Cultural heirs to Elizabethans and Puritans, those moving into the hinterlands sensed an 'errand into the wilderness' and felt a compelling need to control all that was beastly—sexuality, vice, nature, and colored peoples."[32]

White supremacists first entered Texas when the Mexican government in 1821 granted colonization rights to Moses Austin. Stephen F. Austin later recalled the purpose of this immigration: "[I wanted] to redeem Texas from the wilderness. . . . My object, the sole and only desire of my ambitions since I first saw Texas, was to redeem it from the wilderness—to settle it with an intelligent honorable and interprising [*sic*] people" (p. 3).

Of course, what Austin meant through his frontier rhetoric was a "whitening" of Texas. As De León suggests, Austin wanted to make the Texas frontier "a cultural and racial copy of the United States" (p. 3). In Austin's words, "I wished a great immigration from Kentucky, Tennessee, every where, passports, or no passport any how."[33]

As these white settlers arrived, many came with their white supremacist attitudes. Indeed, they also brought xenophobic attitudes against Catholics and Spaniards as well as supremacist contempt for Indians and blacks. According to De León, "Mexicans were doubly suspect, as heirs to Catholicism and as descendants of Spaniards, Indians, and Africans" (p. 4).

As a result of these sentiments, hundreds of native Mexicans in Texas fell victim to lynch laws and ruthless attacks by white settlers and the Texas Rangers. In response to Webb, De León wrote: "From a small body of volunteers charged with scouting against Indians in the 1820s, it became a corps that enjoyed the tacit sanction of the white community to do to Mexicans in the name of the law what others did extra-legally" (pp. 75–76).

Hinojosa's historical series[34] negates many of the "disinterested" and "objective" narrative versions of Texas history. In addition to Chicanos being subdued, ranches stolen, and the frontier somehow "won," he allegorizes the period's pernicious underside.

Two distinct south Texas worlds are at the center of his new narrative: a Mexican ranch society in which old guard Texas-Mexicans such as Esteban Echevarría, Evaristo Garrido, Manuel Guzmán, and Braulio Tapia regard with pessimistic resignation a degenerating way of life where people seem helpless to control their fate; and an Anglo-Texan, white supremacist farm society. The testimony of Earl Bennet, a Texas Anglo, is representative of the blatant white supremacist attitudes in the series: "The trouble with Mexicans is that if we give 'em a raise, they'll either get lazy or they'll quit on you; just like that. Looky here: they make as much as they want, and if we step in and give them some more, why, they'll just blow it away. You know they 'git drunk' and play them some rancheras on the juke box there and adiós mi dinero boys. And that's no lie: I know what I'm talking about" (p. 72).

Clearly, the *Klail City Death Trip* series is about these two societies, but only gradually does the author provide the explosive historical setting in which these tensions and conflicts become fully evident. Thus, to fully explicate Hinojosa's emergent Chicano historical novel, let me place the literary text within a broader U.S.-Mexican Border cultural context.

In his penetrating book *Anglos and Mexicans in the Making of Texas, 1836–1986,* David Montejano has demonstrated that the central history of Nuevo Santander and south Texas focuses on the gradual erosion of native Mexican class order.[35] Around the time of the 1848 annexation there existed in south Texas a landed Mexican elite, an entrepreneur Anglo mercantile clique, a class of autonomous but impoverished Mexican *rancheros,* and a working class of Mexican peones. In Montejano's view, the next fifty years witnessed "the gradual erosion" of this order. The reasons are complex, but according to him Mexican rancheros could not compete in the booming cattle market and, as a result, were gradually "eliminated" (p. 51). Although some Chicanos kept their Rio Grande Valley lands through intermarriages, other Mexican elites held on to their properties through political alliances with Anglo white supremacists. In Hinojosa's new narrative, the unscrupulous Leguizamón family, his version of Faulkner's Snopes clan in Mississippi, keep their land in this way. Cattle society thus became the region's dominant social and economic institution, and as a result, Montejano concludes, the relations binding the Anglo patron and his Mexican workers were "circumscribed by paternalism, reciprocal obligations, and permanency" (p. 82).

At the turn of the century, however, when irrigation techniques, refrigerated railcars, and other innovative technologies made farming profitable in the arid frontier Border lands, second-generation Anglo elites initiated what Montejano terms "an agricultural revolution." For economic reasons, the ranch country traditionally belonging to Chicanos was cleared, making room for Anglo farmers and a growing economy of underclass agricultural workers, and "market development for the Mexican community signified a collapsing of the internal class structure" (p. 74).

As Hinojosa shows us again and again, the new relations between the Anglo-Texas farm owners and Chicano workers are largely impersonal. With the triumph of farming over ranching, a striking segregation of the races emerged. In this respect, Hinojosa seems to agree with Montejano that "so effective were . . . paternalistic work arrangements that they survived as a feature of South Texas ranch life well into the twentieth-century" (p. 81).

Because Hinojosa's fictional world of Belken County has taken shape gradually, critics and scholars have been slow to realize that an analysis of his work dramatizing a profound alienation in south Texas society should include not only critical interpretations of individual texts but consideration of the whole corpus of the series owing to recurrent characters, scenes, retelling of historical events, and repetition of themes.

As it stands, Hinojosa's series is both integrated and disintegrated. Each narrative composes an integrative creation at the same time that it works out its own individual detachment from it.

In the fifteenth- and sixteenth-century Hispanic chronicle traditions of Peréz de Guzmán and Hernando del Pulgar, in the transgeographical tradition of Martí's "Nuestra América," the Chicano literary tradition of Paredes's *"With His Pistol in His Hand,"* and in the traditions of the disintegrating Americas of Faulkner and García Márquez, Hinojosa's new narrative through its doctrine of the "political unconscious" counters historical amnesia by restoring to the materiality of its signifiers the buried reality of south Texas history. As the author has said:

> For me and mine, history began in 1749 when the first colonists began moving into the southern and northern banks of the Rio Grande. That river was not yet a jurisdictional barrier and was not to be until almost 100 years later; but, by then, the border had its own history, its own culture, and its own sense of place: it was Nuevo Santander, named for old Santander in the Spanish Peninsula.[36]

The *Klail City Death Trip* series, like García Márquez's new narratives about Macondo, is the overall title of a number of multidimensional historical novels. It is first an ascent insofar as the Chicano community struggles, lives, and survives in a segregated society; and second, it is a descent from its Nuevo Santander past insofar as the old and new guard Chicano Borderers grow more alienated and marginalized by an Anglo farm society and economic world. This profound alienation, or breakdown of kinship, in Mexican ranch society can be discerned in many sections of the series, but it is especially dramatized in *Claros Varones de Belken/Fair Gentlemen of Belken County.* In a moving section, "Con el pie en el Estribo" ["Going West"], where Esteban Echevarría, one of the novel's principal "native informants," confides to Rafa Buenrostro, one of the novel's principal narrators-social historians:

> Casa sin corredores, calles sin faroles, amigos que mueren, jóvenes que ya no hablan espanol ni saben saludar. . . . Je! desaparece el Valle. . . . Los bolillos con sus propiedades, sus bancos y contratos. Si. Gente que no reconoce un choque de mano como cosa

> legal. . . . Pa'qué le sirve a uno vivir ochenta y tres años si todo lo que uno vio nacer está enterrado? Los Vilches? Muertos! Los Tuero? También! Los Buenrostro se acaban y las familias fundadores se secan como las hojas del mesquite doliente. (Homes without porches, streets without lamp lights, friends who've died away, and youngsters who no longer speak Spanish. . . . Hah! The Valley's no longer, no longer the Valley, folks. The Anglos and their landed property, their banks, their legal contracts. Sure. People who know nothing of the legally binding handshake. . . . What's the use of reaching eighty-three if everything's gone up in smoke? The Vilches? Dead. The Tueros? They're dead too! The Buenrostros are almost gone and the founding families are drying up like leaves on a dying mesquite tree.) (p. 207)

Echevarría's task here is to restructure the problems of ideology, the unconscious, desire, and cultural production around the process of oral narrative. Like Faulkner's and García Márquez's characters, Hinojosa's Echevarría indulges in an ideological nostalgia for an idyllic past where "ese Río Grande . . . era para beber y no pa' detener los de un lado contra el otro" ("that Rio Grande, which was for drinking, not for keeping those on one side away from the others on the other side") (p. 206), and where Chicanos defended their homes, families, and communities, with pistol in hand, if necessary. In other words, many of Hinojosa's old guard Chicanos want to stop the clock of Anglo farm society time, or regard with pessimistic resignation the breakdown of their Mexican ranch way of life. Thus, thematically, tradition in the past versus "reification" in the present and future is a basic idea of the series.[37]

Stylistically, the author uses his dialogical imagination to depict a changing historical materialism in south Texas. Numerous characters reveal themselves through what Mikhail M. Bakhtin calls "heteroglossia," that is, discourses from varied strata of society.[38] Indeed, Hinojosa employs a multiplicity of characters and storytellers, making many of them recurring personae, because he wants to resist monologism and closure: "I don't work," he tells us, "as if life begins here and ends there, A to Z. . . . My novels don't end—they are open-ended, and you never know what is going to happen to these people later on. . . . I pick them up at different stages of their lives because that's how you run across people."[39] It should be stressed, then, that the essence of Hinojosa's new narrative does not lie in its plot. As the author says, "My stories are not held together by the *peripeteia,* or plot, as much as by *what* the people who populate the stories say and *how* they say it. . . . (p. 21) But there are countless dramatic incidents in the narrative, unexpected changes of direction in peoples' lives within a segregated society, and revelations of further depths in the collective Border character.

Hinojosa's first published text, *Estampas del Valle y Otras Obras* (1973), introduced elements that recur in nearly all of his later work—Klail City, a fictional town in the Rio Grande Valley, in the midst of a larger North American *société de consummation;* political and racial feuds that intermarriages and barbecues cannot heal; and the Rio Grande Valley Borderlands, which become objects of material desire and social struggle.

Structurally, *Estampas del Valle* comprises four discontinuous parts: twenty portraits of the Valley and its people by the participant-observer Jehú Malacara; six documents describing Baldemar Cordero's fatal stabbing of Ernesto Tamez; a chronicle of brave, loyal, and "treacherous" Texas Mexicans; and Rafa Buenrostros (another central participant-observer) remembering his school days and the Korean War.

As with most of the nine narratives, *Estampas del Valle* gives a fleeting perspective of the characters' lives; Braulio Tapia, Evaristo Garrido, and Don Manuel Guzmán, like Echevarría, are connected to the specific Border history of Mexico and south Texas: "Estos viejitos . . . nacieron en [los] Estados Unidos pero guerrearon en la Revolución igual que tantos otros de la misma camada y calaña, como se dice. Los padres de esta gente también nacieron en este pais así como los abuelos [aquí se habla ya de 1765 y antes]." ("These old men . . . were born in the United States but fought in the Revolution as so many others of the same age and breed. The parents of these men were also born in this country as were their grandparents [and here we are referring to 1765 and before]" (p. 105).

Again and again in *Estampas del Valle,* historical materialism through legal and mythic discourse is dramatized, and land-grabbing by both unscrupulous Anglos and Mexicans (emblematized by the Leguizamón family) is spelled out: "Los primeros Leguizamón llegaron a Belken County en 1865, despues de atole, como quien dice, y se asentaron en lo que son ahora Bascom y parte de Flora. . . . Los primeros Leguizamón supieron defenderse solos a puro pulso contra la bollida que vino al Valle con la biblia en una mano y el garrote en la otra. . . . En esos tiempos Javier Leguizamón pertencía al bando de la raza que se granejaba con los bolillos. Tuvo buenos resultados, recibió bastante tierra en la punta oeste del condado." ("The first Leguizamón arrived in Belken County after 1865; after all had been said and done with, as they say. Some wound up in what is now called the town of Bascom, and others settled near Flora. . . . The first Leguizamóns were tough enough to hold on against the Southern Anglos, many of whom came to the Valley holding a Bible in one hand and a club in the other. . . . At that time, Javier Leguizamón belonged to a small group of Mexicans who sided with the Anglo Texans. His early profits amounted to a fair-sized chunk of western county land") (pp. 111–12). This technique of uncovering the political, socioeconomic, and historical unconscious of the Rio Grande Valley informs almost every line of the series. Moreover, this political struggle between a white supremacist farm society and a native Mexican ranch society motivates Hinojosa's dramatized cultural conversations with Paredes, Rivera, and Webb.

Klail City y sus alrededores (1976), the next sociopoetic and aesthetic development in Hinojosa's new narrative, more than any of the author's works, can be read independently; it is his most finished piece of fiction. Perhaps for this reason *Klail City* is a compendium of the formal and ideological achievements that the author discovered in the creative illuminations of *Estampas del Valle* and that he would relentlessly pursue throughout his early career. It is a virtual handbook of ethnopoetic and folkloric techniques, one that displays all of his talents as the text drives itself to the limits of postmodernist narrative form: collage and metafiction. *Klail City,* in short, is another beginning for Hinojosa's great unfinished cultural conversation of history in a segregated society.

Add to all of this Hinojosa's well-known rhetoric—its mix of wit, "el choteo" (Mexican male jive), and pathos, its oral expansiveness, and its dialogic novelistic form—and one can begin to understand what makes Hinojosa's Texas-Mexican narrative of higher quality. In the novel's ironic and hyperbolic prologue, the narrator tells us: "El número de bolillos que se ven en estos escritos es bien poco. Los bolillos están, como quien dice, al margen de estos sucesos" ("The number of Texas Anglos who appear in these writings is relatively small. The Texas Anglos are, so to speak, marginal to these events") (p. 11). Given our knowledge of south Texas history—the domination of Texas Anglos over Chicanos—we can detect irony whenever the text appears to offer judgments with which one differs. Thus, from the start, situational and verbal irony are seen to be the author's favorite tropes. Like Paredes before him, Hinojosa's irony is employed to deconstruct established authority in south Texas the authority of U.S. white supremacy.

Generally, *Klail City* is obsessively concerned with the problematics of power, with disjunctive class and race relationships. At one extreme, Esteban Echevarría's oral tales at "El Oasis cantina" (the chronotopic patriarchal center of the novel where the knots of Hinojosa's new narrative are often tied and untied) lead to one of the text's most socially symbolic sections—"Echevarría tiene la palabra"—and to the central cultural conversation of the series: the uses and abuses of Texas Ranger power in south Texas. Echevarría's listeners at the cantina, in effect, are a composite of the old guard, male-centered audiences Hinojosa visualizes as his readers. Through the presence of Echevarría's companions, a friendly commerce of oral storyteller and listeners is restored in our postmodernist world. An intimacy of communication, Echevarría's living voice, and the setting that awakens it profoundly affect the atmosphere of *Klail City.*

In "Echevarría tiene la palabra," for example, we not only learn about the insensitive and mendacious former Texas Ranger George "Choche" Markham and the bitter rivalry over Chicano ranch lands between the Buenrostro and Leguizamón families, but we are given Hinojosa's most explicit response to Webb's one-dimensional view of the "quiet, deliberate, gentle" Rangers:

> Amigo de la raza, ya quiserian raza! Choche Markham es bolillo y rinche. . . . La bolillada se cree que los rinches son gallones; me cago en los rinches y en sus pinches fundas contoy pistolas. . . . A ver? Qué le paso hace unos diez-quince años? Ehm? Cabrón se quiso meter en el asunto aquel de los Buenrostro y los Leguizamón. . . . Cabron vino echando madres y diciendo que el iba a arreglar a la raza y todo el pedorron. Pura madre. Los Leguizamón mataron a don Jesús mientras dormia y que hizo Choche Markham—les pregunto, raza— . . . pos ya saben: no hizo nada. No hizo una chingada. . . . Y por qué? . . . [N]o lo hizo por miedo de ir solo y por los favores que le debía a los Leguizamón. (A friend of mexicanos? Not quite. Choche Markham is a Texas Anglo and a Ranger. . . . All the Texas Anglos think the rinches are hot shit.

> Let me tell you: the whole mess of them and their guns and holsters too are full of shit. Shit hooks, that's what they are. . . . Let's see. Look at what happened ten-fifteen years ago. Hey? The son of a bitch said he was going to straighten out the Buenrostro-Leguizamón affair. . . . Son of a bitch raised hell and bragged about straightening us out. Bullshit. The Leguizamóns still went right out and killed Don Jesús while he slept, and what did Choche Markham do? I ask you, what did he do? . . . Well you know what he did. Nothing. Not one fucking thing. . . . And why not? . . . Because he was afraid to go by himself and because the Leguizamóns own him). (pp. 18–20)

Just as Paredes was right on target in debunking the sacrosanct Texas Ranger mythology, so Hinojosa deconstructs the "rinche" mystique, emblematized by Choche Markham. *Klail City*'s form and content, its craft and materiality, like Echevarría's tales themselves, work in dialectical accord, at once engagingly distinct and emotionally inseparable.

Hinojosa remarked that he wrote *Klail City* to keep the memory of his youth alive. *Klail City,* indeed, searches for the aura of the past through its adroit use of at least four generations of historical storytellers, of whom Esteban Echevarría, Jehú Malacara, Rafa Buenrostro, and Aureliano Mora are exemplary. For example, in Mora's confession to Don Manuel Guzmán, the author, following Martí's rhetorical insights in "Nuestra América," articulates one of the underlying themes of the series and of *Klail City* in particular:

> Es que somos griegos, don Manuel. Griegos en casa de romanos. . . . [T]enemos que educar a los romanos . . . los bolillos . . . que son lo mismo. . . . Somos griegos, don Manuel, y el dia vendrá cuando la raza vive en el condado del Belken como lo hacía antes de que llegaron estos desgraciados." (We're Greeks, don Manuel. Greeks in the lands of Romans. . . . We have to educate the Romans . . . the Texas Anglos . . . they're one and the same. . . . We're Greeks, Don Manuel, and the day will come when Mexicanos will live in Belken County like they did before these wretched Texas Anglos came here.) (p. 137)

To be sure, Hinojosa's critical commentary is Martiano here, but Mora, over eighty years old, supplements Martí's rhetoric by clearly spelling out a belief held by many native Chicanos on the Border: Chicanos are a conquered people economically forced to serve the high barbarism of the conquerors.

As such, *Klail City* projects a world of tragic realism in which the ultimate entanglements of alienation and desire are so anguished as to appear almost beyond salvation. Hinojosa's development of what can be described only as the "political unconscious" of south Texas, however, becomes powerful, moving, and brilliant in its scandalous historicizing of the Chicano's psyche, senses, and self.[40]

Korean Love Songs, one of the least studied books in the series, is a remarkable account of a fragmented, personal, and complex hierarchy—army life during the Korean War.[41] In it, Rafa Buenrostro attempts to narrate in a *corrido*-like fashion his thoughts on the global conflict. When he is about to return to Klail City, what he calls "the slice of hell/heaven/Purgatory and land of our Fathers," he tells us in documentary fashion:

> I'm through here, and I'm through with skull in place.
> In time, the U.S. Army will tell us how many men
> It lost here; for now
> I'll tell you how many friends I lost:
> Chale Villalón and Pepe Vielma,
> Cayo Díaz and a kid named Balderas. . . . (p. 53)

Hinojosa's *corrido* of global resistance is not intended for an elite audience. There is a simplicity in these poetic lines memorializing the hundreds of human beings undocumented in the cultural conversations of American history. With the deaths of friends like Chale, Pepe, and Cayo, Rafa Buenrostro returns home, like many American GIs before him, to a changing, (post)modernist Texas society where Esteban Echevarría's idyllic world is dying "like the leaves of a diseased mesquite tree."

Although *Claros Varones de Belken/Fair Gentlemen of Belken County* was accepted for publication by Justa Publications in the late 1970s and was to follow *Korean Love Songs* chronologically in the series, it was not published until 1986, when Bilingual Press produced a bilingual version, translated by Julia Cruz. The reasons for this problematic situation in Latino publishing in the United States need to be carefully explored, but this is not the place for it. Suffice it to say that, as the author explained in an interview, "the contracts were signed, but Justa Publications suffered some reversals . . . y allí se quedó. Nothing was done with it."[42]

As in his previous narratives, Hinojosa in *Claros Varones de Belken* uses strategies of ellipsis, concealment, and partial disclosures—a discourse that experimental anthropologists and cultural studies critics would recognize as their own—to characterize his vast chronicle about U.S. Border history and culture. The message of partiality resonates throughout this novel and the series. Although a fragmented and decentered postmodernist narrative, the novel, like the entire series, is a chronicle written within certain formal generic constraints. As Hayden White suggests, the chronicle form is superior to the annal form of historiography in "its greater comprehensiveness, its organization of materials by 'topics and reigns' and its greater narrative coherence."[43] For White, "the chronicle also has a central subject—the life of an individual, town, or region, some great undertaking, such as war or crusade; or some institution, such as a monarchy, episcopacy, or monastery" (p. 16). Finally, White contends that unlike most historical narratives, the chronicle "does not so much conclude as simply terminate; typically, it lacks closure, that summing up of the 'meaning' of the chain of events with which it deals that we normally expect from the well-made story" (p. 16).

What thus appears to be fragmented and postmodern is really formal and generic. *Claros Varones de Belken* begins in medias res, and though it promises closure, it does not provide it. Like most chronicles, then, Hinojosa's texts have a central subject: the conflicts and local wars of Esteban Echevarría, the race wars and Texas Ranger wars in south Texas, and the "global" wars of Jehú Malacara and his cousin, Rafa Buenrostro, in Korea. Hinojosa consciously situates his work in a tradition of chronicle-writing as biographical sketches by alluding in his own title to Hernando del Pulgar's medieval Spanish chronicle, *Claros Varones de Castilla.* The chronicle is thus a highly self-conscious and fashioned discourse. Pulgar who was a chronicler and author of numerous letters, some of which became independent essays, was one of the first Spaniards deliberately to write chronicles as a form of biography. Pulgar dedicates his work to the most eminent figures of the noble class and of the clergy in Juan II's and Enrique IV's court. As Hinojosa scholars such as Rosaura Sánchez, Yolanda Broyles, and Héctor Calderón have suggested, Hinojosa subverts the lofty tradition of the Spanish chronicle by focusing not on the power holders in south Texas, but on the powerless, not on the colonizers, but on the colonized men of Belken County. Like Plutarch and Pulgar before him, Hinojosa is interested in rendering the so-called cardinal virtues of prudence, temperance, fortitude, and justice, so it is not coincidental that many of his male characters are named for such values—Prudencio (prudence), Buenaventura (good fortune), Malacara (bad face), Buenrostro (good face), and el Chorreao (dirty and unkempt).

Claros Varones de Belken comprises eight fragmentary sections. As the author tells us early on, "En este cronicón se contaran, entre cosa varia, casos en las vidas de Rafa Buenrostro, Esteban Echevarría, Jehú Malacara, y P. Galindo" ("In the lengthy chronicle, among sundry things, events in the lives of Rafa Buenrostro, Esteban Echevarría, Jehú Malacara, and P. Galindo will be related") (p. 15).

Although we learn much about Rafa Buenrostro and Jehú Malacara (for instance, that Rafa is made a widower at eighteen when his wife tragically drowns at a local resaca; and we see how Jehú uses his spare time reading the Bible while in the army, or attending the College of William and Mary part-time), the real foci are the Border characters P. Galindo and Esteban Echevarría. In fact, the several retellings by Galindo, Rafa, and Jehú of Echevarría's peaceful death under a mesquite tree give the narrative its coherence.

As in *Estampas del Valle* and *Klail City y sus alrededores*, P. Galindo is absorbed in writing. Like an indigenous ethnographer (an insider talking back), he fleshes out interpretations, records important events (such as Jehú's cure from "susto"), and fills in the gaps left in the earlier chronicles. As an observer-participant, his sketches and short stories of south Texas Border culture are experimental, and as "un hombre recto" the texts are always properly ethical. Perhaps an alter ego of Hinojosa himself, Galindo avoids a smoothed-over, monological form and presents his writings as literally pieced together, full of lacunae in their own right—what we might call "history with holes."

Functioning as a Klail City insider, then, Galindo offers us new ways of seeing and understanding Chicano Border culture. Very much a traditional participant-observer, often locked in to visual description, he also explores the consequences of positing cultural facts as things heard: Esteban Echevarría's oral tales at the local cantinas and the various *corridos*, tangos, and boleros in south Texas that record the Río Grande Valley's emergent cultural resistance.

What is most significant is that Hinojosa, through P. Galindo, uses techniques of digression and incompleteness—Echevarría's oral narratives—to impart oppositional historical knowledge to younger Chicano kinsmen such as Rafa and Jehú. An episode recalled by Rafa is particularly illuminating:

> Esteban Echevarría told me that when he was still young, the Seditionists rode down Klail's main street; they rode in after dark and camped out at the park that divides Anglo town from Mexican town. . . . They passed through, according to Esteban, without fanfarrón, as if on a Sunday ride. . . . That same day, later on, Ned Baker arrived in Klail with sixty deputies or so: policemen, marshals, constables, county officers, rangers, and the usual hangers-on. When Baker asked Esteban what he knew, Echevarría said, "They went through here. . . ." (p. 34)

This short section presents the reader with a highly compressed view of one of the most dramatic events in the history of the Southwest, the armed insurrection of south Texas Chicanos in 1915 and their defeat by the Rangers. While many of Hinojosa's readers may miss the author's historical allusion, Rafa knows the complete story: the seditionists drawn heavily from the Chicano communities along the border had joined together to regain land lost to Anglo-Americans by their parents and grandparents. In Echevarría's reconstruction, the Rangers do not merely suppress the seditionists; they pave the way for Anglo-American domination of south Texas. Thus, Hinojosa stresses the value of local knowledge and local history: that is, a recognition of class actors such as Echevarría to shape local cultures. Nor is the larger context forgotten, for the outside world of commodities segregating Klail City into Anglo-American and Chicano zones of core and periphery is always there, affecting local matters. As David Montejano sees it, the seditionists' acts of revolt, "simply stated, were a response on the part of Texas Mexicans to the new farm developments" (p. 125). What Hinojosa thematizes in his chronicle are the oppositions Echevarría expresses in his childhood memory of the seditionists' ride: Mexicans versus Anglo-Americans, seditionists versus Texas Rangers, and newcomers versus old-timers. At the center of these oppositions are the opposed views of economic development. *Claros Varones de Belken*, like the rest of the series, thus articulates a cultural poetics that is not only visually prefigured, but is an interplay of oppositional histories, economies, voices, songs, and inflected utterances.[44]

What we see and hear before us is a "plural poesis" of south

Texas Border culture. Formally, the book dramatizes the author's passion for chronicles and for freedom in the most radical of literary genres—the novel. Eschewing proto-structuralist notions, Hinojosa, through Galindo, Rafa, and Jehú, is not after a unified system. Rather, he pursues aggregates of forces, suggestive metaphors, the possibility of an artistic social act doing something not systematic and predictable, but something new, unusual, and unexpected. Put succinctly, *Claros Varones de Belken* is a fluid narrative that exemplifies Hinojosa's larger designs, for the chronicle formally represents a certain impulse that the author has been emphasizing since at least 1973. In "The Sense of Place" (1985), he puts it this way: "As the census rolls filled up in the works, so did some distinguishing features, characteristics, viewpoints, values, decisions, and thus I used the Valley and the Border, and the history and the people. The freedom to do this also led me to use folklore and the anthropology of the Valley and to use whatever literary form I desired and saw fit to tell my stories: dialogs, monologs, imaginary newspaper clippings, and whatever else I felt would be of use" (p. 23). In other words, Hinojosa's "gran cronicón," like García Márquez's *Leafstorm*, "Big Mama's Funeral," and *One Hundred Years of Solitude*, reflects the aggregate forces Bakhtin called polyphony, dialogism, heteroglossia, and carnival.

To be sure, Hinojosa sees his "gran cronicón" participating in Southwest cultural conversations, where Border culture is a serious contest of codes and representations. More specifically, *Claros Varones de Belken* is part of the Chicano response to the white supremacist scholars of the 1930s and 1940s who represented a popular, romanticized history of the Border. My own view is that Hinojosa, like Paredes, strips away the mythical aspects of the Southwestern periphery by dramatizing this history in economic and sociological terms. The fullest description of his counterdiscourse can be found in a section of the novel called "Going West," where Esteban Echevarría tells Rafa about social change, economic development, and ethnic relations in Belken County:

> Before there was such a thing as Belken County or a Klail City and the rest of it, there were people, Rafa, people. Fields and small towns and that Rio Grande, which was for drinking, not for keeping those on one side away from the others on the other side. No, that came later: with the Anglos and their civil engineers and

> all those papers in English. . . . Valley people, Rafa, this Valley of ours used by them as pawns; Valley people who tilled the land but lost it little by little. (pp. 206, 208)

This conversation fairly describes what historians call the transformation of a precapitalist, agrarian society into a modern commercial order. Hinojosa thus directs the reader's attention to familiar actors and events in the loosening of the Chicanos' hold on the land. In *Claros Varones de Belken* we see how an organic class society, where a certain social order and class relations made sense to a people, shattered under the pressures of market developments and the politics of new class groups.

If the *Klail City Death Trip* series is a history of the Río Grande Valley, that is, a fictional text with a deep historical, structural, poetic, and sociolinguistic content, then the author's use of language should necessarily register the transitory linguistic changes for the Chicano and Texas-Anglo communities. Hinojosa's project succeeds admirably in representing the Valley's linguistic evolution by dramatizing the range of verbal contacts and linguistic expansion in south Texas. The following passage is exemplary of his linguistic project: "El campaign manager raza de Ira, need I say it? es none other than Polín Tapia. Pasó por el banco esta A.M. Picking up orders from Noddy & some dinero; . . . Los años no pasan por ese hombre—ni las indirectas tampoco, pero eso es harina de otro costal. Una vez, allá cuando tú y yo tendríamos unos doce años, Bobby Campbell me pregunto: Is Polín Tapia the mayor of Mexican town?" (p. 29).

Mi querido Rafa, Hinojosa's explicitly bilingual cultural conversation, is written in two parts. The first half of this epistolary novel contains twenty-two letters written by Jehú to his cousin Rafa, who is recovering from war wounds at the veterans' hospital in William Barrett, Texas. Now an aspiring loan officer at the Klail City Savings and Loan, Jehú tells Rafa about local gossip and reports on the nefarious manipulation of the local elections by his boss (Albert "Noddy" Perkins).

For the first time in the series we are taken to the site of south Texas financial power: the Klail-Blanchard-Cooke capitalists. As an employee of the families' savings and loan, Jehú gives us insight through his letters into how the ruling class uses and abuses the lower classes—mostly Chicanos—in south Texas. We also learn much about Noddy Perkins, his daughter Sammy Jo, and of Jehú himself. Although Jehú is fired and then rehired by Noddy Perkins, he eventually decides on his own to leave his banking job for Austin and the university—where Webb and Paredes are engaging in heated discussions.

The second half of the book consists of a series of interviews conducted by the indigenous south Texas ethnographer, P. Galindo. Both Texas-Anglos and Chicanos are asked what they think of Jehú's mysterious and sudden departure, for one, it is assumed, does not simply walk away from an important banking job in a segregated society in the 1950s. Throughout this half of the novel, Galindo remains carefully neutral about Jehú's life and career as a banker, insisting that he has no opinion.

Rites and Witnesses fills in the gaps left open by the narrative: 1959–60 Klail City and the world of the Korean War. Like Hinojosa's earlier texts, this book collects vignettes, dialogues, and reportages about Chicano life in and beyond the Río Grande Valley. In the first part, "The Rites," Hinojosa describes the fields of death that Chicanos and other young men entered in Korea. Many of those killed in action, the narrators tell us, had obscure burials, no formal rites, or formal ostentation. In the second (testimonial) half of the novel, "The Witnesses," Hinojosa juxtaposes the camaraderie that existed among all the soldiers in Korea to the blatant feelings of white supremacy in the Rio Grande Valley, of which the following testimonial by the Texas Ranger, George Markham, is representative: "Mexicans! What the hell do they know? Why, if it hadn't been for me, they'd all been rounded up for sure. Damfools. . . . First thing they see is this circle star of mine, and right away: Pinche rinche! Well, I'll pinchy-rinchy them goddammit. I'm their friend. What the hell do they know. . . . Why, I married a Mex, didn't I? . . . Bunch-a goddam ingrates" (76).

Rites and Witnesses ends by recapitulating one of the major scenes in the series: the Rangers' murder of the three Naranjo brothers in 1915. Abel Manzano's reconstruction of this crime directly counters Webb's version in *The Texas Rangers:*

> [Near] El Carmen Ranch . . . the Texas Rangers shot the three Naranjo brothers in 1915. In cold blood. At night. And in the back. I was the same age as Jesus Christ then, and I found them where they were left: on the Buenrostro property; the Buenrostros were

> blameless, and they had nothing to do with that. They were left there until I cut them down. With this. Look.
>
> It was the Rangers who took them from the deputies, and it was the Rangers who executed them. I have heard *now* and for the last twenty years, that Choche Markham had nothing to do with the shooting. . . .
>
> I am saying it *now, right now* that Choche Markham was one of the seven Texas Rangers who took the Galveston Ranch hands from the Relámpago jail; they were going to Ruffing, but they never got there; listen to this:
>
> En el camino a esa ciudad mentada
> En un domingo por la noche con nubarrón
> Estos rinches texanos de la chingada
> Mataron a más mexicanos del Galvestón. . . .
>
> Yes I covered the bodies with the tarp from my roll and took them to Santa Rita Mission—near El Carmen, by the bend of the River, and they were buried there. . . . (pp. 109–11)

U.S. Border history is clearly a serious contest of codes and representations, and Hinojosa's chronicle necessarily involves the rehistoricizing of the mythic subject and a historical account of its making.

Unlike Hinojosa's earlier books in the series, *Rites and Witnesses* is written entirely in English, reflecting the fact that Jehú Malacara and Rafa Buenrostro are now participating fully in the cultural conversations of the United States. As the author said in an interview, "In the first two or three works I focus mainly on the Texas-Mexican. But as both Rafe Buenrostro and Jehú Malacara grow up and go into the Army, the University of Texas and the workplace, they're coming into the Texas Anglo world."[45]

Hinojosa's *Partners in Crime: A Rafe Buenrostro Mystery* deserves some comment because in this postmodernist novel we can sense the full emergence of a mass-cultural discourse—a first-rate murder mystery—but juxtaposed with it, the full blossoming of the author's radical critique of late capitalism. *Partners in Crime*—set in Klail City; Barrones, Tamaulipas, Mexico; and, to a lesser extent, Jonesville-on-the-River—describes a brutal murder and then a group "matanza" (massacre) in October 1972 and Rafe's role in solving the murders of two Mexican nationals, César Becerra and Andrés Cavazos de León, and a Texas Anglo, Gus Elder. The conventional patterns and motifs of the genre are all here: shrewd detectives (a

Chicano, a Texas Anglo, and a Mexican), naive disciples, the "who's next" series, and misleading but genuine clues. Hinojosa's sleuths are Rafe, who is a lieutenant in the Belken County Homicide Squad, and Captain Lisandro Goméz Solís, Cuerpo de Policia Estatal, Sección del orden público of Barrones. An unnamed narrator tells the story, and his curiosity and growing awareness of the complexity of the murders underscores Hinojosa's concern with truth and falsity. When the mystery is finally solved, we are given a clear message: beware of meaning.

Partners in Crime continues to focus on the lives of his participant-observers, who are now in their late thirties. What is especially valuable about the novel is that we learn significant details about our protagonists' pasts. We discover, for example, that Rafe, after his junior year, decided to enter the university's law school. He borrowed money from his brothers, Aaron and Israel, to study for the bar exam, passed it, and then, to everyone's dismay, decided to become a Belken County policeman. We also learn that Jehú, after his resignation as a loan officer, had gone to Austin, where he attended graduate school. He dropped out three years later, returned to Klail City, and was rehired by Noddy Perkins as vice president and cashier of the Klail City First National Bank.

Where in the earlier texts, Mexican oil and south Texas cotton had generated revenue for the Klail-Blanchard-Cooke family's bank to control and manipulate, in the 1972 world of *Partners in Crime* multinational "racketeers" are forcing their way into the Belken County economy—what Noddy Perkins symptomatically reads as "someone trying to fiddle with our money." Hinojosa's motif of death and loss is dramatized in *Partners in Crime* by using the exchange value of marijuana and cocaine, their transformation of the Río Grande Valley economy, their fragmentation of the family unit (working class and bourgeois), and their disruption of traditional values. Throughout this fast-paced narrative, Hinojosa's ideological perceptions are at their sharpest, for the communal world forged by Guzmán, Mora, and Echevarría, among many others, and the bourgeois-entrepreneurial world produced by the Klail-Blanchard-Cooke family has been displaced by the world market of racketeering, which is the author's critical metaphor for late capitalism and the end of reason in south Texas.[46]

With the same effect as the traditional historical novel, Hinojosa's *Klail City Death Trip* series invents a body of characters and discourses that reflect the ways of a south Texas culture and the people who constitute it.[47] In few ethnopoetic American novels do we find so many characters whose changing fate and collective self-revelation we follow through so many years and through such extraordinary vicissitudes. Rafe Buenrostro, Esteban Echevarría, Jehú Malacara, Choche Markham, Sammy Jo Perkins, Irene Paredes—these are figures whose histories of collective and social destiny prove unforgettable. And there are literally hundreds of other characters whose experiences in new situations offer further insights into the clashing cultural conversations in American society.

The series simultaneously functions as historical record, genealogy, and a rousing cultural critique of Texas Ranger mythography and of south Texas history. Like other classical historical works, it is the creation of its own public, its own audience in the creation of self-consciously "historical subjects."

Chicano Cultural Studies in the 1990s

> Ay! Este recuerdo pasado/me ha sangrado el corazon . . ./solo un mesquite ha quedado.
>
> —Famous *décima cantada* on the Texas-Mexican Border

This chapter traces a small group of south Texas writers and cultural studies intellectuals between 1958 and 1991—a period of progress in Chicano self-consciousness. But let me be clear about this intellectual and artistic flourishing. First, the emergence of Chicano oppositional thinking in south Texas is more than a literary movement; it also represents an outpouring of art as in the silk screens and paintings by Amado Peña at El Taller Gallery in Austin, in history (Arnoldo De León, Emilio Zamora, and David Montejano), musicology (Manuel Peña), in ethnography and folklore (José E. Limón and José Cuellar), and in feminist cultural criticism (Pat Mora and Evangelina Vigil).[48] To be sure, Gloria Anzaldúa argues convincingly in her experimental autobiography, *Borderlands/La Frontera: the New Mestiza* (1987), that an autonomous, internally coherent patriarchal universe no longer seems tenable in the postcolonial world of the Border. Unlike Paredes's, Rivera's, and Hinojosa's Border zones, Anzaldúa's "la frontera" is a space, consciousness, and eruption where "Los atravesados . . . [the] squint-eyed, the perverse, the queer, the troublesome, the mongrel, the mulatto, the half-breed, [and] the half-dead reside."[49]

What is experimental is the author's effort to explore mestiza conventions, idioms, and myths, what she calls the "Shadow Beast" within herself. At the heart of her dissent from racialist purity and patriarchal postmodernity is her deep hostility to the process of late capitalism. For Anzaldúa, multinational capital and agribusiness have an impact on the physical world of the Borderlands that is just as devastating as their effects on Chicano workers and landowners. In the chapter "The Homeland/Aztlán," she describes how for the south Texas white agribusinessmen, nature—the Borderlands—exists solely as commodity. On Anzaldúa's native farmlands in Hidalgo County, the use value of natural objects has been consumed by their exchange value. Moreover, she shows this destruction of nature actually coming to pass through the speculations of Anglo farmers and ranchers who almost literally carry the Border landscape off to market: "In the 1950s, I saw the land cut up into thousands of neat rectangles and squares, constantly being irrigated" (p. 9).

As Anzaldúa's description of agribusiness practices on the landscape makes clear, her quarrel with multinational capitalism is in large measure represented in a nationalist allegorical mode. In *Borderlands/La Frontera,* she exposes the primordial crime of capitalism—not so much wage labor but the gradual displacement of the older forms of collective life from a Borderland now seized and privatized. As Fredric Jameson stressed in "Third World Literature in the Era of Multinational Capitalism" (1986), "It is the oldest of modern tragedies, visited on Native Americans yesterday, on the Palestinians today."[50] This "oldest of modern tragedies" is significantly reintroduced by south Texas writers such as Anzaldúa and Hinojosa where native Borderlands were seized and privatized by Anglos, their Texas Rangers, and their lawyers. As Anzaldúa tells us, her grandmother "Mama Locha . . . lost her terreno. For a while we got $12.50 a year for the mineral rights of six acres of cemetery, all that was left of the ancestral lands. Mama Locha had asked that we bury her there beside her husband. . . . But there was a fence around the cemetery, chained and padlocked by the ranch owners of the surrounding land" (p. 8). Anzaldúa's national Border allegory determines a remarkable generic transformation of the author's experimental narrative: suddenly, at the beginning of her life history, we no longer are in a prototypical conversion/autobiographical confession mode, but in ritual. *Borderlands/La Frontera* foretells the utopian deconstruction of patriarchy in south Texas, even as it reaches back to touch the oldest of modern tragedies on the Border.

The Chicano Border narratives by Paredes, Rivera, Hinojosa, and Anzaldúa thus challenge the authority and even the future identity of monocultural America. Contemporary Chicano/a criticism in the Borderlands appears in several forms, traditional and innovative, postmodernist and gendered. As an academic practice, Chicano cultural studies, like Hinojosa's use of the participant-observer, simply examines thinking and writing in diverse ways. In this expanded sense, these four writers are resounding ethnographers who happen to be what social scientists call "native informants." Finally, Chicano cultural studies in the 1990s, a Border zone of conjunctures, must aspire to be regionally focused and broadly cosmopolitan, a form of life and travel in our global Borderlands.

II

Magical Narratives

4 The Real and the Marvelous in Charleston, South Carolina
Ntozake Shange's *Sassafrass, Cypress & Indigo*

It is probably true that critics of African and Afro-American literature were trained to think of the institution of literature essentially as a set of Western texts.
—Henry Louis Gates, Jr., *The Signifying Monkey*

While Ntozake Shange has been widely praised for her oppositional feminist "combat-breathing" poetics in her explosive Broadway choreopoem, *For Colored Girls Who Have Considered Suicide/When the Rainbow Is Enuf* (1976), and for her powerful "lyricism" in *Sassafrass, Cypress & Indigo* (1982), her use of Afro-Caribbean and Latin American magic realism has received little attention, owing to an inadequate understanding of a vast and rich literary and cultural movement in the Americas that began over forty years ago.[1]

The reasons for this state of affairs are complex. Henry Louis Gates correctly claims that critics of African American texts are trained to think of "the institution of literature essentially as a set of Western texts."[2] W. Lawrence Hogue, moreover, contends that a primary reason for the dearth of comparative cultural pan-American studies is that most critics in the United States are "silent on the production . . . of texts."[3] In *Discourse and the Other: The Production of the Afro-American Text* (1986), Hogue critically judges various African American interpretive practices, ranging from Amiri Baraka's "advocacy of a nationalist Afro-American literature" (p. 11) in the 1960s to Robert Stepto's proto-structuralist attempts in the 1970s "to isolate an Afro-American cultural myth, the pregeneric myth, and [use] it to define an Afro-American literary tradition" (p. 13). Hogue also analyzes the more recent attempts by Houston Baker, Jr., and Barbara Christian, who in their critical practices have created what Hogue calls a powerful but incomplete "theory of the Afro-American literary tradition." Although Hogue is generally sympathetic to Baker's early "anthropology of art," he points out the following problem in Baker's seminal study of African American literature, *The Journey Back:* "He ignores," Hogue writes, "the fact that Afro-American myths, stereotypes, and cultural forms are not innocent, that they are bound culturally and historically—even within Afro-American reality—and therefore have political and ideological functions" (p. 15). More important for Hogue, "Baker's anthropology of art is silent on literary production" (p. 16). To be sure, Hogue's self-conscious analysis is itself silent on Baker's sophisticated and powerful reading of the "blues vernacular" in *Blues, Ideology, and Afro-American Literature* (1984) or his magisterial reading of Caliban's "triple play" in *Modernism and the Harlem Renaissance* (1987). (In chapter 6, "The School of Caliban," we will return to Baker's enormous contributions to the comparative cultural studies project.)

Hogue turns his Foucauldian hermeneutics of suspicion to Barbara Christian's ground-breaking book, *Black Women Novelists: The Development of a Tradition, 1892–1976.* Although Hogue praises Christian's attempt to account for how "certain ideological and literary forces" produce the image of black women in American society, he finds troubling "gaps" and "silences" in her discourse. He contends: "Without discussing the issue of literary production, Christian's critical practice cannot fully explain how images of black women are tied to the production of literary texts, or why certain black women novelists are published and promoted, others published and excluded, and still others aborted at editors' and publishers' desks" (p. 19). As with Baraka's, Stepto's, and Baker's earlier studies, Hogue believes that Christian's analysis of "canon formation" is unconsciously "informed by an external ideological discourse" (p. 20). In contradistinction to Baraka, Stepto, Baker, and Christian, Hogue argues that certain African American writers are published and promoted in the mainstream canon "because they reproduce certain sanctioned . . . stereotypes and conventions." "Others," he argues, "[are] published and ignored because they fail to reproduce sanctioned literary myths and conventions" (p. 21).

Instructive gaps and silences in Hogue's lucid analysis of contemporary African American women's fiction, however, can be found. In his chapter "Sixties' Social Movements, the Literary Establishment, and the Production of the Afro-American Text," for example, he asserts that the radical "feminist discourse" of the 1970s "produced texts such as Toni Morrison's *The Bluest Eye* and

Sula, Alice Walker's *The Third Life of Grange Copeland* and *The Color Purple,* Ntozake Shange's *For Colored Girls,* and Gayl Jones's *Corregidora* that produced new myths about black women . . ." (p. 62). Unfortunately, what Hogue's Foucauldian analysis was not in a position to recognize was how some African American writers such as Morrison and Shange were profoundly engaged in a bold cultural conversation with the Afro-Caribbean and Latin American tradition of magic realism. A writer such as Shange thus creates texts that are "double voiced," to use Gates's term, in the sense that her literary antecedents are both black and *mestizo* (African American and Latin American) novelists.[4] By examining the historical and ideological intertextual forces that produced her magic realism in *Sassafrass, Cypress & Indigo,* we can supplement previous studies of African American literary production. To be sure, Shange's new narrative is a "mulatta" text, with a two-toned heritage. She speaks in an always distinct and resonant voice, a voice that "signifies" on black male vernacular and *mestizo* Latin American magic realist traditions.

Shange has been actively engaged during the 1980s and into the 1990s with a group of committed artists and intellectuals associated with the Casa de las Américas. She has traveled extensively throughout the Americas and read her works in Brazil, Haiti, Cuba, and Nicaragua. Her books *A Daughter's Geography* (1983) and *See No Evil* (1984) speak eloquently of her political interests in Castro's and the Sandinistas' revolutions.

In a 1985 interview at the University of Houston, Shange insists that she moved there "to escape the celebrity status" she received after the successful Broadway production of *For Colored Girls* and to be closer to the Latin American cultures of resistance.[5] In Houston, she tells us, she could "find another version of reality" (p. 2). In *Sassafrass, Cypress & Indigo,* she is directly concerned with this different "version of reality," whose depth and complexity cannot be fully presented by existing U.S. ideological and literary labels and categories. Her novel is concerned with both the Afro-Caribbean and Latin American mythical thought systems outside those appropriated by the dominant official Western society. Before discussing the merits and demerits of magic realism in Shange's new narrative, we must look afresh at the problems, theoretical and historical, involved in *lo real maravilloso* (marvelous realism) and *el realismo mágico* (magic realism).

Some Concepts and Definitions of Magic Realism

What is the history of the Americas but the chronicle of *lo real maravilloso?*
—Alejo Carpentier

[M]agic realism . . . is to be grasped as a possible alternative to the narrative logic of contemporary post-modernism.
—Fredric Jameson, "On Magic Realism in Film"

It is generally accepted that the magic realist movement led by Carpentier, García Márquez, Fuentes, and, more recently, Allende has had a powerful influence in the 1980s on a diverse group of U.S. writers: Gary Soto (*The Tale of Sunlight*), Alberto Ríos (*Whispering to Fool the Wind*), Helena María Viramontes (*The Moths*), Paul Theroux (*The Mosquito Coast*), and Dennis Johnson (*Fiskadoro*). But the possibility that magic realism functions as a force or as a discursive formation in contemporary African American literature has not been fully explored.

As Jameson has noted, "the concept of magic realism raises many problems, both theoretical and historical."[6] We will not here retrace the rich polemical debate among Latin American and U.S. scholars over the concept "magic realism," for Fernando Alegría, González Echevarría, and Amaryll Beatrice Chanady have written cogent and useful critical surveys of the debate.[7] Rather, my task is to make the demanding argument about magic realism available to readers who have heard of its importance but who have so far been baffled.

According to González Echevarría, magic realism as a concept appears in "three different moments" in the twentieth century.[8] The first appeared during the avant-garde 1920s in Europe "when the term is used by Franz Roh in his *Nach-Expressionismus: Magischer Realismus* (1925) and when the Surrealists, especially Breton in the first *Manifesto* (1924), proclaim the 'marvelous' (*le merveilleux*) an aesthetic category and even a way of life" (p. 109). The second moment was in the late 1940s when the expressions "*el realismo mágico*" and "*lo real maravilloso*" were used by the Latin American writers-intellectuals Arturo Uslar Pietri and Alejo Carpentier to measure, compare, and evaluate indigenous Latin American cultural art forms.[9] Whereas Pietri adopted Roh's term "magic realism," Carpentier, the more influential writer and sophisticated theoretician, adopted in González Echevarría's view "the Surrealists' version and create[d] the term 'marvelous American reality'" (p. 110).

A third period of magic realism began in 1955 when the Latin American scholar Angel Flores published his influential essay, "Magic Realism in Spanish American Fiction." For González Echevarría, this third phase continued through the 1960s "when criticism searches for the Latin American roots of some of the novels produced during the 'boom' and attempts to justify their experimental nature" (p. 111). As will be seen, there was a "fourth phase" as Ntozake Shange and Arturo Islas, among others, expanded the tradition of magic realism in new and political (often "Signifyin[g]") ways.

Flores argued that what distinguishes magic realism from other realisms is that it attempts to transform "the common and the everyday into the awesome and the unreal."[10] Furthermore, he emphasized the connections between magic realism and examples of European modernist aesthetics practiced by Kafka and Chirico.

In 1967 Luis Leal joined the growing debate by attacking Flores's essay. In "El realismo mágico en la literatura hispanoamericana," he argued that magic realism was, for all intents and purposes, an exclusively New World literary movement. Included in his school of Latin American magic realist writers were Arturo Uslar Pietri, Miguel Angel Asturias, Carpentier, Lino Novas Calvo, Juan Rulfo, Felix Pita Rodríguez, and Nicolás Guillén. According to Leal, the following is the basic difference among the competing schools of "magic realism," "realism," and "surrealism":

> El mágico realista no trata de copiar (como lo hacen los realistas) o de vulnerar (como lo hacen los surrealistas) la realidad circundante, sino de captar el misterio que palpita en las cosas. (The magic realist does not attempt to copy [like the realists] or make the real vulnerable [like the surrealists], but attempts to capture the mystery which palpitates in things.)[11]

But Leal's essay ignores the profound impact Surrealism, European Modernism, and Ethnography had on the generation of writers he analyzes, especially Asturias and Carpentier.[12]

Carpentier made the connections in the famous prologue to his revolutionary Afro-Caribbean novel, *El reino de este mundo* (1949), and reprinted an expanded version in *Tientos y diferencias* (1964). To the rhetorical question, "What is the history of the Americas but the chronicle of *lo real maravilloso?*," he suggests the ideology that lies at the center of his early magical narratives: how to write in a European language—with its Western systems of thought—about realities and thought structures never before seen in Europe. In the oxymoron *lo real maravilloso,* Carpentier is concerned not only with African magic (*obeah*), but with the perceptions and ideas of the world underlying the horizon of Afro-Caribbean magic. For the first time in 1949 he asks these questions: what is the New World African, Amerindian, and *mestizo* heritage of the Caribbean? And how can it function as an ideology, a stylistics, and point of view?

In Paris, Carpentier was introduced by Desnos to André Breton and began his bold cultural conversation with European Modernism and Surrealism. Throughout his Parisian stay, Carpentier was concerned with the role of art in revolution, as well as with what constituted Surrealism. Not surprisingly, he was attracted to the Surrealist's attack on human consciousness—which was part of their larger assault on all forms of bourgeois established order. As we know from their much-quoted maxim, knowledge for these Europeans is the sound "boom," and everyone is entitled to a "boom" of his or her own making.[13] Carpentier, thus, was initially fascinated by Breton's attempts to break through "the provoking insanities of realism."[14]

He learned much from the Surrealists' experiments, which he employed to explore a kind of second reality hidden within the world of dreams and the unconscious. By whatever means, chiefly automatic writing and the imitation of dreams, the individual, according to the Surrealists, must strive to achieve "surreality," which Breton saw as the absolute of the unconscious.[15] Surrealism thus led Carpentier to see afresh "aspectos de la vida americana que no habia advertido," as he was to confess.[16]

But what led to Carpentier's "break" with Breton's Surrealism? Emir Rodríguez Monegal argues convincingly that "political tensions" which arose among the Surrealists themselves caused Carpentier to become alienated from them.[17] González Echevarria suggests in *The Pilgrim at Home* that Carpentier went his own way because European Surrealism clashed with the Cuban's "Spenglerian conception of man and history he had absorbed through avant-garde journals like the *Revista de Occidente*" (p. 122).

Thus, in spite of his early fascination with Surrealism in general, and with Breton in particular, Carpentier never became a committed disciple. Unlike Breton and the Surrealists, he argued in his prologue and the essay "De lo real maravilloso" that the "second reality" the Surrealists explored in automatic reality is merely part of the everyday world. Further, as a follower of Spengler's *Decline of the West* (in Spengler's universal history there is no fixed "center"), Carpentier eschewed Breton's and the Surrealists' Eurocentric doctrines of the marvelous and argued that all things of a truly magical nature are, in fact, found within the reality of the Caribbean Americas—not the "boring" cities of Europe. According to Carpentier, the "discovery," conquest, and colonization of the New World are magical events in themselves:

> Open Bernal Díaz del Castillo's great chronicle [*True History of the Conquest of New Spain* (1552)] and one will encounter the only real and authentic book of chivalry ever written: a book of dust and grime chivalry where the genies who cast evil spells were the visible and palpable *teules,* where the unknown beasts were real, where one actually gazed on unimagined cities and saw dragons in their native rivers and strange mountains swirling with snow and smoke.[18]

For Carpentier, then, Bernal Díaz del Castillo's chronicle of the Spanish Conquest of Mexico is an exemplary magic realist narrative because Díaz (unwittingly) had written about the clash of cultures—Old World and New World—and had described, in great detail, the superposition of one layer of reality on another. Thus envisaged, in Bernal Díaz's narrative armored Spaniards led by Cortés wander over "magical" deserts and cross over barren peaks, some of which burst into flame at their approach. Further, Díaz describes the Aztecs assailing the Spaniards with blood rituals of human sacrifice. At the end of their travels (travails), Cortés enters a great supernatural New World city, heaped with flora, floating in the midst of a blue lake.

Forming a background for Carpentier's theory is what he sees as the "fecundity" of the New World landscape. His concept of "marvelous reality" thus can be summarized in his own words:

> Due to the untouched nature of its landscape, its ontology, the Faustian presence of the Indian and the Black, the revelation inherent in the continent's recent discovery and the fruitful cross-

> breeding this discovery engendered, America is still very far from exhausting its wealth of mythologies. Indeed, what is the history of America if not the chronicle of marvelous reality? (pp. xiv–xv)

In outlining his theory of *lo real maravilloso,* Carpentier posits the following conditions that must be met for the marvelous to exist (pp. x–xi):

(1) that *lo real maravilloso* unmistakably emerges as such only when it arises from an unexpected alteration of reality (a miracle),

(2) a privileged revelation of reality,

(3) an unaccustomed or singularly enhancing illumination of the riches of reality that had passed unnoticed,

(4) an expansion of the scales and categories of reality, now perceived with a particular intensity by virtue of an exaltation of spirit that leads to a kind of liminal state.

Carpentier thus set up an antithesis between Surrealism and magic realism. He unfavorably compares Surrealism with a privileged New World aesthetic grounded in a reality that is inherently magical. To be sure, Carpentier's thesis rests on the claims that New World artists and people experience the marvelous in their daily existence and therefore have no need to invent a domain of fantasy. Thus, on the basis of local New World privilege, he rejects Surrealism as sterile and legitimizes the mode of writing he elects: "a chronicle of the marvelous real."

More recently, García Márquez in *El olor de la guyaba (The Fragrance of the Guava)* also anchored his notion of magic realism within a local Afro-Caribbean context:

> I believe that the Caribbean has taught me to see reality in a different way, to accept supernatural elements as something that is part of our daily life. The Caribbean is a distinctive world whose first magic piece of literature is *The Diary of Christopher Columbus,* a book which speaks of fabulous plants and mythical worlds. Yes, the history of the Caribbean is full of magic.[19]

Although García Márquez's use of magic realism includes Carpentier's familiar tropes of the supernatural—one of the foundation concepts of magic realism—his version differs from Carpentier's in this important way. García Márquez's concept of magic realism presupposes the narrator's identification with the oral expression of popular cultures in the Third World *pueblo.* In other words, the narrative dramatization of magic realism is usually expressed through a collective voice, inverting, in a jesting manner, the values of the official culture.

Finally, at a recent PEN conference, Fernando Alegría, the noted Chilean literary scholar and writer, expanded the debate by arguing audaciously in his essay "Latin American Fantasy and Reality" (1987) that "reality" in the Caribbean and in Latin America "is neither marvellous nor magical."[20] For in reading Carpentier or Asturias, Alegría contends, "we come to realize [that their realism] is a truthful image of economic injustice and social mockery which passes off as authoritarian democracy in Latin America." To support his ideological reading of magic realism, Alegría turns to an interpretation of García Márquez's "puzzling speech," "The Solitude of Latin America," given at the 1982 Nobel Prize awards, where García Márquez spoke specifically about politics and economics on a global scale, emphasizing the heated quarrel between the superpowers, the United States and the Soviet Union. According to Alegría, García Márquez addressed these issues "to clear up the legend of magical realism in his own fiction." Further in Alegria's view, García Márquez wanted once and for all to "acknowledge the basic reality lying at the bottom of the mythical world of Latin America." He used "statistics," Alegría suggests, to give his audience "stuffed into their fancy-label penguin suits, an astonishing, brutal image of a continent torn asunder and bathed in blood" (pp. 117–18):

> There have been 5 wars and 17 military coups; there emerged a diabolic dictator who is carrying out, in God's name, the first Latin American ethnocide of our time. In the meantime, 20 million Latin American children died before the age of one—more than have been born in Europe since 1970. Those missing because of repression number nearly 120,000. . . . Numerous women arrested while pregnant have given birth in Argentine prisons, yet nobody knows the whereabouts and identity of their children, who were furtively adopted or sent to an orphanage by the order of the military authorities. . . . Nearly 200,000 men and women have died throughout the continent, and over 100,000 have lost their lives in three small and ill-fated countries of Central America: Nicaragua, El Salvador, and Guatemala. . . .
>
> I dare to think that it is this outsized reality, and not just its literary expression, that has deserved the attention of the Swedish Academy of Letters. A reality not of paper, but one that lives within us and determines each instance of our countless daily

> deaths, and that nourishes a source of insatiable creativity, full of sorrow and beauty, of which this roving Colombian is but one cipher more, singled out by fortune.[21]

Alegría is correct when he redefines García Márquez's version of magic realism as a truthful vision of "outsized reality." Perhaps it was "The Solitude of Latin America" that led Jameson in his essay dedicated to Fernández Retamar and the Cuban Revolution to theorize and define magic realism as a formal mode "constitutively dependent on a type of historical raw material in which disjunction is structurally present; or, to generalize the hypothesis more starkly, magic realism depends on a content which betrays the overlap or the coexistence of precapitalist with nascent or technological features."[22]

It is precisely this "articulated superposition of whole layers of the past within the present" in Shange's *Sassafrass, Cypress & Indigo* that aligns her with such committed magic realist authors as Carpentier, García Márquez, and Islas.

Feminist Culture and Magic Realism

> Where there is a woman there is magic.
> —*Sassafrass, Cypress & Indigo*

What are some of the rules of the black vernacular "Signifyin[g]" formation that produces Shange's radical-feminist text, written in a magic realist style? What are the statements and concepts that inform the author's controversial "mulatta" poetics?[23]

In Claudia Tate's *Black Women Writers at Work* (1983), Shange specifies her concern for a particular African American vernacular and "Signifyin[g]" practice:

> My lower case letters, slashes, and spelling [were] influenced by Leroi Jones's *The Dead Lecturer* and *The System of Dante's Hell* and Ishmael Reed's *Yellow Book Radio.* I like the kinds of diction Ishmael uses, and I like the way Leroi's poems look on the page. . . . I like the idea that letters dance, not just that words dance; of course, the words also dance.[24]

Shange's African American tradition is close to music, an insight she thematized in *For Colored Girls,* where she uses popular Motown music, oral speech, feminist poetry, and dance to critique patriarchy in the United States. Therefore, one statement or concept that informs Shange's work in general, and *Sassafrass, Cypress & Indigo* in particular, is her attempt to deconstruct traditional modes of representing discourse on the page. In other words, Shange's novel does not always read like a Western traditional novel, but it is designed to challenge the traditional notions of realism.

Another statement that informs the book's production is the need, according to Shange, for black women to insert themselves into the cultural conversations of U.S. history. As she said in response to the "media blitz" that followed her Broadway production: *For Colored Girls* "is a record of me once I left my mother's house. I was raised as if everything was all right. And in fact, once I got out of my house, everything was not all right."[25] In addition, Shange believes that her generation of black women were brought up to be silent in the face of male oppression. Her mother, she suggests, failed to pass on to her certain truths about male violence. In her work, then, Shange reproduces a version of the black female experience designed to encourage women of color "to tell their stories." Because she sees herself responsible for letting others abuse her, she now sees her power as an artist as an attempt to encourage women to refuse victimization.

Sassafrass, Cypress & Indigo represents the author's commitment to radical feminism: her struggle to articulate repressed and silenced black females' stories and voices. As Barbara Christian says of the African American women's fiction of the 1970s and 1980s, Shange, Morrison, Bambara, Walker, Lorde, and Marshall "explor[ed] these themes—that sexism must be struggled against in black communities and that sexism is integrally connected to racism."[26] The novel, as Hortense Spillers suggests, is structured with "the allusive echoes of the Moirae, the three women of fate in classical mythology, who weave the thread of human life, or the natural objects and substances to which the names of the sisters refer. . . ."[27] In other words, Shange's narrative attempts to make a new mythos of the black female self. By way of discrete chapters on each of the three sisters, Sassafrass, Cypress, and Indigo, and through Hilda Effania's letters, she traces the process of change in the lives of these women.

Finally, Afro-Caribbean and Latin American magic realism inform significant parts of *Sassafrass, Cypress & Indigo.* When asked about her use of magic realism in the novel, Shange matter-of-factly responded that her character, Indigo, was her attempt to "Signify" on García Márquez's wonderful character Remedios the Beauty in *One Hundred Years of Solitude.*[28] Shange's mulatta text therefore is double-voiced and talks to other works in a process of intertextual revision. Indigo is a magic realist character with a difference.

Sassafrass, Cypress & Indigo, published in 1982 at the peak of both the "fourth moment" of magic realism in the Americas and the women of color movement, begins:

> Where there is a woman there is magic. If there is a moon falling from her mouth, she is a woman who knows her magic, who can share or not share her powers. A woman with a moon falling from her mouth, roses between her legs and tiaras of Spanish moss, this woman is a consort of spirits. Indigo seldom spoke. There was a moon in her mouth. Having a moon in her mouth kept her laughing. Whenever her mother tried to pull the moss off her head, or clip the roses round her thighs, Indigo was laughing.
>
> "Mama, if you pull 'em off, they'll just grow back. It's my blood. I've got earth blood, filled up with the Geeches long gone, and the sea."[29]

Not since the first half of Jean Toomer's *Cane,* or García Márquez's descriptions of Remedios the Beauty, have readers seen such an urgently passionate discourse that captures and celebrates female gender. Through etymological wordplay and word associations, Shange introduces the highly charged leitmotifs that characterize Indigo's section in the novel: mouth, moon, blood, spirits, and magic. Throughout the novel's first section, she represents Indigo as in touch with her emergent female sexuality and with the beginning of magic realism—for Indigo "is a consort of the spirits" (p. 3).

Like Carpentier's magical character Mackandal in *El reino de este mundo,* Shange's Indigo can compel the wind to blow a white woman's hat off (pp. 71–72); she can "move the razors off the roosters [and] put them in the palms of onlookers" to let them "know the havoc of pain" (p. 44); and she can, in García Márquez's sense, "see reality in a different way, to accept supernatural elements as something that is part of our daily life."

Indigo, as an incarnate of magic realism, thus can see things in Charleston, South Carolina, in ways that her sisters, Sassafrass and Cypress, could never see. For example, Shange tells us of Mrs.

Yancey's courtship by Uncle John, a local junk man and connoisseur of magic realism in the black community. Although most of their courtship is ordinary, Indigo arrives on the scene and experiences a profound transformation:

> Everybody knew Uncle John lived in his wagon, but nobody had ever seen what Indigo saw. Uncle John went over to his wagon, pulled out a fine easy chair and set it by the curb, then motioned for Mrs. Yancey to have a seat. Next thing Indigo knew, he had spread a Persian rug in the middle of the street, set a formal table, pulled out a wine bucket, and started dinner on the stove at the back of his wagon. . . . Out of nowhere the guys from the Geechee Capitans, a motorcycle gang of disrepute led by Pretty Man, came speeding down the street. Uncle John didn't exhibit much concern about these young ruffians. . . . He looked up waved his hand, and the Geechee Capitans, who had never done a good turn by anybody in the city of Charleston, South Carolina, made road blocks on either side of Uncle John's parlor. . . .
>
> When Uncle John pulled out a Victrola, played a Fletcher Henderson 78, and asked Mrs. Yancey to dance, Indigo knew it was time to go home. There was too much magic out in the night. (pp. 13–14)

In this passage we see a characteristic of Shange's magic realism: her new narrative is informed throughout by an element of the unexpected, of chance, of the ordinary experience that is not ordinary, and, finally, of the opaque daily event that must be interpreted (Indigo suggests that there was too much magic in the night) to be truly seen.

But what accounts for Indigo's "consorting" with the magical, supernatural, and spiritual worlds? Shange provides the reader with two answers. First, Indigo is initiated into the world of magic realism by Uncle John when he "tells [her] some matters of the real of the unreal" (p. 26). Specifically, Uncle John suggests to Indigo that one way of experiencing magic is by understanding the African American vernacular uses of music, especially, "the blues:" "What ya think music is, whatchu think the blues be, & them get happy church music is about, but talkin wit the unreal what's mo' real than most folks ever gonna know" (p. 27). Thus building on the rich African American blues tradition, Shange joins Richard Wright, Ralph Ellison, Sherely Anne Williams, Amiri Baraka, Henry Louis Gates, and Houston Baker in celebrating the strengths and beauties of the blues vernacular tradition that arises, in Le Roi Jones's term, out of the depth of the black soul.[30] But it must be emphasized, Shange celebrates the blues with a "Signifyin[g]" difference—the blues constitute "talkin wit the unreal." Throughout *Sassafrass, Cypress & Indigo,* Shange shows us how Indigo "colored & made the world richer what was blank & plain. The slaves who were ourselves knew all about Indigo & Indigo herself" (p. 40).

Shange also posits a second reason for Indigo's intimacy with magic and the supernatural. Throughout the novel, the author suggests that women in and of themselves are magical subjects. As Hortense Spillers argues, "There is a rhetoric appropriate to Shange's realm of women, a set of gestures and desires that distinguishes female from male, even though the latter is ultimately absorbed by the womb." Indigo grounds it at a more basic gender level when she has a conversation with one of her dolls about her "Marvelous Menstruating Moments": "When you first realize your blood has come, smile; an honest smile, for you are about to have an intense union with your magic" (p. 19). Like many contemporary feminist anthropologists such as Carol Delaney and Emily Martin, Shange criticizes traditional understanding of menstruation not solely as the negative, polluting phenomenon described by males but as a magical and potentially positive experience with deep implications for the spiritual lives and power of women.[31]

The first fifty pages of *Sassafrass, Cypress & Indigo,* then, in magical and radical feminist rhetoric tells the story of Indigo's creating, nurturing, and celebrating her feminine essence. Clearly, one aspect of this magic realism is associated with the author's belief that Indigo is special because her gender allows her to fully experience her "blood earth." The other element is her mastery of music, for she captured through her violin "the hum of dusk, the crescendo of cicadas, swamp in light wind, thunder at high tide, & her mother's laughter down the hall" (p. 36). However, it must be stressed that Shange's discussion of what accounts for Indigo's "consorting" with the magical finally leaves the reader with these questions unanswered: Why should the blues provide a privileged means of access to the "unreal?" And if the "magical" somehow inheres in an essentialized notion of femaleness, then how does Shange explain why the "source" for magic realism within the Latin American grain is emphatically male—Carpentier, García Márquez, and Fuentes?

The other major sections of *Sassafrass, Cypress & Indigo* concentrate on Hilda Effania's middle daughter, Cypress, a ballerina who uses her training in traditional dance "to find out the truth about colored people's movements." Unlike Indigo, who stays with her mother in Charleston, Cypress moves to San Francisco, and then to New York, using her love for dance to "take on the struggle of colored Americans" (p. 135).

When Cypress finally settles in New York, she enters into a community of Third World lesbian dancers called the Azure Bosom. Cypress delights, for the first time, in female sexuality. Some of these women, Shange writes, "were super chic and independent ones like Celine . . . others rounder than Xchell and more bangled than Cypress. . . . [There were] women like Smokey Robinson and women like Miriam Makeba" (p. 145). As Barbara Christian has noted in "No More Buried Lives," the Azure Bosom is "rooted in the image of the Haitian Voodun, Erzulie. . . ."[32] Shange protests the abuse of women's bodies and allows women collectively "to linger in their own eroticism, to be happy with loving themselves" (p. 144). Yet her vision of Cypress's world is not idealized; for at their parties Cypress realizes that the celebrations were "more like a slave market where everybody is selling herself" (p. 145). Shange's radical-feminist poetics, at least in this section of the novel, bring into consideration the issues of race, class, and gender. This is especially true of Cypress's utopian dream near the end of the novel. In her dream, Cypress survives a nuclear war, and "somehow the men and women are separated." The women survivors are "left to contend with the fruitlessness of the soils, the weight of the skies" (p. 203). In a wonderful narrative of condensation, displacement, and revision, Shange constructs and then deconstructs Cypress's desire for an essentialized and idealist feminist world. To clearly understand Shange's cultural critique of radical feminism, let me quote from most of Cypress's dream:

> Cypress was initiated into the new world—not quite as herself. All vestiges of male-dominated culture were to be "rehabilitated" out of her psyche; the true matriarch was to be nurtured. . . . But here there were no patriarchs, ordering and demanding. Here there were only Mothers and Daughters. "Mothers" were supreme; there was no higher honor than to be deemed "Mother," yet this had nothing to do with biological offspring. Women who had no children were of a higher caste than the "bearers," as they were called. The "bearers" were never seen in public assemblies,

> nor were they allowed to wear bright colors, because they might bear sons. (p. 203)

On one level, then, the creation of a new social form is explicitly drawn out in Cypress's dream vision. Women in this world might genuinely learn to love each other. But Shange's narrative is not ahistorical. Throughout Cypress's dream, the author reminds us of the painful lessons of the logic of postmodernist societies—namely, that our postmodernist culture is always a sign of the internal and superstructural expression of class, race, and economic domination.

This explains why Cypress's dream also emphasizes that the underside of postmodernism is always blood, torture, death, and horror. Thus, some of the women in Cypress's dream are "breeders," and they make up an imprisoned class. And the majority of the bearers in Shange's brave new world are Latinas and black. Male babies are murdered, and males captured in the periphery are incarcerated in glass cages. Shange's novel, thus, represents the African American historical experience not as one continuous development, centered on one object, but as a double-voiced vision of the American historical past made up of different experiences. This is especially true of her sections on Sassafrass, the oldest daughter. Like Indigo and Cypress, Sassafrass is an artist—a weaver of cloth and a poet. But unlike her sisters, she desires to return to social forms and modes of production that are explicitly precapitalist:

> As she passed the shuttle through the claret cotton warp, Sassafrass conjured images of weaving from all time and all places: Toltecas spinning shimmering threads; East Indian women designing intricate patterns for Shatki, the impetus and destruction of creation; and Navajo women working on thick tapestries. (p. 92)

Pervaded with images of weaving and symbols of kinship, the world, as Sassafrass imagines it, assumes a different social form.

Although Sassafrass attends an expensive boarding school in New England, the Callahan School, she eschews traditional bourgeois ideologies by moving in with her lover, Roscoe Mitchell, in Los Angeles. Mitch, a black nationalist who shoots heroin and often imagines himself on the same bandstand with John Coltrane, turns out to be given to violence. This section of the novel is the most violent, in which Sassafrass must pay a high price for her independence. After putting up with Mitch's head-bashing for too long, she convinces him to join her in entering The New World Found Collective, a religious Afro-Caribbean commune, in Louisiana. Here, she is finally free to practice the Bembee religion in a community where social unity and spirituality can be achieved. In illuminating African-oriented religions like *vodoo* in Haiti, *santería* in Cuba, *espiritismo* in Puerto Rico, and Shango and Pocomania (both in Trinidad), Shange attempts, in this final section, to bring the history and cultural identity of black people in the Caribbean, Latin America, and U.S. Southern states closer together. At the end, Sassafrass tries "everything to be a decent *lbejii,* a Santera. She desperately wanted to make *Ocha.* To wear white with her *elekes.* To keep the company of the priests and priestesses. The New World Found Collective where she and Mitch had been living for over a year offered spiritual redemption, if little else" (p. 213).

Although many readers find Shange's novel depressing (Spillers writes that her "particular strength is the lament, and the lament is an apparently limited, probably even sentimental form"),[33] its ending is a socially symbolic celebration of the unity of black people in all the Americas. Her emphasis on the Bembee religion, on *santería,* and other rituals allows for another reading of the African American historical past. Shange's description of Sassafrass's African-based religious experiences, in the end, offers an alternative to the Eurocentric understanding of America. Blacks as a people in the Americas, she reminds us, have experienced a history according to different circumstances. This strong understanding of a non-European America in her narratives has helped make her work especially attractive to Cuban and Nicaraguan audiences. In a speech commemorating the fifteenth anniversary of the Bay of Pigs victory, Castro affirms Cuban solidarity with African cultures and acknowledges that Cubans are an Afro-Latin people.[34] Like him, Cuban and Nicaraguan readers of Shange can recognize that Cuba's revolutionary experience and black heritage constitute a bond with African and Caribbean nations.

Finally, since place and territory are crucial in Shange's work, the Caribbean should be understood not as some vague politico-geographic region, but as what Wallerstein calls "the extended Caribbean," a coastal and insular region stretching from southern Virginia to easternmost Brazil.[35] The Caribbean social space that Sassafras desires at the end is the tropical belt defined ecologically or meteorologically. For Shange, then, the extended Caribbean is a historical and magical entity that can offer us a new way of imposing an imaginary coherence on the black experience of dispersal and fragmentation. It is only from this position that we can properly understand the traumatic character of the New World primal scene—where the fatal encounter was staged between Africa and the West.[36]

5 The Hybridity of Culture in Arturo Islas's *The Rain God*

In recent years critical interest in the theorizing of ethnic, Third World, and "minor" literature has increased.[1] For the most part, however, this new writing has tended not to emphasize what Charles Newman in *The Post-Modern Aura* calls "the new agencies of production, transmission, and administration of knowledge as dominant cultural institutions,"[2] according to which the distinctions between minor and major work is posited. This is the case with William Boelhower's *Through A Glass Darkly: Ethnic Semiosis in American Literature,* whose first chapter, "A Modest Ethnic Proposal," valuably traces, with the help of Henry James, the identity crisis of Americans and concludes that "everybody in America is willy-nilly an ethnic subject."[3] Throughout his study, however, Boelhower defers analysis of the canon's ideological function and blurs the opposition that continually haunts his work, namely, the collapsing of a radically minor literature into one that seeks a major function. Likewise, Werner Sollors declares in *The Invention of Ethnicity* that ethnicity is an invention, a cultural construction. To be sure, Sollors's analysis of U.S. mainstream and minority discourses has a structuralist slant, for even if Puritan and minority discourses differ in their application, he claims they are the same in their grammar.[4] Puritan and what he calls "non-WASP" discourses all find redemption in representing themselves as outside, radical dissent.

To produce an adequate understanding of ethnic, minor, or Third World writing, it is necessary to understand the criteria that determine the constitution of a canon at every juncture and to grasp those criteria in relation to the ideological forms that legitimate domination at any given time. Arnold Krupat's *The Voice in the Margin* goes a long way toward engaging this issue. What Krupat effectively demonstrates is how Anglo-American New Critics consistently chose to privilege texts "that could accommodate the wider context of international—or at least of Western—literature."[5] In other words, Anglo-American New Critics, for Krupat, defined international literature as independent of all socio-temporal determinant—"as if one actually could read globally (and timelessly), passing directly to the highest levels of generalization (linguistic, philosophical), by passing the mean and ordinary local—as if rhetoric were a matter of figures and of no occasions" (p. 183).

Indeed, rhetoric and literary history are more than a matter of figures or tropes. Rather, literary history tells us how writers' works are packaged, distributed, sold, or censored in the postmodern marketplace. This chapter contests Boelhower's and Sollors's poststructuralist generalizations about ethnic literature by discussing the editorial deliberations of some mainline editors and reviewers (male and female) who read Arturo Islas's *The Rain God* (1984) within an Anglocentric monocultural matrix, thereby refusing to see his magical narrative as a novel with a difference. To put it in Krupat's terms, *The Rain God* reveals the local and ordinary but accommodates its own cosmopolitan critical context. A study of the editors' and reviewers' reading practices will reveal the complex ideological calculations and negotiations of one part of the Anglo-American middle class as it attempts to define itself within the already established taste hierarchy.[6] By tracing some deliberations of the editors who read Islas's novel in manuscript, we can learn something of the taste and ideological and ethnic assumptions of those who, in Janice Radway's and Richard Ohmann's words, control "the gate, deciding not only what cultural creations will be formally produced but also which among those will be distributed" "in an urgent or attractive way."[7]

I

New York publishers who read *The Rain God* in manuscript largely directed their attention to Islas's Chicano background and the ethnic cultural gaze in his work. This narrow view overlooked the complex literary and crosscultural influences from both North America and Latin America that shape his writing. Put differently, white middle-class editors refused to consider his narrative as part of the hemisphere's pan-American traditions.

In a letter from Frances McCullough, senior editor at Harper & Row, on December 30, 1975, to John Meyers, Islas's agent, Ms. McCullough made this comment: "I think what's wrong with the characters is tha[t] they are so busy conveying a cultural message that they have no time to be real people. This is true also of the plot; whatever happens has a heavy cultural message but you don't feel its weight in terms of the people's lives."[8] This characteristic reading of Islas's fiction precisely addresses the problem that Chicano and Chicana writers are confronted with in New York: the ethnic "cultural message" label imposed on them by mainline editors draws simplistic attention to their "otherness," while their place in U.S. society and the relation of their work to global literature tends to be undervalued.

The temptation to examine Islas's work only for its "insider" Chicano cultural message has been considerable. Two examples are enough to show the shortcomings of this approach. A reviewer, Raymond Mungo, suggested that the Chicano essence of *The Rain God* is the author's "striving for the key to some Castañedan, soulful mystery in the lives of these [Chicano] people."[9] Likewise, Carol Fowler used similar racial criteria in her 1985 review. She claimed that Islas's Chicano characters "seem" to have "a sense of clannishness stronger than Anglo families. . . ."[10] The suggestion that his work reflects some aboriginal "soulful mystery" or some "clannishness" betrays an insufficient understanding of the background to his writings. Such critical stances lead to an unbalanced and restricted view of his importance as an American writer with a difference and give rise to pernicious stereotypes.

Henry Louis Gates, Jr., has convincingly argued that the trope of "race" is an important concern of many U.S. writers and thus demands our critical attention.[11] And since Chicano and Chicana identities are shaped in the tension between cultures—U.S. and Mexican—they embrace elements from different backgrounds. In other words, Islas does not work in an artistic vacuum. He is free to incorporate what he chooses from outside his immediate "Latino" cultural sphere.

The value of Islas's *The Rain God* lies not in the author's depiction of traditions alien to American readers but in the specific way he bridges the gap between North American and Latin American cultures and unites, like Shange, literary and transnational traditions. The "ethnic" label used by New York editors therefore detracts from these qualities.

Islas's personal background and his academic interest in American literatures—he was a professor of English at Stanford University and had served as visiting professor of creative writing at the University of Texas, El Paso—explain why his work is marked by crosscultural hybridization. Yvor Winters and Wallace Stegner, two of his Stanford mentors, and such writers as Faulkner, Wallace Stevens, Maxine Hong Kingston, Juan Rulfo, and García Márquez have left their mark on his double-voiced writing. He used his own experience of migration to create an ideal of himself out of his Mexican and American background, his knowledge of "New World" Amerindian cultures, his experiences in postmodern American society, and his study of classic American literatures. All of these factors must be considered when assessing his fiction.

Another reason editors were incapable of acknowledging the true character of his novel was their fear that *The Rain God* would be bought by only a limited number of Chicano readers. Henry William Griffin, a senior editor at Macmillan, put it this way in an April 5, 1976, letter to Bob Cornfield, Islas's agent at the time: "Interesting, very interesting indeed, but I'm afraid our sales force would be very hard put to sell a thousand copies."[12] Seven years after its publication by Alexandrian Press, *The Rain God* has sold approximately ten thousand copies.[13] One can only imagine how many copies might have been sold if the book had been published, distributed, and marketed with understanding by the mainline big boys in New York.

Comments such as Mr. Griffin's have led Islas to remark that "the constant observation from New York was that publishers felt there was no audience for this work—no market. And market is really the word because it means money."[14] Although Islas does not deny that his novel is about Chicanos and Chicanas who live in a Southwestern Border town, he says over and over again that "it was not intended solely for a Chicano audience."[15] But after eight years of struggle with unresponsive New York publishing houses (he submitted his novel to more than twenty), he gave up trying to convince them that his story about the Angel family would have "universal" appeal. "I finally decided to stop banging my head against the wall."[16]

To his credit, Islas claims that his comments aren't "sour grapes." But he does point out that people he went to school with at Stanford, who are now editors in New York, have consistently ignored Chicano and Chicana writers: "I know that world. I went to Stanford with a lot of the [people] who are editors, and it's a very circumspect and provincial world; they publish their own. . . ."[17]

Certainly, Islas is not the only Chicano writer who is angry and distressed at traditional U.S. publishers. Rudolfo Anaya, professor of English at the University of New Mexico and author of the best-selling *Bless Me, Ultima* (Quinto Sol, 1972), says that "a lot of Chicano writers have been out there for fifteen or twenty years, producing good work, getting nominated for National Book Awards and recognition around the world. But they can't get New York publishers even to look [at their work]. It makes me wonder if the system is fair. . . . We've been waiting for our turn and it hasn't come."[18]

Brad Chambers, director of the New York Council for Interracial Books for Children, agrees with Islas's and Anaya's criticisms. He calls Chicano writers' lack of access to New York publishers "shocking and shameful," and he argues that "a lot of it is based on the fact that publishing houses are based in the Northeast and there is very little awareness of Mexican-American, Chicano [and Chicana] realities."[19] To support his claim, Chambers points to a creative writing contest that his council conducted for more than a decade as an attempt to bring unpublished African American, Chicano, Puerto Rican, Asian-American, and Native American writers to the attention of major publishers. "In 10 years, not a single winner in the Chicano category was picked up by a major house and published," he says. He emphasizes, however, that "it worked for winners of every other category. It did not work for Chicanos. And several were really quality work." In other words, those who create subjects privileging the WASP, Eastern, male outlook have primary claim to attention in the U.S. literary canon. Those who attend to African American, Native American, and Puerto Rican subjects come next, Chambers suggests. A distant last are works attentive to Chicano and Chicana subjects.

Finally, Al McDonald, who has described himself as the only senior African American editor "in all of New York," said this about the "brown barrier" in the New York publishing world: the problems Chicanos and Chicanas face with major houses are symptomatic of American publishing, an "insular" business that breeds a "homogeneity among editors" and often "ghettoizes" minority discourses. He gives this advice: "The trick is not to publish a book that's black or Chicano but a book that everybody should read for its literary value, its honesty, its power."[20] But Islas's *The Rain God* was not picked up by a major publisher precisely because its so-called "brown" cultural elements are what attracted most of the attention of the editors.

So far we have examined how the dominant institutional practices caused Islas's *The Rain God* to be rejected as an American novel with a difference. To show specifically how New York publishers influence Chicano texts and determine which images of the Chicano and Chicana will appear in them, let me examine how these institutional practices produced, in an exploitative manner, two novels by and about Chicanos: José Antonio Villareal's *Pocho* (Doubleday, 1959) and Edmundo Villaseñor's *Macho!* (Bantam Books, 1973).[21]

As the title suggests, *Pocho* is Villareal's attempt to write about the "pocho" (an Americanized Mexican) experience in California. In so doing, the author (unwittingly) projects a stereotypical view. The opening scenes of the novel, for example, as Evangelina Enríquez has pointed out, introduce us to Juan Rubio, an arrogant, callous *macho* who has been a soldier in Pancho Villa's army and has now returned to Juarez.[22] He enters a cantina complete with a mariachi band playing sentimental ballads and a young girl dancing a *tapatio* on a tabletop. Juan takes a fancy to the señorita and orders her to sit and drink with him. She obeys nervously, for she knows that her lover is nearby. Juan, however, kills the boyfriend and literally pulls the señorita out of the saloon and into a hotel room. She dutifully removes his boots, and after their lovemaking tells him that he does not even know her name. "What does that matter?" he answers, thinking, "in a cantina, as in bed, courtesy was nonexistent" (p. 2).

As we gather from this scene, *Pocho* is marked by the protagonist's clichéd Mexican male values. An ex-revolutionary, he leaves Mexico and becomes a farmworker in California. In struggling to exist in the United States, he tries to retain his Mexican cultural values in the rearing of his family. Richard Rubio, Juan's son and the *pocho* in the family, experiences the novel's basic tensions: either assert an Americanized individuality, or succumb to the burden of machismo and cultural nationalism imposed on him by his father and his community.

In much the same way, Edmundo Villaseñor's *Macho!* hailed by Bantam Books as "The First Great Chicano Novel"—although by 1973 "greater" Chicano novels such as Tomás Rivera's *Y no se lo tragó la tierra* and Rolando Hinojosa's *Estampas del Valle* had already been published by Chicano presses—confirmed popular views of the Chicano family that had made *Pocho* the first Chicano novel to be published by a major New York house. *Macho!* focuses on one year in the life of Roberto García, a Tarasacan Indian boy from Michoacán who is forced to cover for his father's poor work in the fields. As with a principal character in *Pocho*, the father in *Macho!* is a misogynist and a drunk. The novel stresses the isolation and "backwardness" of the protagonist's village, where strict obedience to old customs makes the atmosphere suffocating for the younger generation. After a night's brawl in a cantina, Roberto, seeking material wealth, emigrates to the United States following the example of the norteño, Juan Aguilar. In the United States, Roberto becomes acquainted with Cesar Chávez, the Chicano labor leader. But Roberto is turned off by Chávez, since he is primarily concerned about his parents and his family's suffering in Mexico.

Macho! thus describes the young field hand's disillusionment with life as a migrant farmworker in the United States.[23] Roberto has several negative encounters as a worker: he is cheated by a Mexican *coyote* (labor contractor) who breaks his promise to obtain legal status for Roberto; he is humiliated by immigration officers when he crosses the border; he is initiated into the endless cycle of dawn-to-dusk work in the California fields.

Clearly, Roberto García, like Juan Rubio in *Pocho*, is a one-dimensional character: he blindly follows the cult of machismo, which Villaseñor posits as the essence of the Mexican's value system. One example will suffice to point out the author's limited understanding: "Roberto got the first whore of his life, and then the next morning he felt bad and went to church and lit three candles and prayed a long time, but by afternoon with a few beers and money in his pocket it was all much better inside his soul, and he went back to the cantina with the woman" (p. 85). As this representative passage shows, Villaseñor's language, a poor Hemingway imitation at best, is stiff and awkward. Throughout the novel, his Chicano and Chicana characters sound like Hollywood stereotypes.

This brings us back to the original question about Arturo Islas's *The Rain God*. Why were Villareal's and Villaseñor's Chicano novels published by major New York houses and Islas's refused? Can we say that Villareal's and Villaseñor's books were simply better written? Or can we best answer if we shift from the purely "literary" to an extradiscursive examination of definitions, assumptions, and criteria used to determine the values of "ethnic" American texts?

The rejection of *The Rain God* by New York publishers can best be explained, first, by acknowledging that the novel does not stereotype Islas's Chicano and Chicana characters. More significantly, it did not conform to the editors' ideas about ethnic American literature's intrinsic "themes." It did not indulge in determinism, survival, the immigrant experience, and violence as Villareal's and Villaseñor's texts did. Unfortunately, these so-called "ethnic themes" are still part of reality as defined by the ruling ideological apparatus. Briefly, Villareal and Villaseñor were writing according to New York editors' standards about certain U.S. ethnic themes—social maladjustment, the individual and his environment, the pathological character of the Chicano family, illegals, violence, and criminal behavior—that dominant cultural practices define as worthy and "universal." Thus, it was Villareal's and Villaseñor's ability to produce cultural objects whose effect and function generated a popular American mythology and cultural view of Mexicans and Chicanos that made *Pocho* and *Macho!* the first Chicano novels to be published in New York.

To show how Islas's work can be read as a direct refutation of the New York publishing world's view of Chicano literary and cultural practices as well as a narrow U.S. sense of literary and historical "tradition," the following sections draw upon Islas's letters and interviews to trace the classical Anglo-American and Latin American literary backgrounds of *The Rain God*. In other words, Islas dissents from the consensus ideology of classic American literature that projects onto the vast and diversified body of literature a totalizing cultural homogeneity.[24]

II

Two statements by Islas in a letter to his agent are particularly pertinent to an initial understanding of *The Rain God*. He suggests that his novel is in the U.S. Southern tradition of Faulkner's classic *Absalom, Absalom!* (1936): "I am chronicling," he writes, "the life of a historical creature who happened to live at a time when he was taught to hate what he perceived himself to be."[25] In the same letter Islas elaborates: "[Miguel Chico is] my Quentin Compson; he would say in exactly the same tone Quentin uses at the end of *Absalom!*: 'I don't hate Mexicans! I don't hate Anglos! I don't hate gays'!"[26]

In *The Mind of the South*, W. J. Cash notes of U.S. Southern writers—and Islas, like García Márquez and Fuentes, stresses an affinity with them: "[they are] romantics of the appalling," who only hate the South "with the exasperated hate of a lover who cannot persuade the object of his affections to his desire," much as "Narcissus, growing at length analytical, might have suddenly begun to hate his image in a pool."[27] Presumably, what Islas wants us to see is that his central consciousness, Miguel Chico, like Faulkner's Quentin Compson, comes under Cash's definition. There is every reason to see, at least on a first reading, the novel as a compressed exploration of Miguel Chico's narcissistic hatred and resentment. Put differently, Miguel Chico exemplifies what Nietzsche saw in intellectuals as a form of profound *ressentiment*.[28] He suffers in a "psychological" sense from the destructive envy of the have-nots for the haves.

Seen in this light, Islas would have readers center the novel's interest on Miguel Chico. Those who do so, he believes, will see the primary importance he places on the contemplative mind and its exploratory, interpretive acts. Hence, early in the novel he describes the protagonist as central consciousness:

> He, Miguel Chico was the family analyst, interested in the past for psychological, not historical reasons. . . . he preferred to ignore factors in favor of motives, which were always and endlessly open to question and interpretation. . . . [He] wanted to look at motives and at people from an earthly, rather than outworldly, point of view.[29]

Clearly, the hero's central consciousness is the fixed point of view from which readers overhear the various generations of the Angel family. It follows that instead of attempting to give readers an "ethnic cultural message," as many editors in New York narrowly claimed, Islas's Chicano narrative is in the long tradition of psychologically complex novels, for *The Rain God* constantly draws attention to its ideas and labyrinthine methods. The central task of Miguel Chico as "family analyst" therefore is clear: to penetrate and attempt to see below the surface of things and so arrive at psychological judgments. Like a bookish Henry James character, he is "affected with a certain high lucidity."[30] For Islas, his character becomes not simply exceptionally intelligent and sensitive with a "value intrinsic," but, as in James's best work, as "a compositional resource" of the highest order. From the point of view of structure, Islas obviously places Miguel Chico and the play of his impressions and reactions at the book's center to make for a unity and intensity of focus that could not be easily achieved by other means. But his interest in such a character clearly extends beyond his structural use, for, like Henry James before him, he sees the "large lucid reflector" as no less than "the most polished of possible mirrors of the subject."[31]

As a consequence of this method, the novelist seems to withdraw from the action, allowing his intense perceiver to discover the subject for himself and in the process reveal it to the reader. Miguel Chico's function is to create the story out from its particulars by gradually perceiving the full significance of events in which he is involved. A word of qualification about Miguel Chico is in order here, for like John Marcher in James's classic tale, "The Beast in the Jungle," in which Marcher spends most of his time staring his fate (in the person of May Bartram) in the face and failing to get the point precisely because it so apparent, Miguel Chico often tends to (mis)read experience. Miguel Chico, Islas writes, "was still seeing people, including himself, as books. He wanted to edit them, correct them, make them behave differently. And so he continued to read them as if they were invented by someone else, and he failed to take into account their separate realities, their differences from himself. When people told him of their lives, or when he thought about his own in the way that is not thinking but a kind of reverie outside time, a part of him listened with care. Another part fidgeted, thought about something else or went blank, and wondered why once again he was being offered such secrets to examine" (p. 26). In *The Rain God,* as in James's fiction, failure to get the point that directly confronts one is often a matter of life and death.

Another source of difficulty for early mainline reviewers and readers is Islas's use of chronological dislocation—the free, wandering flow of mind, back and forth in time, over names and events known to the narrator but not to us on a first reading. Early reviewers, like the editors at major publishing houses, were baffled by these techniques in Islas's art. "The first 78 pages," one wrote, "seemed to me nothing more than a long introduction to the scores of characters in the novel, in which each is described but not given enough depth or color to be believable. The net effect is one of wholesale confusion as the reader tries to memorize dozens of names and figure out their relationships in this fictional middle-class Mexican-American family."[32] Capable of such remarks, the reviewer seems never to have read a Faulkner or García Márquez novel!

Additionally, the work of Wallace Stevens, Yvor Winters, and Wallace Stegner probably has most affected Islas's preoccupation in *The Rain God* with morality, postsymbolist technique, male utopias, and death. During his undergraduate and graduate studies in English and American literature at Stanford, Winters and Stegner undoubtedly were his most important artistic and scholarly influences. The full extent of his indebtedness to Winters can be appreciated only if we recall the most basic of Winters's powerful literary theories. Winters, as Terry Comito explains in his book *In Defense of Winters* (1986), was concerned with a moral evaluation of literature.[33] In Winters's view, literary works of art enable people to come to a rational and emotional understanding of the human condition and allow writers to make moral judgments. Above all, writers are to avoid producing obscure and confused works of art.

Islas profited immensely from this great dictum: "It ought to be possible to employ our sensory experience . . . in an efficient way, not as ornament, and with no sacrifice of rational intelligence."[34] In this regard, central to Islas's *The Rain God* is what Winters termed "controlled associationism," or a "postsymbolist method." This Wintersian technique is to establish a theme or introduce an abstract idea in conceptual terms. Such a rational framework is then entwined with sharp sensory details. The controlled association of abstract theme with imagery charges images with meaning. For Winters and, by extension, for Islas, the writer's moral attitude is defined not only by the logical content of the work, but by the writer's emotional reaction to its ideas.

Many of Islas's literary preferences—his interest in antiromantic American literature, or his deep admiration for Stevens—were first induced by Winters. Stevens's influence on *The Rain God* has not been noted by either his mainline or his brown "inside" reviewers and critics. Briefly, Stevens's entire poetic enterprise, as Daniel Hoffman pointed out, can be seen as a heroic and brilliant attack against the emptiness of "heaven," where "the death of one god is the death of all."[35] For Stevens, the withering away of traditional religion leaves the poet-artist of the twentieth century with only the impoverished earth and what Stevens termed "the gaiety of language." This is one of *The Rain God*'s central issues.

Specifically, Stevens's classic poem "Sunday Morning" (1915) informs much of Islas's thinking about traditional religion, for the poem as Stevens said in one of his letters "was simply an expression of paganism. . . ."[36] Like "Sunday Morning," *The Rain God* mounts a counter-rhetoric against the words of idealism (holy, divinity, lord, Jesus, soul) by bringing those words into his Chicano narrative and to the Southwest desert: freedom is rain, soul is sexual passion, the lord is the Amerindian Tlaloc (the rain god), and angels are well-built young men.

Stevens's "Sunday Morning," moreover, argues in provocatively erotic language, what Frank Lentricchia calls a "gutsy, wet, blooming passion," that the Christian myth has outlived its usefulness, for just as Jove stayed inhuman in the clouds only until he could move among us, so a later God-myth went unrealized until "our blood" mingled with Christ's at Bethlehem and the shepherds discerned it in a star.[37] Today, Stevens contends, the myth of Christ is as obsolete as the myth of Jove. Like Stevens, Islas argues in *The Rain God* that we are unable to look beyond the human for our gods. Thus, he suggests, even the gods need human flesh.

In short, Islas, like Stevens, gives his idealist readers a lesson: we must avoid abstraction, fixed principles, and closed systems. Throughout *The Rain God* he challenges the legitimacy of universals, repeatedly offsetting images of hollow spiritual categories with a wet, blooming imagery of a vibrant sexual world. To be sure, Islas, like Stevens, replaces what he sees as the desolate Christian mythology with one of his own: he inverts the procedure of Christianity in which people reach toward paradise in humble supplication. Naked in the desert, gay Uncle Felix, the rain dancer, in a male utopian vision chants not to paradise but from paradise, not in supplication but in triumph, projecting himself from the center of the world, not from its margins.

At the same time, Islas supplements Stevens's "pagan view" by interpolating an indigenous brown poem by the great Amerindian King Nezahualcoyotl:

> All the earth is a grave and nothing escapes it;
> nothing is so perfect that it does not descend
> to its tomb.
> Rivers, rivulets, fountains and waters flow,
> but never return to their joyful beginnings;
> anxiously they hasten on to the vast realms
> of the Rain God.

As they widen their banks, they also fashion
the sad urn of their burial.
Filled are the bowels of the earth
with pestilential dust once flesh and bones,
once animate bodies of men who sat upon thrones,
decided cases, presided in council,
commanded armies, conquered provinces,
possessed treasure, destroyed temples,
exulted in their pride, majesty, fortune,
praise and power.
Vanished are these glories, just as the fearful smoke
vanishes that belches forth from the infernal fires
of Popocatepetl.
Nothing recalls them but the written page. (p. 162)

In the Amerindian view, men and women hold an insignificant place in the world. The very world in which people make their brief struggle is seen as no more than an ephemeral shape, one experiment among others, and like them doomed to catastrophe. King Nezahualcoyotl's poem, like *The Rain God,* is haunted by the idea of death as total annihilation. For Nezahualcoyotl and Islas, religion and the art that expresses religion crush men and women with the harshness of a fate beyond their control.

Lastly, Islas owes something to Wallace Stegner, his dissertation advisor at Stanford. Like Stegner, he yearns for the day when the American West will have not only writers but all the infrastructure of literary life—a book publishing industry, a range of literary and critical magazines, and a reviewing corps not enslaved by East Coast opinions, support organizations such as PEN, and all the rest. Thematically, *The Rain God,* like the best of Stegner's narratives about the American West, takes life from the memory of formative events in a specific landscape characterized by migration. For them, the American West is an arid country, and aridity enforces space, which in turn enforces mobility and travel. In contradistinction to the settled communities of New England and the Midwest, the oasis space of the American West, they claim, does something to vision. It makes the country itself formidable and ever-present, and in the words of Stegner "it tends to make humans as migratory as antelope."[38] It is therefore true to say that Islas belongs to that large family of U.S. writers—from Willa Cather to N. Scott Momaday—whose works have been defined by motion and desire. Both Stegner and Islas ransack their memories, submitting them back to a special place and to the unforgettable time of childhood, followed by their achieving adulthood and deciding to become writers.

Similarly, Islas's autobiographical impulse in *The Rain God* owes much to Stegner's influence, for both writers deal with youth, initiation, and disillusionment. If Islas's affinity for Stevens was induced by Winters, his affinity for Cather was initiated by Stegner. Lines of kinship can be drawn between *The Rain God* and *My Ántonia.* Presumably, Islas read Stegner's essay on Cather, where he argued that Cather discovered her true voice when she began to write about the region and people she knew best. Then, Stegner avers, she wrote "spontaneously because she was tapping both memory and affection."[39]

A significant technical device that Islas draws from Cather and Stegner is the point of view from which *My Ántonia* and *Angle of Repose* are told. Each of these writers has in common the use of the narrative mask that enables Jim Burden, Lyman Ward, and Miguel Chico to exercise the author's sensibilities without obvious self-indulgence. In the processes of understanding and commemorating characters such as Ántonia or Mama Chona, the narrators locate themselves.

III

If Islas belongs among those U.S. writers whose works have been defined by region, his double-voiced novel also has direct lines of kinship to the Latin American new writing by Paz, Rulfo, and García Márquez. Throughout Islas's desert tale, there are New World-Amerindian qualities that clearly identify the book with the Latin American and, more specifically, the Mexican-Amerindian obsession with death. Islas digs deeply into the reality of his Chicano Border culture by showing how the Angel family fits together in a Mexican cultural pattern.

Foremost in this Amerindian-New World context is the author's assumption that the moment of death does nothing to inhibit communication. This characteristic, an important theme in Rulfo's classic Mexican novel *Pedro Paramo* (1955) and in García Márquez's *One Hundred Years of Solitude* (1967), stems from the New World idea of *almas en pena* (souls in torment) that wander the earth even after death. Comprehension of such an unaccustomed reality requires a reading more like the lyrical experiences of poetry than of the dialogical novel. Clues of all kinds are therefore important—repeated images, references to unreal events—not to remake the novel into a realistic experience, but to establish the relationship for a magic realist appreciation of the work.

At the novel's end, for example, Islas writes of Mama Chona's familiarity with *almas en pena:* "In the daytime, usually before the late afternoon meal, she would ask, 'Where is your father?' The first time she asked, Mema, surprised, told her straightforwardly that he was dead. Without blinking, Chona retorted, 'Yes, but why doesn't he come to see me? Where is he?' " (p. 172). On another occasion, Mama Chona, like Úrsula Buendía in *One Hundred Years of Solitude,* matter-of-factly reveals to Mema that she has visited with her dead husband, Carlos: "I saw your father today. He was with that woman Josefina. They came to see me together, can you imagine? I knew he was seeing a great deal of her, but it was shameless of him to bring her here when there are children in the house. I will not forgive him for that" (p. 172).

Mama Chona, to be sure, is not the novel's only character conversant with the Amerindian spiritual world. Nina, Miguel Chico's godmother, also is intimate with the supernatural: "The otherworldly side of her," Islas writes, "came to the surface before her son's death, and she explored it with the care and precision she used to prepare the annual income tax accounts of various business firms in town" (p. 33). Like the best magic realist writers, Islas often turns his back on realism. But it is important to note how, like García Márquez, he extends a magic realist situation to the edge of comedy and parody:

> It was not until she discovered the spirit world that Nina began to recognize that death might not exist as she imagined it in her terror. At the bi-weekly seances in the basement of her friends' Mexican food restaurant, her nose itched from the Aqua Velva they sprinkled into the air to induce serenity, Nina gradually became aware of two women waving at her from a strange and unknown region. They were about the same age and Nina saw with joy that one of the women was her sister, Antonia, who had died in her late twenties. The other woman was her mother, who at twenty-nine had died giving birth to Nina. (p. 34)

The comical "Signifyin[g]" distortion of reality at the séance—induced by the sprinkling of after-shave in the air—conveys an absurd and humorous effect. Indeed, this humorous critique of the magic realist tradition informs much of this comic-tragic novel. For example, when Juanita, Nina's sister, begins attending Nina's "classes in mind control," Islas "Signifies" on García Márquez's fantastic world in *One Hundred Years of Solitude*, where one character literally ascends to heaven. Like García Márquez's writing, Islas's prose style is usually plain, exact, and easily leaps into the comical and the exuberant. Although Nina's séance is accurately described, and with a wonderful, inventive touch, his desert tale in the end is always brought back to ordinary experience.

As his title suggests (Tlaloc in Amerindian religion), Islas's novel is preoccupied with the Amerindian beginnings of Chicano culture in the United States. Originally *Día de los Muertos (Day of the Dead)*, the book challenges American literature's very concept of "tradition" and deconstructs the one-dimensional (linear) view of history on which it is often predicated. Freed from strictly national U.S. genealogical imperatives, tradition in Islas's sense of the Americas can be perceived as a system of affinities independent of racial, ethnic, national, or linguistic criteria. The author thus combines historical with literary revision by demonstrating the impact of what Bakhtin called hybridization on literary production, specifically on questions of American literary canonization.[40] Translating cultural interaction into an exchange of literary forms, Islas, like Shange and Hinojosa, invalidates distinctions and proposes his own distinctive U.S.-Amerindian mythology of writing.

III

Caliban and Resistance Cultures

6 The School of Caliban

> A new turbulence is at work everywhere, and Caliban is wide awake.
> —George Lamming, *The Pleasures of Exile*

> Caliban can still participate in a world of marvels. . . .
> —Aimé Césaire, quoted in Munro's *Kas-Kas*

> I lack language./The language to clarify/My resistance to the literate.
> —Cherríe Moraga, *Loving in the War Years*

> Caliban is in control, metamorphosing a linguistics of mastery with masterful sound.
> —Houston Baker, Jr., "Caliban's Triple Play"

The title of this final chapter has several related senses essential to my comparative cultural analysis of Latin American, Afro-Caribbean, African American, and Chicano/a writers. The phrase suggests a group of engaged writers, scholars, and professors of literature who work under a common political influence, a group whose different (imagined) national communities and symbologies are linked by their derivation from a common and explosive reading of Shakespeare's last (pastoral and tragicomic) play, *The Tempest*. The phrase also emblematizes not just the group's shared subaltern subject positions, but the "schooling" that their enrollment in such an institution provides.

At the outset, let me emphasize that it would be gratifying if my study of Caliban in the Americas contributed in even a small way to developments in literary studies on both sides of the Atlantic known as the New Historicism in the United States and as Cultural Materialism in England.[1] My belief is that both the new U.S. and British ideological scholars would profit immensely in a comparative global cultural studies perspective from reading the various works by members in the School of Caliban, for they tell us much about the colonial encounters of the First and Third Worlds. Unfortunately, both the New Historicists and the Cultural Materialists have signally ignored Lamming's, Césaire's, and Fernández Retamar's appropriations of *The Tempest*. Regrettably, they have tended to listen exclusively to Prospero's mastery of voice; for, after all, he speaks their language of empire. Before we turn to the writers from Our America who have suffered colonial usurpation, and at the same time who have reversed the power-subject positions in *The Tempest*, let me briefly focus on some New Historicist and Cultural Materialist readings of Elizabethan drama and of *The Tempest*.

In U.S. universities, Shakespeare always stands alone. Without a doubt, he is the preeminent "monumental" figure in the West, what Rob Nixon calls the cultural gold standard of literature and literary value.[2] Typically, Shakespeare is separated not only from his global contemporary peers, but from the most general historical ground. In my first undergraduate survey course in Shakespeare at Yale in 1974, my young professor centered exclusively on New Critical and (post)structuralist "close readings" of several plays, demanding that we allow the texts, like well-wrought poems, to speak for themselves. To be fair, she suggested that most of Shakespeare's plays were related to the world of dreams and that psychoanalysis could provide us with a way of dealing with Shakespeare's overdetermined texts.[3]

Today, much of what goes on in the New Historicist classroom argues against the formalist idea of Shakespeare's plays as well-wrought poems, or as overdetermined dreams, for literary works can no more transcend history than can real people. Steven Mullaney and Stephen Greenblatt, exemplars of the New Historicism, have radically changed the direction of Shakespeare criticism and pedagogy by setting his plays in the context of the social drama out of which theater in Elizabethan England arose. In *The Place of the Stage* (1987), for instance, Mullaney begins his analysis of Elizabethan theater by turning to "the city itself and pursuing terms such as 'situation' and 'place' with as much literal-mindedness as can be mustered—more than might seem appropriate to readers trained, as I was, to regard plays as poems, and drama as primarily (if not entirely) a literary phenomenon."[4] What Mullaney contends is that "drama, unlike poetry, is a territorial art. It is an art of space as well as words, and it requires a place of its own, in or around a community, in which to mount its telling fictions and its eloquent spectacles" (p. 7).

Mullaney's reading of Elizabethan drama as a spatial "territorial art" inextricably connects to the high French theory of Michel Foucault. Foucault's writings, particularly those devoted to madness and prison, stand behind Mullaney's New Historicism. As with Foucault's reading of leprosy in the Middle Ages, Mullaney sees popular drama as taking place on "the margins of the city" where "forms of moral incontinence and pollution were granted license to exist beyond the bounds of a community they had, by their incontinence, already exceeded" (p. 9). Mullaney's work thus owes much to Foucault's analysis of the politics of space and to the topology of contestatory power in civil society.

Stephen Greenblatt, however, is the real center of the New Historicist movement in the United States, for he alone was responsible for naming the school.[5] Although this is not the place for a complete review and analysis of Greenblatt's enormous contributions to Renaissance literary studies, this section focuses on his method of reading Shakespeare by looking at his idiosyncratic reading of *The Tempest*, "The Land of Cockaigne," in his book *Shakespearean Negotiations* (1988). Greenblatt's New Historicist readings of Shakespeare are by now familiar. Usually he begins by seizing on something extraordinary, obscure, and unexpected: prison treatises, diaries and autobiographies, New World pamphlets and exotica, reports on diseases or hangings. As Walter Cohen says, the New Historicist "strategy is governed methodologically by the assumption that any one aspect of society is related to any other. No organizing principle determines the relationship: any social practice has at least a potential connection to any theatrical practice."[6]

More precisely, Greenblatt's characteristic move is to begin from a colonialist episode and proceed to the Shakespearean text. For example, in his reading of *The Tempest* the flow is from the cultural to the literary. He starts by discussing a story told during a sermon by Hugh Latimer, a Protestant martyr, which demonstrates the use of what Greenblatt terms "salutary anxiety" to manipulate a condemned woman. Greenblatt shows how salutary anxiety is at work in *Measure for Measure* and in a fully developed manner in *The Tempest*. It is precisely in *The Tempest*, he asserts, "when . . . Shakespeare reflected upon his own art with still greater intensity and self-consciousness than in *Measure for Measure*, he once again conceived of the playwright as a princely creator of anxiety."[7]

Why is "salutary anxiety" important for Greenblatt, and how does it operate in *The Tempest?* In Latimer's narrative, anxiety is produced through his withholding of a royal pardon for the condemned woman until he can convince her to abandon her belief in the Catholic doctrine of purification for women after the birth of a child. Latimer thus created a state of anxiety for the woman who was convinced that she was doomed to execution. Greenblatt tells us of another creation of salutary anxiety by James I, following the execution of three men allegedly involved in a conspiracy against him. Three more men were scheduled to die by hanging; however, at the last moment the sheriff informed them of their pardon. To be sure, the first executions had created a real state of anxiety among the masses; however, they were becoming resentful as executions appeared to be increasing. The king's pardoning of the last three prisoners evoked a response from the populace—thereby, according to Greenblatt, strengthening his power.

In "The Land of Cockaigne," Greenblatt uses these examples to demonstrate how the controlled management of anxiety will provide the desired effects in the people. Thus, anxiety must be controlled to achieve its results. As Greenblatt puts it, "managed insecurity may have been reassuring not only to the managers themselves but to those toward whom the techniques were addressed" (p. 137). Once the definition and practice of salutary anxiety is established, he proceeds to analyze it in theatrical and literary terms. He analyzes controlled anxiety's place in *The Tempest,* then deals with the reciprocal nature of art and life by discussing the influence of William Strachey's famous letter regarding the shipwreck of the *Sea-Adventurer,* bound for Jamestown colony, on Shakespeare's play. Shakespeare did not simply use Strachey's letter as a source grounded in the literature of voyaging; rather, for Greenblatt, a cultural phenomenon engaged both Strachey and Shakespeare: namely, the production of anxiety for managing a group of people or a situation. In Greenblatt's words, "the conjunction of Strachey's unpublished letter and Shakespeare's play signals an institutional circulation of culturally significant narratives. And as we shall see, this circulation has as its central concern the public management of anxiety" (p. 149). For Greenblatt, it is not simply that works of art borrow a situation from the real and fictionalize it; he sees the relationship between literature and history as more subtle. In his reading of Latimer's story of the condemned woman, he suggests, "if the practice he exemplifies helps to empower theatrical representation, fictive representations have themselves helped to empower his practice" (p. 147).

Greenblatt ends his New Historicist reading of *The Tempest* by telling the story of the explorer H. M. Stanley and his colonialist "encounter" with the Mowa people of Africa. Stanley claims he had to burn his copy of Shakespeare to appease the "natives" and to save the more important notes and maps they had seen him writing in his tent.[8] Because Stanley's notebook survived with its essential information about the region and its people, the colony of the Belgian Congo could be established. Greenblatt notes that although other discourses (in this case Stanley's notes and maps) are more directly responsible for the management of power, they might not survive without fictional discourse. Stanley's and Shakespeare's discourses, Greenblatt believes, are equally important in establishing and maintaining a state of power.

In contrast to this Foucault-inspired New Historicism in the United States, Cultural Materialism in England addresses other issues in Shakespeare studies: monumentalism in English studies, colonial discourse, and ideology. As Raymond Williams, one of the founders of the Cultural Materialist school, suggests: "There is a shift, beyond the world of world-pictures, and equally beyond the close readings of dramatic poems, to attention to the basic forms of drama itself."[9]

In explicit opposition to the monumentalist New Historicist readings by Greenblatt and Mullaney, the English Cultural Materialist readings by Barker, Hulme, and Hawkes condemn Shakespeare for producing an essentializing colonialist discourse. The case against Shakespeare has been most powerfully argued in two new readings of *The Tempest:* Barker and Hulme's "Nymphs and Reapers Heavily Vanish: The Discursive Contexts of *The Tempest*" (1985) and Terence Hawkes's *That Shakespeherian Rag* (1986).[10]

Barker and Hulme begin their critique by arguing that the Swan of Avon today is made to participate in the construction of a mythic English past "which is picturesque, familiar and untroubled" (p. 192). That is, they read the play through poststructuralist lenses: *The Tempest,* they contend, is two irreconcilable dramas that radically explode and deconstruct one another. Prospero's play is obsessed with legitimating his power by securing recognition of his claim to Milan; in contrast, Caliban's play dramatizes Prospero's suppression of Caliban's mutiny, which allows Prospero "to annul the memory of his failure to prevent his expulsion from the dukedom" (p. 201).

If the New Historicists tend to rewrite *The Tempest* as Foucauldian allegory, the Cultural Materialists allegorically rewrite the play as poststructuralist critique. For Barker and Hulme, Prospero needs to establish his version of the past, which no one on the island is able to question. Moreover, Prospero usurps Caliban's indigenous authority; Prospero needs to make Ariel and Caliban slaves; Prospero needs to suppress the matriarchal order of Caliban's mother, Sycorax. Finally, they criticize Prospero's princely Manichaean aesthetics: his dualistic categories of "Others" on the island as rapists or virgins, friends or foe; and his division of the shipwrecked voyagers into clearly defined groups of aristocrats and plebeians. In brief, Barker and Hulme suggest that *The Tempest* does not simply reflect colonialist practices within a New World context, but that Shakespeare's play should be seen as an "intervention" in an ambiguous and contradictory "colonial discourse"—promoting a colonialist ideology.

Hawkes in *That Shakespeherian Rag* develops a similar Cultural Materialist critique of *The Tempest* in a chapter entitled "Swisser-Swatter: Making a Man of English Letters." Like Barker and Hulme before him, he addresses the complexity of the playwright's colonialist discourse. For Hawkes, as for Barker and Hulme, "colonial discourse" loosely signifies a cluster of linguistically based practices unified by their common deployment in managing colonial relationships and power.

Hawkes's analysis of the way Shakespeare constructs the threatening "other" is especially revealing. He begins by focusing on Trinculo's unsettling question, "What have we here? a man or fish?" (2.2.24). For Hawkes, the question is asked in the colonialist's language par excellence. Throughout his discussion, he shows how the query "focuses exactly on that vexing boundary and from the perspective of a European signifying system the lineaments of an exotic, aboriginal or Indian culture" (p. 51).

Of course, Shakespeare describes Caliban in other ways: "Legg'd like a man! and his fins like arms!" (2.2.34); "no fish" (2.2.36); "some monster of the isle with four legs" (2.2.66); "a plain fish" (5.1.266); and a "mis-shapen knave" (5.1.268). Nevertheless, as his name suggests, he is a "cannibal," a figure, which as Hawkes and other Cultural Materialists emphasize, has taken shape in colonial discourse: ugly, devilish, ignorant, gullible, and treacherous—according to a history of Europeans' descriptions about him. For the Cultural

Materialists, Caliban bears the colonialist inscription: savage, deformed, slave—a multiple burden of Old World Mediterranean and New World Atlantic descriptions. He is seen as the monster that all the characters make him out to be, Hawkes suggests.

We began this book with Fernández Retamar's reworking of *The Tempest,* so it is only fitting to return to that point of departure. Admittedly, Fernández Retamar was not the first writer from Nuestra América to rewrite Shakespeare's "colonialist narrative" to meet contemporary political and cultural needs. George Lamming from Barbados was one of the first great investigators of Caliban's mastery in the New World. His chief subject in the autobiographical text *The Pleasures of Exile* (1960) is a "descriptive reflection" on the predicament of a group of writers from the English-speaking Caribbean who arrived in Great Britain as part of what Lamming calls a "larger migrating labor force."[11] His text, moreover, focuses "on the colonial character of their relation to the metropole" (p. 6).

Along with Fernández Retamar, Lamming is the supreme commentator, the one author from Our America, who pulls Old World colonialist and New World colonized writing into a coherent and continuous line; this is the role he has played in Fernández Retamar's larger constructions of the literatures of the Americas.[12] Lamming delivers an exciting postcolonial autobiography by exploring his and a group of Caribbean writers' experiences in Britain within *The Tempest*'s frame of reference. It is the frame, Lamming stresses, "within which the meaning of our total experience, at the time, could be located" (p. 6). Lamming's revisionist tactic is to rewrite *The Tempest* from the colonialist subject's standpoint. Rob Nixon suggests that Lamming and other Caribbean and African writers "on the one hand . . . hailed Caliban and identified themselves with him; on the other, they were intolerant of received colonial definitions of Shakespeare's value."[13] Lamming recalls how his teachers in Barbados

> followed the curriculum as it was. He did what he had to do: Jane Austen, some Shakespeare, Wells's Kipp, and so on. What happened was that they were teaching exactly whatever the Cambridge Syndicate demanded. That was the point of it. These things were directly connected. Papers were set in Cambridge and our papers were sent back there to be corrected. We had to wait three to four months. Nobody knew what was happening till they were returned.[14]

In describing his own childhood cultural dependency, Lamming directly challenges colonialist readings of *The Tempest*. In his chapters "A Monster, A Child, A Slave," and "Caliban Orders History," he suggests that European and British colonialism provides Shakespeare's dominant discursive contexts. *The Tempest* is simply "an expression of the perfect colonial concern" (p. 96). At the same time, the play is about Caliban's enslavement as the means of supplying food and labor on which Prospero and his daughter, Miranda, are completely dependent. "It is in his relationship to Caliban, as a physical fact of life that we are allowed to guess some of Prospero's needs," Lamming writes. "He needs his slave. Moreover, he must be cautious in his dealings with him, for Caliban contains the seed of revolt" (p. 98).

What is especially significant in this reading is that *The Tempest* describes colonialist hegemony in the New World through Prospero's native violence, for Prospero is always trying to perform his colonialist legitimacy through what Lamming calls "sadism": "After the slaves were encamped in Haiti, torture became a common method of persuading them to work. In some cases they were roasted, others were buried alive up to their neck[s], their heads smeared with sugar that the flies might devour them; they were . . . made to eat their excrement, drink their urine, lick the saliva of other slaves" (p. 98). Likewise, in Shakespeare's play, Lamming asserts, "there is a similar sadism in Prospero whenever he is moved to threaten Caliban for his rebellion" (p. 99). To support this reading, he cites the following:

> Prospero: For this, be sure, tonight thou shalt have cramps
> Side stitches that shall pen thy breath up; urchins
> Shall, for that vast of night that they may work,
> All exercise on thee; thou shalt be pinch'd.
> As thick as honeycomb, each pinch more stinging
> Than bees that made them. (1.2.325–30)

Prospero's sadism, Lamming contends, has been signally ignored by European and North American critics, who have tended to listen exclusively to Prospero's voice. In other words, *The Tempest* has been interpreted through critical practices that are complicitous, whether consciously or not, with a Eurocentric colonialist ideology.

But what changed this colonialist interpretation of *The Tempest?* According to Lamming, two world historical events destroyed Prospero's domination in the New World: "a profound revolutionary change initiated by Toussaint L'Ouverture in the Haitian war of independence" and Fidel Castro's overturning of Prospero in Cuba in 1959. As Lamming states, "The Caribbean remained, for Europe and the United States, an imperial frontier until, like a bolt from the blue, Fidel Castro and the Cuban revolution reordered our history, and called attention to the obvious and difficult fact that people lived there. The Cuban revolution was a Caribbean response to that imperial menace which Prospero conceived as the civilizing mission" (pp. 6–7).

For Lamming, Prospero's defeat by Caliban in the Caribbean can no longer be glossed over. Unlike the colonialist Prospero who "forgot that foul conspiracy/Of the beast Caliban and his confederates/Against my life": (4.1.139–41), the postcolonial Prospero no longer can contain Caliban's revolt and can no longer complete, in a smoothed-over narrative, the colonialist project. Prospero's version of history, after the Cuban Revolution, can thus no longer remain authoritative:

> The dialogue which Caliban now offers Prospero is an important occasion; for it is based upon and derives from a very great drama. I would describe that drama as the release of two-thirds of the world's population from the long and painful purgatory of unawareness. . . . The world from which our reciprocal ways of seeing have sprung was once Prospero's world. It is no longer his. Moreover, it will never be again. It is ours, the legacy of many centuries, demanding of us a new kind of effort, a new kind of sight for viewing the possible horizons of our own century. (p. 203)

The establisher of Caliban's coherence and continuity in the New World, Lamming also functioned as the agent who gave Caribbean and U.S. minority discourses a bold new protagonist.

Since 1939, Aimé Césaire with his famous anticolonialist "Notebook of a Return to the Native Land," a poem about his native Martinique, about colonial oppression, and African sources (written, at times, in the language of Rimbaud), has communicated the urgent need for decolonization and used his aesthetics of Negritude to counter Prospero's ideology of racial superiority. Throughout his career (he has held elected posts as mayor of Fort-de-France and deputy to the French National Assembly), Césaire has oscillated between the political periphery and center.

Aesthetically, he has been central in producing an alternative art aimed back at France and the metropole. Together with his collaborator, Michel Leiris, he opened a debate in the 1950s with the First World that has continued during subsequent decades. In 1969, he focused the debate by freely rewriting *The Tempest* with his own play entitled *A Tempest*. As with his earlier poetry and essays, he remains concerned with these questions: How has European knowledge about the world been shaped by a totalitarian will to power? How have Western writers been enmeshed in colonial situations?

Like Lamming, Césaire makes Caliban the central protagonist in *A Tempest*, what one could call a noninstrumental protagonist. "I was trying to de-mythify [Shakespeare's] tale. To me Prospero is the complete totalitarian. I am always surprised when others consider him the wise man who 'forgives.' . . . Prospero is the man of cold reason, the man of methodical conquest—in other words, a portrait of the enlightened European."[15] Not surprisingly, Césaire's protagonist "is the man who still is close to his beginnings, whose link with the natural world has not yet been broken. Caliban can still participate in a world of marvels, whereas his master can merely 'create' them through his acquired knowledge. At the same time, Caliban is also a rebel—the positive hero, in a Hegelian sense" (p. 176).

Like Shakespeare's *The Tempest*, Césaire's *A Tempest* has a shipwreck, an irritable father, and a character who manipulates the plot. The old conventions are here, but mainly Césaire "writes back" at an imperial discourse from the position of a Caribbean Caliban whose actuality has been distorted and denied:

> Prospero, you're a great magician:
> you're an old hand at deception.
> And you lied to me so much,
> about the world, about yourself,
> that you ended up by imposing on me
> an image of myself:
> underdeveloped, in your words, incompetent,
> that's how you made me see myself!
> And I loathe that image . . . and it's false!
> . . . .
> And I know that one day my bare fist, just
> that, will be enough to crush your world. The
> old world is falling apart![16]

Most significant is Caliban's refusal to see himself within the European "signifying system." At the beginning of Césaire's play, Caliban, like a Malcolm X, challenges Prospero by saying:

> Call me X. That would be best. Like a man
> without a name. Or, to be more precise, a
> man whose name has been stolen. You talk about history . . .
> well,
> that's history, and everyone knows it! Every time you
> call me it reminds me of a basic fact, that fact that you've
> stolen everything from me, even my identity.
> Uhuru! (1.2.18)

Throughout *A Tempest,* Caliban offers his searing and defiant counter to Prospero: he reminds him again and again not only of his Afro-Caribbean roots ("Call me X"), but of how he showed him all the marvelous qualities of the isle.

In Césaire's play it is also remarkable how Caliban contests its true beginnings. We are made aware that he has his own story and that it does not begin where Prospero begins. A theatrical space of resistance is opened, a gap that allows us to see that Prospero's narrative (or Shakespeare's narrative) is not simply history, not simply the way things were, but a particular version. In his own space, Césaire's Caliban, or rather "X," is allowed to tell his story with grace and wit. Césaire's account is remarkable because Prospero and Caliban are seen not only as archetypes of the colonizer and colonized, as the Cultural Materialists emphasize in their allegorical rewritings of *The Tempest,* but Prospero in Caliban's response is represented by Césaire as a colonial historian, and such a convincing and subtle historian that other histories have to fight their way into his official document.

In brief, *A Tempest* is a Caribbean landscape in which ideological and cultural transformations occur. The play makes demands. As with Césaire's poetry, readers must search for dictionaries in several languages, to encyclopedias, to atlases, and to African sources. To complicate matters, he even counters Prospero's white magic and the tradition it reflects. Against the Western cultural complex network of Neoplatonism, hermeticism, and occult philosophy, he offers the reader Afro-Caribbean *lo real maravilloso;* he counters Prospero's magic with "Eshu," an African god. In the end, he forces his audience to construct readings that are familiar to New Historicists and Cultural Materialists but that must be shaped from a comparative global cultural situation. Césaire's world, like Lamming's and Fernández Retamar's, is Caribbean—hybrid and heteroglot.

Like Lamming and Césaire, Fernández Retamar institutionalized a powerful reading of *The Tempest* in his pamphlet *Caliban*, but this time he went further than the others by presenting a severe cultural critique of Borges, Fuentes, and Rodríguez Monegal.[17] His adamantly anticolonialist form of pan-American studies puts forward a radical criticism of alterity that merits close scrutiny, for *Caliban* may be read as a long meditation on the problem of cosmopolitanism itself as well as in mapping out the paradoxes of the dialectics of otherness.

First and foremost, Fernández Retamar is a loyal, though critical, disciple of the Hegelian Fanon of *Black Skins/White Masks* (1952). This does not mean, however, that his interpretive essays tend only toward a dialectical and psychoanalytical reading of colonialism and racism. His theories, to be sure, tend to agree with Fanon's deconstruction of the neutrality of language, for in *Caliban* he offers an astute and painful elaboration of what it means to speak the language of the dominant class: "Right now, as we are discussing [a recent polemic regarding Cuba], as I am discussing with these colonizers, how else can I do it except in one of their languages, which is also our language, and with so many of their conceptual tools" (p. 11). Within this Fanonian reading of language and domination, Fernández Retamar shows in a starkly private discourse how the master (Prospero) imposes his language, his system of thought and values, and even his conceptual models on the indigenous inhabitants of the Americas (Caliban). The slave thus becomes trapped within these systems of thought and behavior.

Like Lamming and Césaire before him, Fernández Retamar claims that Caliban and not Prospero or Ariel is "our symbol," for "we, the mestizo inhabitants of these same isles where Caliban lived, see with particular clarity [the following]: Prospero invaded the islands, killed our ancestors, enslaved Caliban, and taught him his language to make himself understood. . . . I know no other metaphor more expressive of our cultural situation, of our reality" (p. 24).

Caliban, in its most general intention, popularized and completed a total shift in perspective about the Americas that Lamming and Césaire had begun—in opposition to ruling culture or hegemony in the New World—for no longer are we to see history from the viewpoint of that familiar protagonist, Prospero, but rather we are to rethink our American culture and identity from the perspective of the Other—Caliban—a protagonist excluded, ruled, and exploited. As inhabitants of the same geopolitical space as Caliban, we are to resist what Stephen Greenblatt has described as Prospero's refashioning of our inner lives and thus fight against Prospero's "disciplinary techniques" of mind control, coercion, and anxiety.

Caliban is also about the role of pan-American writers and intellectuals in a postcolonial world—how intellectuals and writers in their work in and on culture choose either to involve or not to involve themselves in the political work of social change and criticism. Said differently, intellectuals (Ariels), according to Fernández Retamar, can side either with Prospero and help fortify ruling culture, or side with Shakespeare's "mis-shapen knave," Caliban, "our Symbol," and help resist, limit, and alter domination in the Americas. In this chapter we will examine four contemporary Chicano/a and African American narratives by Rodriguez, Galarza, Moraga, and Baker in light of this Calibanic frame of reference.

While much has been written about Rodriguez's autobiography, *Hunger of Memory* (1982), little has been written about Galarza's *Barrio Boy* (1971), Moraga's *Loving in the War Years* (1983), or Baker's *Modernism and the Harlem Renaissance* (1987).[18] However, much of what has been written about Rodriguez and what has not been written about Galarza, Moraga, or Baker lacks a Calibanic viewpoint. Written against the background of contemporary American history and the global movement of change, the experimental narratives of these four writers of color reflect the impact of events in Our America. Their context is ethnocentric, homophobic, and racist America: concrete and intolerably continuing. My view is that their narratives are written, considered, and experienced by Caliban who desires either to participate in the historical process of hegemony or to participate in resistance to domination.

Within this Calibanic context, for whom do they write? In what circumstances? The answers to these questions can provide the ingredients for making a politics of interpretation. But if we do not want to answer in a dishonest and abstract way, we must show why these questions are relevant to the present, for as this book has mapped out, writing, criticism, and cultural studies are not merely related to but are integral parts of the currents and practices that play a role in the postcolonial world.

Rodriguez's controversial *Hunger of Memory* should be analyzed because the dominant U.S. literary public has by now legitimated his work.[19] In the words of Ramón Saldívar, "Rodriguez has become in the span of a few years' time the voice of 'Hispanic America' as his many short articles on a variety of topics and in various publications, such as a recent one in the *Wall Street Journal* on language policy indicate."[20]

Hunger of Memory is his first attempt at full-scale autobiography. His prologue, aptly called "Middle-Class Pastoral," eloquently answers the question "who writes?": "[A] dark-skinned . . . comic victim of two cultures . . . a middle-class man" (p. 3). His chapter "Mr. Secrets" answers the question for whom is the writing done?—"I write today," he tells us, "for a reader who exists in my mind only phantasmagorically. Someone with a face erased; someone of no particular race or sex or age or weather. A gray presence. Unknown, unfamiliar. All that I know about him is that his society, like mine, is often public, *'un gringo'* " (p. 182). Yet, paradoxically, he pretends to join Caliban's school of cultural resistance that Lamming, Césaire, and Fernández Retamar have described: "I have taken Caliban's advice. I have stolen their books. I will have some run of this isle. . . . (In Beverly Hills will this monster make a man?)" (p. 3). Can our misshapen, suburban knave pass himself off so easily as a writer-intellectual who leans toward Caliban and against Prospero?

Instead of writing in straight narrative, Rodriguez adapts the structure of focusing on specific subjects. He presents chapters on the Borgesian-like public and private self, on Catholicism, the scholarship boy, Mexican braceros, eroticism, jogging, on the small world of academia in the San Francisco Bay area, and on Sunday brunches. This structure of cohesive, yet autonomous, essays allows him to meditate on the brutal process of his own "normalization," summarized in the subtitle, *The Education of Richard Rodriguez*.[21] Far from celebrating his Americanization, however, Rodriguez's autobiography is a highly marketable lyric of rhetorical angst. The main subject is his estrangement from his working-class parents because of his education at Stanford, Columbia, and Berkeley, and his subsequent rise in the ruling culture: "What preoccupies me is immediate," he writes, "the separation I endure with my parents in loss. This is what matters to me: the story of the scholarship boy who returns home one summer from college to discover bewildering silence, facing his parents. This is my story. An American story" (p. 5). Nevertheless, he never makes clear in his confession why his gain—becoming a public citizen—should be his parents' loss of a son. His father, for instance, asks perhaps the book's most important question: "I don't know why you feel this way. We have never had any of the chances before" (p. 172). Rodriguez's ahistorical autobiography, one may conclude, sins against his father's historical insight.

What is even more unsettling in *Hunger of Memory* is the author's claim that education necessarily causes alienation, when his thesis is demonstrably false: education does not have to cut us off from our world, community, and family. Rather, education can provide critical understanding. As postcolonial intellectuals—as Ariels—who have a choice to make between hegemony and Prospero on the one hand, and Caliban and resistance on the other, we must involve ourselves in the political work of social change. As Frank Lentricchia has said in *Criticism and Social Change:* "We might do it very well because we have the technical knowledge of the insider. We have at our disposal an intimate understanding of the expressive mechanisms of culture."[22]

Although Rodriguez continually tells us that he suffers from a sense of the subaltern's lack of advantage, from the evidence it is clear that he suffers more from a profound sense of snobbery and bad taste. As he tells us freely with his own pen, "I am filled with the gaudy delight, the monstrous grace of the nouveau riche" (p. 137). In Lamming's, Césaire's, and Fernández Retamar's sense, Rodriguez is not a Calibanic protagonist; rather, he has become, in Renato Rosaldo's words, "an icon of collaboration with the English-only movement and the conservative right wing."[23]

Furthermore, Rodriguez's autobiography is not depicted in the "biographical time" that chronicles its subject in what Mikhail Bakhtin has called "the flow of history";[24] but, as Ramón Saldívar suggests, it is structured "on the archetypal pattern of redemption, albeit in Rodriguez's case a secular redemption" (p. 28). In other words, in *Hunger of Memory* (as in Christian hagiography) Rodriguez narrates only the extraordinary, "unusual" moments of his Chicano life. He eschews the whole of human life. What he in fact dramatizes are two images of the self: that of the sinner before rebirth and that of the saint after crisis and rebirth, joined by a period of purification through redemption. It is therefore not surprising that he is last seen leaving the last supper with his family at Christmas—ready to redeem our Chicano sins of barbarism and ready to be reborn as the hero of the conservative English Speaking Union and its ilk. *Hunger of Memory* in my view is significant not for its poetic representation of the adventures of language acquisition, but rather for its dramatization of the *muy mal educado*—the case history of ruling cultural normalization in the United States.

Against this background of the alienated Ariel writer-intellectual who sides with the disciplinary techniques of Prospero, we may better understand Galarza's *Barrio Boy,* Moraga's *Loving in the War Years* and Baker's *Modernism and the Harlem Renaissance* as signs of independence from their enslavers. Of all the recent autobiographical/critical/testimonial narratives written by Chicanos and African Americans, these three express the most valid and serious reversal of trends and influences: in the past from the metropole to the barrio, now from the politicized and feminist barrio to the metropole. In these three books, Caliban who represents the negative of the master-slave relationship, assumes powerful consciousness. Caliban curses the oppressor, be it Díaz's Mexico or Teddy Roosevelt's America in Galarza's case, the bourgeois categories of family and lover for Moraga, or the white New England monumentalists for Baker.

Of all the interesting Chicano activist-historians, (with the possible exception of Américo Paredes), Galarza's is the surest literary gift and the most committed intellectual ambition. So it is natural to think of him as a great historian—and not merely because we recognize him as an artist. As Alfred Kazin said in his book about classical American writers, *An American Procession:* "A great historian is not the most *immediately* influential writer of history, not the most painstaking specialist in history, but the writer who, within the discipline of scholarship, has more than any other created our image of History. The great historian, the great dramatists and analysts of history, are closest to what history means to us. Since History, as an intellectual order in the mind, is the creation of historical *writers,* it follows that it is such writers who have made history."[25] This is precisely what Galarza accomplishes in *Barrio Boy;* he creates our activist image of Chicano history.

Barrio Boy is so accomplished, subtle, and persuasive in its own historical way that it takes Galarza's more famous social-science books under its wing.[26] It has gathered his life, his emergent oppositional values of cultural resistance and struggle, his contempt for ruling-class authority into a single document of the great transformation of Mexican life after the Mexican Revolution, a document that also offers itself as the key to the transformation of Mexicanos into Chicanos. His account of his "double acculturation," it can be argued, has already become the great historical allegory of his epoch.

"History," said Fredric Jameson, "is what hurts, it is what refuses desire and sets inexorable limits to individuals as well as to collective praxis."[27] Galarza, throughout his remarkable life, believed that. As he said in one of many letters to his sister, Nora Lawson:

> As far back as I can remember, people have come to me for help. Most of what I have learned has been in one way or another related to personal and collective problems that these people posed. . . . I don't know how many opportunities I have had to make money, as for instance the job of assistant manager for Standard Oil in Venezuela when I was barely out of college. Each time such a chance has come my way, my problem was whether I should take it so that I might be able to do something for those I loved—sending you to college, for instance. But I have always resolved the conflict against the advantages to my family, and always because I could not see myself cutting myself off from the other world that really bore me—my mother's world and that of her people.[28]

Barrio Boy succeeds as a work of Calibanic history precisely because Galarza can present the actors of history who taught him how to serve his people. His book, nominally intended as oral "thumbnail sketches" for his wife and daughters, is a committed scholar's inside story of the emergence of a leading demographic group in California whose members personify a new type of cultural citizen. Once you become aware of the autobiography as a dialogue spoken to the masses of young men and women who like Galarza had been uprooted by the Mexican Revolution to travel north from Mexico, you find nothing strange in thinking of him as the master of his literary trade and the willing agent and maker of our history. How crafty he is in the driving spirit of struggle against ruling-class authority both in Mexico and the United States. In the full freedom of cultural conversation, he plays and replays his life as a young child and rehearses facts. Broadly speaking, he seeks to create a travel narrative, to prove a case against the "psychologists, psychiatrists, social anthropologists and other manner of 'shrinks' [who] have spread the rumor that these Mexican immigrants and their offspring have lost [their] self-image" (p. 1). Everything in the life of young Ernesto—his countries, Mexico and the United States; his ancestors; his generation; and his particular subject, an individual's participation in one of the grandest migrations of modern times—finally arranges itself as a wonderful travel narrative to produce a particular effect. Chicanos have never lost their sense of self; they have always been the agents who built the greatness of America through their labor and struggle.

Galarza's purpose was always to write Calibanic history. In *Barrio Boy,* he cleverly turned himself into a character, not the mature scholar-activist Dr. Ernesto Galarza, but "little Ernie" who "was never told, and . . . never [was] asked, about getting into the *lucha*" of history (p. 229). He became, however, inextricably and willingly involved, first as a witness to history, then as a chronicler of history through memory. So *Barrio Boy* always draws on history to portray young Ernesto as a type of new global citizen. He is by turns an example of the human species in the revolutionary Americas, the barrio boy who did odd jobs (drugstore clerk, messenger, field and cannery worker, court interpreter) in the ghettos of the United States, the translator of North American ruling culture to his proletarian Mexican family, the sensitive, Gramscian "organic intellectual" fighting for farmworkers' rights in the labor camps of California. As he says at the book's end: "When troubles made it necessary for the *barrio* people to deal with the American uptown, the *Autoridades,* I went with them to the police court, the industrial accident office, the county hospital, the draft board, the county clerk . . ." (p. 256).

More than anything else, *Barrio Boy* is the story of young Ernesto's working-class acculturations in Mexico and in Sacramento. Born in a small village "in the wild, majestic mountains of the Sierra de Nayarit" (p. 3) in 1905, he records his life story in its geopolitical context. Caught up in the unsettling events of the Mexican Revolution (1910–17), he, his mother, and his uncles, migrate in stages from one workplace to another—Jalco, Tepic, Mazatlán, Nogales—finally settling in the Sacramento barrios. What we read in the autobiography's five parts are in fact the stages of a travel narrative—a narrative of the road that forms the organizing centers for the development of his private and political self.

The earliest episodes are set about 1905 in Jalco, and the latest centers on his first summer as a migrant labor organizer in rural California, daydreaming of the high school he will attend in the fall. The most enjoyable episodes are his vividly recorded adventures on the road (chapters 3 and 4). In these middle chapters, young Ernesto encounters people of all social classes, religions, ages, and nationalities at the height of the Revolution. This is important for us, because, as Ramón Saldívar suggests, as the Mexican Revolution shattered the rigid boundaries of prerevolutionary society, Ernesto was able to experience first-hand the breakdown of social distance between the individual and the collective.[29] His acculturation was shaped in the midst of these revolutionary experiences. His book, it can be argued, describes these complex intersections of the self in both a private and public revolutionary world.

Throughout his early acculturation, aided with *dichos, corridos,* proverbs, legends, and folklore told to him by his mother and her mountain people, Galarza's sense of self is strong, resilient, and historical. Like his Uncle José, he is never silenced by society or made into a passive victim. Rather, like his uncle, he is self-assured and always vocal. He speaks the "vernacular rhythms" of Caliban. As Galarza says of Uncle José: "He imitated pig grunts, Relámpago's [the community mule's] braying, Coronel [his rooster] sounding his morning call. . . . Out of the double row of small sequence holes of his harmonica, José sucked and huffed the repertoire of *corridos* and lullabies and marches he carried in his head" (p. 48). Thus, *Barrio Boy* is a celebration of orality, strength, and struggle, what his mother called *"hacerle la lucha,"* literally "to do struggle," for "every morning," she taught him, "was a new round in the match between us and the city" (p. 134).

In broad terms, *Barrio Boy* is about the author's education in resistance to entrenched authority in both Mexico and the United States. Even language itself, Ernesto philosophizes, gives us clues to the intense battle between those who had authority and power and those who had none: "I came to *feel* certain words rather than to know them. They were words which came from the lips of jalcotecanos with accents of suspicion, of fear, and of hatred. Those words were *los rurales*, the *jefe político*, the *señor gobernador, las autoridades, el gobierno.* When a stranger rode into Jalco, people stopped talking. Every detail about him and his horse was observed for a clue as to whether he was one of the *autoridades*" (p. 59). In the early sections, then, we catch glimpses of an emerging political consciousness, an ideology of cultural resistance to power of every kind. Later on, he continues to question power by following the example of his Uncle José's resistance to religious authority: "[José] composed comical versions of *Dominus vobiscum* and other bits of the ritual. The priest heard about this and expelled him because his translations were disrespectful. One of them was to the effect that if you were an awful sinner, just invite the priest to dinner" (p. 50). As this passage illustrates, the autobiography is narrated in what Hayden White has defined for historiography as the mode of irony. It is sophisticated, self-conscious, subversive, and skeptical.[30]

Once on the road, uprooted by the Revolution, young Ernesto's acculturation begins to shift from a rural Mexican education to an urban U.S. one. From the dark musty rooms of their first residence in Sacramento, a prison even more confining than the alley [off of which they lived] in Tucson (p. 133), the Galarza family slowly explores its brave new world. "It was a block in one direction to the lumber yard and the grocery store," Galarza writes,

> half a block in the other to the saloon and the Japanese motion picture theater. In between were the tent and awning shop, a Chinese restaurant, a secondhand store, several houses like our own. We noted by the numbers on the posts at the corners that we lived between 4th and 5th streets on L. Once we could fix a course from these signs up and down and across town we explored further. On Sixth near K there was the Lyric Theater with a sign we easily translated into Lírico. . . . Navigating by these key points and following the rows of towering elms along L Street, one by one we found the post office on 7th and K; the cathedral, four blocks farther east; and the state capitol with its golden dome. (p. 197)

As the passage points out, the process of acculturation in the barrio is at first a conscious act of translation. Later, the acculturation becomes an unconscious imaging and projecting of the real that serves as the compass of Mexicans' new identities as Mexicans in the United States. In this manner, "with remarkable fairness and never-ending wonder we kept adding to our list of pleasant and repulsive in the ways of the Americans. It was my second acculturation" (p. 205). Again, Ernesto deciphers who has power and is, at once, skeptical of the class differences between the *ricos* and the *pobres:*

> These were the boundaries of the lower part of town, for that was what everyone called the section of the city between Fifth Street and the river and from the railway yards to the Y street levee. Nobody ever mentioned an upper part of town; at least, no one could see the difference because the whole city was built on level land. We were not lower topographically, but in other ways that distinguished between Them, the uppers, and Us, the lowers. (p. 198)

Galarza, to be sure, never quit fighting this invidious difference between the "uppers" and the "lowers."

Two more examples of Caliban's resistance to domination are Cherríe Moraga's autobiography, *Loving in the War Years,* and Houston Baker, Jr.'s literary study, *Modernism and the Harlem Renaissance.* As Moraga makes patently clear in her title, her points of reference are not language or discursive signs, but the battle of an ideological "war of positions." Her monument of the self as it is becoming has the form of dispatches from the war front because she wants to deal with gender, empowerment, sensuous culture, and the libidinal economy, not relations of meaning. Neither Rodriguez's dichotomy between the public and private self, nor Galarza's semiotics of resistance, can totally account for the intrinsic intelligibility of conflicts that Moraga's autobiography records.

Explicitly, the text enjoys a higher degree of critical reflection than either Rodriguez's or Galarza's. In fact, one may read Moraga's experimental narrative (together with Gloria Anzaldúa's *Borderlands/La Frontera*) as the first sustained models of radical Chicana feminist theories. Moreover, such critical reflection encompasses not only literature, but sociology, politics, and the philosophy of desire. She subverts traditional narrative order and coherence by writing in her introduction, "Amar en los años de guerra," that "the selections are not arranged chronologically in terms of when each piece was written [1976–83]. Rather, I have tried to create a kind of emotional/political chronology" (p. i). Traditional historical time and space are immediately displaced and replaced with a bristling "emotional/political" chronotope where the personal is always political. Desire is at the core of the self, of expression, and communication.

In a courageous, frank, and sometimes brutal narrative, Moraga describes growing up in Southern California; in so doing she tells us what it meant to be a Chicana lesbian in the 1970s and 1980s. In celebrating her sexual difference as a source of her creative energy, she traces its beginnings back to her mother. Because she views her Anglo-American father as "bland," passionless, and passive, without a real sense of history, she chooses her mother's working-class Chicana culture. In many ways, *Loving in the War Years* is a socially symbolic critique of the law of the father. "I'd stare across the top of my glass of milk and the small yellow kitchen table," Moraga recalls, "and as far back as I could imagine into that wide rolling forehead, I saw nothing stirring. For the life of me, there wasn't a damn thing happening in that head of his" (p. 8).

The book is also an experimental narrative about her reconciliation with her grandmother and mother—her recognition that these brown women gave her a power of voice. Thus, may her autobiography be read as another powerful meditation on the Ariel-Caliban relationships in Our America, for Moraga demands that for the native intellectual to reject Prospero's influences, she must make a claim toward Caliban's mother, Sycorax. The breakthrough and "breakdown" in her text is her use of this voice to expose the Chicano community's unrelenting homophobia. She elaborates, further, on how this homophobia is related to the struggle of all women of color (p. 124).

Using a remarkable rhetoric of conversion, Moraga establishes a distinction between a naïve self before becoming "a woman[-]identified subject" and one who has been awakened to the evils of racism and heterosexism.[31] As she tells us early on: "When I finally lifted the lid to my lesbianism, a profound connection with my mother reawakened in me. It wasn't until I acknowledged and confronted my own lesbianism in the flesh, that my heartfelt identification with and empathy for my mother's oppression—due to being poor, uneducated, and Chicana—was realized" (p. 52).

What is particularly moving in this autobiography is Moraga's notion that liberation comes only after realizing that class struggle and sexual struggle cannot be separated from racial struggle. Throughout the book, she takes great pains to show how her sexual practice is a "poverty." In addition, the hope that she writes about is continually promoted by a political notion of desire. "My lesbianism first brought me into writing. My first poems were love poems.

That's the source—*el amor, el deseo*—that brought me into politics" (p. iv). Desire, as such, gives her access to a revolutionary energy capable of negating the one-dimensional society of Prospero that has successfully domesticated its opposition.

On another level, Moraga refuses to become part of the heterosexual world, which she sees as a mask for the origins of capitalism. For Moraga, heterosexuality is nothing but the assignment of economic roles: producer subjects and agents of exchange (males) on one side; productive earth and commodities on the other (females). She confronts this commodification by refusing to enter into it and by describing the consequences of that refusal: "Lesbianism as a sexual art can never be construed as reproductive sex. It is not work. It is purely about pleasure and intimacy. How that refutes, spits in the face of, the notion of sex as rape, sex as duty! In stepping outside the confines of the institution of heterosexuality, I was indeed choosing sex freely" (p. 125).

Finally, it is her notion of desire that has crucial consequences for us. If the primary function of memory is to serve the "pleasure principle," as Herbert Marcuse taught us in *Eros and Civilization,* then "memory of gratification is at the origin of all thinking, and the impulse to recapture past gratification is the hidden driving power behind the process of thought."[32] From this point of view, history is that which refuses desire. This historical lesson is the critical reflection of Caliban that Moraga must dramatize. Like Caliban, she "lack[s] language./The language to clarify my resistance to the literate./Words are a war to me" (p. 63). In short, this linguistic reality's paradigm is *The Tempest:* survival, for her, demands that Chicanas resist the master's language; after all, Prospero's conquest of the Americas is fundamentally a male conquest, written from the male perspective. As the work of a Chicana feminist intellectual, Moraga's autobiography may in the end serve as a corrective to Lamming's, Césaire's, and Fernández Retamar's masculinist rewritings of *The Tempest,* for Moraga forces us to return to the question of Ariel's choice between Caliban and Prospero. Before Ariel can choose Caliban, "our symbol," Moraga suggests, Ariel must share in Caliban's subaltern "identification" with Sycorax.

No study of the school of Caliban in the Americas would be complete without a brief discussion of Houston Baker, Jr.'s contributions to cultural studies and to African American cultural forms. In his groundbreaking *Blues, Ideology, and Afro-American Literature: A*

Vernacular Theory (1984), Baker attempts to provide a theoretical framework for African American literature. Using the blues as a vernacular paradigm of American culture, he relates blues themes and attitudes directly to American social and literary history as well as to Afro-American expressive culture.

But his hybrid *Modernism and the Harlem Renaissance* (1987) explicitly joins Lamming's, Césaire's, and Fernández Retamar's works in allegorically rewriting *The Tempest*. As in his earlier studies of African American "vernacular tropes," he focuses on the development of an African American "sound" or "voice." Indeed, he proposes a unique African American brand of modernism against which the Harlem Renaissance can be measured as a resounding success. Said differently, Baker perceives the Harlem Renaissance as a crucial moment in a movement, predating the 1920s, when African Americans embraced the task of self-determination and in so doing created a distinctive form of expression bound up in two strategies: "mastery of form," which camouflages the political task at hand, and "deformation of mastery," through which an artist defies the norm. In rich detail, he traces these strategies to Booker T. Washington's *Up from Slavery*, with its formal mastery of the minstrel mask, and W. E. B. Dubois's *The Souls of Black Folk*, with its evocation and celebration of African heritage and folk traditions. Baker concludes his extended essay, a mixture of cultural analysis and personal testimony, with a reading of the Harlem Renaissance, arguing that Alain Locke's *The New Negro* was the first "national book" in which African American formal mastery of voice and deformation of mastery coalesce.

But how are these African American narratives related to *The Tempest?* And why is Baker's study an example of Calibanic resistance culture? In Baker's view, *The Tempest* is especially significant for vernacular "racial" writing because it contains "the venerable trope of Prospero and Caliban—figures portrayed in terms of self-and-other, the West and the Rest of us, the rationalist and the debunker, the colonizer and the indigenous people."[33] Further, *The Tempest* is simply about "language, writing, ideology, race and a host of other Western signs" (p. 389).

Given his previous work on the blues, it is not surprising that Baker sees Caliban as the first "vernacular" voice represented in Western culture. In his short chapter on *The Tempest*, he contends that we need to respond to the "sound" Caliban offers us, a consideration of what the full politics of deformation and mastery surrounding him amount to.

Baker's rewriting of *The Tempest* is unabashedly political in its presentation of Caliban as an instructor in a first voice, resonant with "a thousand twangling instruments in nature." Like a maroon in Jamaica, or Nat Turner in the U.S. South, Caliban performs a powerful "drama of deformation," Baker asserts. Against the scene of Prospero's "intruding tongue," Caliban talks back through a unique vernacular rhythm. Hence, "what batters our ears—if Caliban is newly interpreted—is a three-personed god of 'natural meanings,' morphophoenemics, and most important, metamorphoses" (p. 56), what he earlier called Caliban's "triple play." Thus, Caliban is a precursor for the "Rest of us" because he "transforms an obscene situation, a tripled metastasis into a signal self/cultural expression" (p. 56). In short, Caliban's triple play is a form of what Baker calls "supraliteracy," that is, "a maroon or guerrilla action carried out within linguistic territories of the erstwhile masters, bringing forth *sounds* that have been taken for hooting, but which are, in reality, racial poetry" (p. 394).

Baker's vernacular reading of *The Tempest* and of the Harlem Renaissance has to be seen as part of a larger project that he has been instrumental in creating: the "writing/righting" of American literature and history, in the broad sense. Such a process involves "talking back" to the masters, not in the hermeneutics of the overseers (deconstruction, the New Rhetoric of the rationalists), but in Caliban's debunking vernacular rhythms.

Hence, the importance of his hybrid narrative where the personal is the theoretical. What we read in *Modernism and the Harlem Renaissance* is a critique of ahistorical, needlessly abstract, formalist theory in the United States. Its style and method—the interplay of scholarly text, personal testimony, and family photographs, the mixture of genres, methods, and styles—capture the complex reality of the African American experience. Quite consciously, he concludes by designing an alternative expression to works of literary criticism or social science. It is a personal rendering of the African American experience brought together by what he calls the "storied sounds that come through my lineage" (p. 100). Only through recognizing the "storied sounds" told to him by his parents and grandparents can we approach the "complex field of sounding strategies in Afro-America that are part of a family" (p. 105).

The Calibanic self that Baker describes does not exist in empty space but in an organic human collective—in what he calls the family. For this reason, the Calibanic self that he lays bare is not alienated from itself; it is in his own folk. "To be exterior meant to be for others, for the collective, for one's own people," says Bakhtin in referring to a certain kind of canonical autobiography (p. 135). We might add that from Galarza's, Moraga's, and Baker's perspective, to be for the collective also means to be for the Calibanic self.

Afterword

Postcolonial Borders, Dissent, and the Politics of the Possible

A radical decentering of postcolonial theory is currently under way in the hybrid works of such writers as Kumkum Sangari, Barbara Harlow, and Norma Alarcón.[1] James Clifford, for example, suggests that "theory, a product long associated with Western discursive spaces—a status that permitted it to speak confidently of 'human' history, culture, psyche, etc.—now is marked by specific historical centers and horizons."[2] If "theory" is no longer at home exclusively in the West, how can our postcolonial Borders bring a repositioning of cultural theory—a contested term used by cultural critics to define any developed comparative knowledge about the histories and forms of collective life?

In turning to experimental texts by Guillermo Gómez-Peña, Renato Rosaldo, and Rubén Blades, each based on the theoretical and political manipulation of a discourse of Borders and dissent, we shift from a totalizing interpretation toward analysis informed by postcolonial location and liminality so that we can begin to remap cultural theory in the Borderlands and further question how the U.S. academy, itself a political institution, can respond to the conditions that generated our oppression.

Guillermo Gómez-Peña's "Border Culture: A Process of Negotiation Toward Utopia" (1986) has an experimental sense about it because he indicates that his cultural group of performance artists from the metropolitan Tijuana-San Diego area (Taller de Arte Fronteriza/Border Art Workshop) forced him to write a different sort of account about Border identities, Border cultures, and Border topography. For him, "existen muchas fronteras. Demasiadas." ("there are many borders. Too many.").[3] His essay therefore deals with what he sees as an infinite number of contrasts and shocks on the Tijuana-San Diego Border: "mariachis and surfers, cholos and punks, second-hand buses and helicopters, tropical whore houses and video discotheques, Catholic saints and monsters from outer space, shanty houses and steel skyscrapers, bullfights and American football, popular anarchism and cybernetic behaviorism, Anglo Saxon puritanism and Latin hedonism. Will they exist in peaceful coexistence or open warfare?" Essentially, what he calls for is a new kind of cultural theory "capable of articulating our incredible circumstances."

His essay does not contain a standard account of the U.S.-Mexico geopolitical Border, for, as he suggests, "the border is not an abyss that will save us from threatening otherness, but a place where . . . otherness yields, becomes us, and therefore [becomes] comprehensible." In contrast to conceptions of the Border as the limits of two countries, he and his Taller de Fronteriza group argue for a more unified Border "as a cardinal intersection of many realities" (p. 1). In short, he focuses on the common ground shared literally by North America and Latin America: "Latin America lives and breathes in the United States and vice versa." The real innovation in Gómez-Peña's new definition of the Border is his attempt to situate the shifting borders of the Americas within a range of "demographic, economic, and cultural" facts. Any account of Border culture should convey for him a sense of what he calls the "borderization" of the American hemisphere: "Whether we want it or not, the edge of the border is widening, and the geopolitics are beoming less precise day by day" (p. 2). What he calls for, then, is a "response from artists" of the Border territories to construct "alternative realities" through interdisciplinary projects, multicultural programs, and internationalist dialogues.

Renato Rosaldo's "Ideology, Place, and People Without Culture" (1988) is similarly an attempt to theorize the Border as a zone of "cultural visibility and cultural invisibility."[4] Rosaldo particularly wants to document "the case of the undocumented workers" in North America. Like Gómez-Peña's and Anzaldúa's accounts, Rosaldo's essay conceives of the Border as "the site of the implosion of the Third World into the first" (p. 78). What is interesting about his article is that he searches for portraits of the cultural "border zones" and eruptions in popular mass media forms as well as in oppositional Chicano literary forms. For example, the reader is encouraged to watch "Miami Vice" to understand how a TV program with its "white zoot suits, high tension mood music, and carefully chosen pastels" disguises itself as "affirmative action heaven, with blacks, Latinos, and whites all playing cops and robbers, vibrantly policing and trafficking drugs together" (pp. 86 and 85). According to Rosaldo, what "Miami Vice" plays out for American viewers is Latin American drugs "invading" North America and Latino drug traffickers "infesting" middle-class white neighborhoods. To be sure, the edge of the Border is widening, but for him "Miami Vice" informs middle-class Americans about the wave of immigrants from the South invading the North and helps explain how new immigration restriction bills in Congress, though unsuccessful, get a boost and how such English-only initiatives as the one in California in 1990 are passed by the electorate.

In addition to seeing the Border as the site of "spatial stereotypes," Rosaldo perceives it as a zone for ludic artistry. In a revisionist reading of José Montoya's classic "El Louie," he characterizes the poem's protagonist as "postmodern" before his time. Louie Rodríguez, he contends, "seeks out incongruity, unlikely juxtapositions [in American culture]: Cagney, El Charro Negro, Bogart, and Cruz Diablo." As such, Louie is not a tragic hero, as many have argued, but rather a liminal Chicano character "playing the role, the cat role, just playing." In brief, "El Louie" "epitomizes the border as a culturally distinct space;" it is at the same time a poem betwixt and between Chicano and Anglo-American cultural traditions and a work of art where Montoya "celebrates polyphony in its polyglot text, and heterogeneity in making Anglo, Chicano, and Mexican elements move together in the dance of life" (p. 86).

The same interplay of locations and hybridity is rearticulated, albeit differently, by the Panamanian salsa composer and singer Rubén Blades in his album "Agua de Luna" (1987). While many electronic mass cultural artifacts supply us with libidinal diversions and distractions mobilized to direct our bodies and minds to advertising messages, Blades's "Agua de Luna" manipulates the powerful apparatuses of mass communications to redirect some of our deepest sympathies. He enters discourses to which masses of young people have access: guitars, congas, and synthesizers. Moreover, as George Lipsitz suggests in his analysis of rock music, Blades's salsa allows listeners "to experience a common heritage with people they have never seen; they can acquire memories of a past to which they have no geographic or biological connection."[5]

If mass cultural forms create conditions of possibility by expanding the present by informing it with memories of the past, Blades's cultural creations can present post-contemporary social contradictions while retaining the potential to play a role in the struggle for hegemony.[6] Blades also traffics in U.S. synthesized jazz fusion and 1950s' doo-wop.[7] Although his fame primarily stems from "Siembra" (Seed), the best-selling album he co-recorded with trombonist Willie Colon in 1978, from his earliest songs Blades has shown a predilection for radically experimenting with the traditional salsa form and content. Still clinging to the tight 3/2 clave, he hybridizes the salsa song by replacing horns with synthesizers and by rewriting mass commercial songs about the guy who betrays his friend, or the woman who left, or simply "let's party" with songs inspired by García Márquez's stories. Blades's new salsa "under-songs," to use William Carlos Williams's memorable term, rely on an eerie juxtaposition of the concrete and the abstract, a willingness to allow his lyrics to link implausible threads and thicken into a braid.[8] Said differently, his "Nueva Canción" becomes transnational rather than foundational. In my view, the interest of the rich salsa songs in "Agua de Luna" lies precisely in demonstrating how resounding poetry and the culture of liberation can exist in a traditional mass cultural form such as the urban salsa song. Blades's songs are worthy of our attention because they mark the point of intersection between his Afro-Cuban musical formation and, the word cannot be avoided, his "magical" sociopoetic idiom. As a hybrid composer, Blades, like Gómez-Peña and Rosaldo, is open to two worlds and is formed within his local and global Borderlands. The hybrid thus becomes through the lived-in simultaneity of the Americas the ground for political analysis and social change.[9]

"Agua de Luna" begins with a haunting rewriting of García Márquez's "Monologue of Isabel Watching It Rain in Macondo" (1955). In the song simply titled "Isabel," he expands the musical boundaries of the traditional salsa song. Instead of the electronic mass cultural topos of sentimental love, he starts with a whirling philosophical song about a woman who cannot bear the pitiless and numbing rain in Macondo, García Márquez's famous territory of the possible. "Isabel," Blades sings, "siente la lluvia en Macondo/dale olor a su soledad/y explicación a su ansiedad" ("feels the rain in Macondo/gives an aroma to her solitude/an explanation to her anxiety").[10] Like García Márquez's magical narrative, Blades's song supplies his listeners with a lyrical story about the politics of the possible ("Todo es posible y nada se pierde en Macondo"—"Everything is possible and nothing is ever lost in Macondo"), a song that turns into an allegory about Isabel's temporal obsessions. As a mode, Blades's electronic mass-media magic realism is attached to the real and to the possible. As in García Márquez's narratives, the brutality of the real is equally the brutality of the immanent. "Claro Oscuro" ("Twilight"), Blades's reworking of García Márquez's "The Sea of Lost Time" (1962), is thus a salsa song that tells the potentially possible story about a desolate pueblo in the Americas: "Del mar," Blades sings, "se derama un viento/que ahuele a ahogado y a rosa; la gente sueña mientras sobre la marea/ se quebra una luna verde./ Y el pueblo entero se esconde 'tras presentimientos/ Y la sombra militar" ("A wind coming from the sea spills a smell of the drowned and of roses./People dream while a green moon breaks over the returning tide and the entire pueblo hides behind its premonitions,/And the Army's shadows").

Whereas "Isabel" and "Claro Oscuro" rely on the traditional salsa 3/2 *clave,* "Laura Farina," a retelling of García Márquez's "Death Constant Beyond Love" (1970), replaces salsa rhythms with *estadunidense,* 1950s' doo-wop. Here, Blades's crossover rhythms drive his song about Senator Onésimo's illicit passion for a young woman, Laura Farina. As with García Márquez's story, Blades unravels the corrupt senator's illusions of politics and love, for, as the song puts it, his heart "[se] falló al momento en que funcionó" ("failed with its first beat").

In "Blacamán," Blades's recasting of García Márquez's "Blacamán the Good, Vendor of Miracles" (1968), the hybridization of tradition and salsa culture becomes most evident. The resemblances to García Márquez's story are clearly striking. Blacamán, a child transformed into a miracle worker by the sadistic torture of his master, has revenge on him. But where Blades's song shows the full extent of its hybridization is in the linkage of the good miracle worker in the Americas, Blacamán, to Caliban. Blacamán employs his magic "para reinventar Caliban." Blades thus uses the metaphors of Blacamán and Caliban in his Nueva Canción as part of the gestalt of the postcolonial Americas, for "Los que eran dueños no lo son ya, se han vuelto sombras de América" ("Those who were masters are no longer; they have become America's shadows").

In light of such decenterings, to "theorize" becomes a newly problematic activity, for theory is now written not from a condition of critical "distance," but rather from a place of hybridity and *betweenness* in our global Borderlands composed of historically connected postcolonial spaces.

Notes

Preface

1. See, for example, José Ballón, *Autonomía cultural de América: Emerson y Martí* (Madrid: Pliegos, 1986); Vera M. Kutzinski, *Against the American Grain: Myth and History in William Carlos Williams, Jay Wright, and Nicolás Guillén* (Baltimore: Johns Hopkins University Press, 1987); *Reinventing the Americas: Comparative Studies of the Literature of the United States and Spanish America,* ed. Bell Chevigny and Gari Laguardia (New York: Cambridge University Press, 1986); Lois Parkinson Zamora, *Writing the Apocalypse: Historical Vision in Contemporary U.S. and Latin American Fiction* (New York: Cambridge University Press, 1989); Alfred MacAdam, *Textual Confrontations: Comparative Readings in Latin American Literature* (Chicago: University of Chicago Press, 1987); and *Do the Americas Have a Common Literature?*, ed. Gustavo Pérez Firmat (Durham, N.C.: Duke University Press, 1990).

2. See Sacvan Bercovitch, "America as Canon and Context: Literary History in a Time of Dissensus," *American Literature,* 28/1 (March 1986): 104.

3. See Immanuel Wallerstein, *The Modern World System I: Capitalist Agriculture and the Origins of the European World-Economy in the Sixteenth Century* (New York: Academic Press, 1974). Though my use of the concept "world system theory" and the base-superstructure doctrine is indebted in the broadest sense to Wallerstein's and Marx's work, I use them in my book as starting points and a problem—an imperative to make connections and linkages, something as undogmatic as a heuristic recommendation to grasp culture and theory in and for itself, but also in relation to its outside context. While it is true that many post-Marxists claim to have buried the base-superstructure model, I agree with Fredric Jameson that it is hard for anyone to find a better and more satisfactory substitute. Everything changes when you grasp the base-superstructure theory "not as a full-fledged theory in its own right, but rather as the name for a problem, whose solution is always a unique, ad hoc invention," (p. 46) Jameson writes in *Late Marxism: Adorno, Or, The Persistence of the Dialectic* (London: Verso, 1990).

4. See George Fredrickson, *White Supremacy: A Comparative Study in American and South African History* (New York: Oxford University Press, 1981): xviii–xix.

5. Myra Jehlen, "The Ties that Bind: Race and Sex in *Pudd'nhead Wilson,*" *American Literary History* 2/1 (Spring 1990): 39.

6. See, for example, Lemuel Johnson, *The Devil, the Gargoyle, and the Buffoon: The Negro as Metaphor in Western Literature* (Port Washington, N.Y.: Kennikat Press, 1971); A. James Arnold, *Modernism and Negritude: The Poetry and Poetics of Aimé Césaire* (Cambridge, Mass.: Harvard University Press,

1981); and Marta E. Sánchez, "Caliban: The New Latin-American Protagonist of *The Tempest,*" *Diacritcs* 6/1 (Spring 1976): 54–61.

7. See Roberto Fernández Retamar, "Our America and the West," trans. Edward Baker, *Social Text* 15 (Fall 1986): 1–25; and "Caliban Revisited," in *Caliban and Other Essays,* trans. Edward Baker (Minneapolis: University of Minnesota Press, 1989): 46–55.

1 The Dialectics of Our America

1. See the critical anthology *Ideology and Classic American Literature,* ed. Sacvan Bercovitch and Myra Jehlen (New York: Cambridge University Press, 1986). See also Bercovitch's *Reconstructing American Literary History* (Cambridge, Mass.: Harvard University Press, 1986) and Mary V. Dearborn's *Pocahontas's Daughters: Gender and Ethnicity in American Culture* (New York: Oxford University Press, 1986). For a general discussion of "ideology" in American literary history, see Bercovitch's "The Problem of Ideology in American Literary History," *Critical Inquiry* 12 (Summer 1986): 631–53.

2. See, for example, Sacvan Bercovitch's comments on "dissensus" in "America as Canon and Context: Literary History in a Time of Dissensus," *American Literature* 58/1 (March 1986): 99–107. See also Bercovitch's "The Problem of Ideology in American Literary History," pp. 632–33. Finally, see Mikhail M. Bakhtin's radical reconceptualization of the novel in *The Dailogic Imagination: Four Essays,* ed. Michael Holquist, trans. Caryl Emerson and Michael Holquist (Austin: University of Texas Press, 1981). According to Bakhtin, the novel is a genre, in contradistinction to such fixed genres as epic and lyric, with the ability to speak out in the most diverse and often conflicting voices. Put plainly, the novel, says Bakhtin, is "dialogic," that is, an interaction of utterances, a "polyphonic" multiplicity of voices and meanings.

3. Some of the more interesting studies in American literary history and canon formation have been done by the Reconstructing American Literature Project, directed by Paul Lauter. For a summary of their project, see Lauter's "Reconstructing American Literature: A Synopsis of an Educational Project of the Feminist Press," *MELUS* 11 (Spring 1984): 33–45. See also Lauter's "Society and the Profession, 1958–1983," *PMLA* (centennial issue; May 1984): 414–26, and his "History and the Canon," *Social Text* 12 (Fall 1985): 94–101. See also Herbert Lindenberger, "Toward a New History in Literary Study," *Profession 84* (MLA): 16–24; Annette Kolodny, "The Integrity of Memory: Creating a New Literary History in the United States," *American Literature* 57/2 (May 1985): 291–307; Juan Bruce-Novoa, *Chicano Poetry: A Response to Chaos* (Austin: University of Texas Press, 1982); Houston A. Baker, Jr., *Blues, Ideology and Afro-American Literature* (Chicago: University of Chicago Press, 1985) and *Modernism and the Harlem Renaissance* (Chicago: University of Chicago Press, 1987); and Jane Tompkins, *Sensational Designs: The Cultural Work of American Fiction, 1790–1860* (New York: Oxford University Press, 1985).

4. See Fredric Jameson, *The Political Unconscious: Narrative as a Socially Symbolic Act* (Ithaca, N.Y.: Cornell University Press, 1981); Frank Lentricchia, *Criticism and Social Change* (Chicago: University of Chicago Press, 1983); Hayden V. White, *Tropics of Discourse* (Baltimore: Johns Hopkins University Press, 1978); and Edward W. Said, *Orientalism* (New York: Pantheon Books, 1978) and *The World, the Text, and the Critic* (Cambridge, Mass.: Harvard University Press, 1983).

5. The following American histories are most relevant to my study: Ronald T. Takaki, *Iron Cages: Race and Culture in Nineteenth-Century America* (New York: Alfred A. Knopf, 1979); Arnoldo De León, *They Called Them Greasers: Anglo Attitudes towards Mexicans in Texas, 1821–1900* (Austin: University of Texas Press, 1983); and Annette Kolodny, *The Land Lay Before Her: Fantasy and Experience of the American Frontiers, 1630–1680* (Chapel Hill: University of North Carolina Press, 1984).

6. Jean Franco, *An Introduction to Spanish American Literature* (Cambridge: Cambridge University Press, 1969): 118.

7. Enrico Mario Santí, "José Martí and the Cuban Revolution," *Cuban Studies* 16 (1986): 139–45.

8. Roberto Fernández Retamar, "The Modernity of Martí," in *José Martí, Revolutionary Democrat*, ed. Christopher Abel and Nissa Torrents (Durham, N.C.: Duke University Press, 1986): 6.

9. Andrés Iduarte as quoted in Ramón Eduardo Ruiz, *Cuba: The Making of a Revolution* (New York: W. W. Norton, 1970): 62.

10. José Martí, *Obras Completas*, 2nd ed. (Havana: Editora Nacional de Cuba, 1963–66): 4, 168. The translation is mine.

11. Ralph Waldo Emerson, "The American Scholar," in *The Collected Works of Ralph Waldo Emerson. I, Nature, Addresses, and Lectures*, intro. and notes by Robert E. Spiller (Cambridge, Mass.: Belknap Press, 1971): 56.

12. José Martí, "The Washington Pan-American Congress," *La Nación*, December 19–20, 1889, in *Inside the Monster by José Martí: Writings on the United States and American Imperialism*, trans. Elinor Randall, with additional trans. Juan de Onís and Roslyn Held Foner, ed. Philip S. Foner (New York: Monthly Review Press, 1975): 355–56. Also relevant here is Abdul R. JanMohamed's analysis of "the manichean organization of colonial society" in his *Manichean Aesthetics: The Politics of Literature in Colonial Africa* (Amherst: University of Massachusetts Press, 1983). According to JanMohamed, the "colonial mentality is dominated by a manichean allegory of white and black, good and evil, salvation and damnation, civilization and savagery, superiority and inferiority . . . self and other, subject and object" (p. 4).

13. See *Granma Weekly Review*, (Havana), May 19, 1968.

14. See José Martí's "Our America," in *Our America by José Martí: Writings on Latin America and the Struggle for Cuban Independence*, trans. Elinor Randall, ed. Philip S. Foner (New York: Monthly Review Press, 1977): 3. All further references to this essay will be paginated in the text.

15. See George M. Fredrickson's *White Supremacy: A Comparative Study in American and South African History* (New York: Oxford University Press, 1981). As Fredrickson tells us, "The phrase 'white supremacy' applies with

particular force to the historical experience of two nations—South Africa and the United States. As generally understood, white supremacy refers to the attitudes, ideologies, and policies associated with the rise of blatant forms of white or European dominance over 'nonwhite' populations. In other words, it involves making invidious distinctions of a socially crucial kind that are based primarily, if not exclusively, on physical characterizations and ancestry. In its fully developed form, white supremacy means 'color bars,' 'racial segregation,' and the restriction of meaningful citizenship rights to a privileged group characterized by its light pigmentation" (p. ix).

16. José Martí, "A Glance at the North American's Soul Today," *La Nación*, January 16, 1886. For an English translation, see *Martí on the U.S.A.*, trans. Luis A. Baralt (Carbondale: Southern Illinois University Press, 1966): 197–98.

17. Carl N. Degler notes in *Out of Our Past: The Forces That Shaped Modern America* (New York: Harper & Row, 1984; 3rd ed.) that "historians usually credit John L. O'Sullivan, spread-eagle nationalist editor of the Jacksonian Democratic organ *United States and Democratic Review,* for originating the phrase. In an article in 1845, justifying America's claims to the Oregon territory, O'Sullivan asserted that the American claim 'is by right of our manifest destiny to overspread and to possess the whole of the Continent which Providence has given for the development of the great experiment of liberty and federated self-government entrusted to us' " (p. 118, n. 4).

18. Martí, *Obras Completas,* pp. 9, 205–6. The translation is mine.

19. André Gunder Frank, *Capitalism and Underdevelopment in Latin America* (New York: Monthly Review Press, 1969).

20. In "Mexico and the United States," first published in the *New Yorker,* September 17, 1979, pp. 136–53, Octavio Paz localizes and supplements Martí's thesis: "The opposition between Mexico and the United States belongs to the North-South duality as much from the geographical as the symbolic point of view. It is an ancient opposition which was already unfolding in pre-Columbian America, so that it antedates the very existence of the United States and Mexico. The northern part of the continent was settled by nomadic, warrior nations; MesoAmerica, on the other hand, was the home of an agricultural civilization, with complex social and political institutions, dominated by warlike theocracies that invented refined and cruel rituals, great art, and vast cosmogonies inspired by a very original vision of time. The great opposition of pre-Columbian America . . . was between different ways of life: nomads and settled peoples, hunters and farmers. This division greatly influenced the later developments of the United States and Mexico. The policies of the English and the Spanish toward the Indians were in large part determined by this division; it was not insignificant that the former established themselves in the territory of the nomads and the latter in that of the settled peoples" (p. 138). More recently, Carlos Fuentes, at a conference at Michigan State University entitled "The Politics of Experience" (October 1985), said this about the essential North-South opposition: "There is a character in *One Hundred*

Years of Solitude who decides that from now on it will always be Monday, and one has the impression in the relations between Latin America and the United States that it is always Monday, that nothing happens because the actual difference is never understood. But if there is a difference, it is the difference as regards the consideration of the past and memory. There is a tendency in this country to look too much towards the future and to forget the past" *Centennial Review* 30 [Spring 1986]: 133).

21. Juan Marinello pointed out that José Martí did not think in "materialist" terms. See his *Once ensayos martianos* (Havana: Comisión Nacional Cubana de la UNESCO, n.d.): 193. But as Fidel Castro justly claimed, Martí was his mentor. A typical statement of Castro's debt to Martí is the following: "I carry in my heart the teachings of the Maestro. Martí is the instigator of the 26th of July Movement," quoted in Ruíz, *Cuba: The Making of a Revolution*, p. 58.

22. See Ernesto Guevara, "The Most Dangerous Enemies and Other Stupidities," in Rolando E. Bonachea and Nelson P. Valdés, eds., *Che: Selected Works of Ernesto Guevara* (Cambridge, Mass.: MIT Press, 1970): 46.

23. Roberto González Echevarría, "Criticism and Literature in Revolutionary Cuba," *Cuban Studies/Estudios Cubanos* 11 (1981): 2. Of relevance here is Judith A. Weiss's summary of the *Mundo Nuevo* and the *Casa de las Américas* conflict. According to Weiss, *Mundo Nuevo*, edited by the eminent Uruguayan writer and critic Rodríguez Monegal, was a right-wing response to the leftist *Casa de las Américas*. See Weiss's *Casa De Las Américas: An Intellectual Review in the Cuban Revolution* (Chapel Hill, N.C.: Estudios Hispanofila, 1977): esp. 18–61.

24. See the following by José David Saldívar: "The Real and the Marvelous in Nogales, Arizona," *Denver Quarterly* 17/2 (Summer 1982): 141–44; "The Ideological and the Utopian in Tomás Rivera's *Y no se lo tragó la tierra* and Ron Arias's *The Road to Tamazunchale*," *Critica* 1/2 (Spring 1985): 100–114; "Ideology and Deconstruction in Macondo," *Latin American Literary Review* (special issue on Gabriel García Márquez) 13/25 (January–June 1985): 29–43; and "Rolando Hinojosa's *Klail City Death Trip Series:* A Critical Introduction," in *The Rolando Hinojosa Reader: Essays Historical and Critical*, ed. José David Saldívar (Houston: Arte Público Press, 1985): 44–63.

25. See Ernest Mandel's *Late Capitalism* (London: NLB, 1975). According to Mandel, "this new period [1940 to 1965] was characterized, among other things, by the fact that alongside machine-made industrial consumer goods (as from the early 19th century) and machine-made machines (as from the mid-19th century), we now find machine produced raw materials and foodstuffs. Late capitalism, far from representing a post-industrial society, thus appears as the period in which all branches of the economy are further industrialized for the first time; to which one could further add the increasing mechanization of the sphere of circulation (with the exception of pure repair services) and the increasing mechanization of the superstructure" (pp. 190–91). Relevant here to my study are Jean François Lyotard's *The Postmodern Condition: A Report on Knowledge*, trans. Geoff Bennington and Brian Massumi (Minneapolis: University of Minnesota Press, 1984); and

Fredric Jameson's "Postmodernism, or the Cultural Logic of Late Capitalism," *New Left Review* 146 (July–August 1984): 53–93.

26. Roberto González Echevarría, "Roberto Fernández Retamar: An Introduction," *Diacritics* (December 1978): 70.

27. See Karl Marx and Friedrich Engels, *The Communist Manifesto,* in Robert C. Tucker's *The Marx-Engels Reader,* 2nd ed. (New York: W. W. Norton, 1978): 477.

28. See Domingo Faustino Sarmiento's *Facundo: Civilización y barbarie* (Buenos Aires: Centro Editor de America Latina, 1979). Sarmiento's hegemonic vision, to be sure, was very powerful among the ruling classes in Latin America; and echoes of *Facundo* can be found in José Enrique Rodó's *Ariel* (1900), another target of Fernández Retamar in *Caliban.* Rodó's *Ariel* was one of the first Latin American appropriations of Shakespeare's *The Tempest.* Rodó glorifies Prospero, whose advice to Latin American intellectuals is to preserve the aristocratic qualities of the mind; admire the greatness of the United States; and preserve the spiritualism of Ariel.

29. Said, *Orientalism.*

30. Roberto Fernández Retamar, "Nuestra América y Occidente," *Casa de las Américas* 98 (1976): 36–57. I cite Fernández Retamar's essay in his collection of essays entitled *Para El Perfil Definitivo Del Hombre* (Havana: Editorial Letras Cubana, 1981): 359. The translation is mine. All further references will be paginated in the text.

31. See E. L. Doctorow's essay "False Documents" in *E. L. Doctorow: Essays and Conversations,* ed. Richard Trenner (Princeton, N.J.: Ontario Review Press, 1983): 16–27. In this essay, Doctorow, like Roland Barthes and Hayden White, García Márquez and Mario Vargas Llosa, Rolando Hinojosa and Ntozake Shange, challenges the distinction, basic to all historicism in all its forms, between "historical" and "fictional" discourse, between what he sees as the "power of the regime" (history) and "the power of freedom" (fiction/narrative). Doctorow's principal aim here is to attack the vaunted objectivity of Western historiography. And this is precisely what he does: he exposes the ideological function of the narrative mode of representation with which it has been associated. Although Doctorow has not been "canonized" by Fernández Retamar and the Cuban-Marxist school of the nueva narrativa, I believe that his works (from *Welcome to Hard Times* [1960] to *Billy Bathgate* [1989]), which are essentially Nietzschean in their semiological method, can be seen as part of the generalized negation by the American *nueva narrativa* that seeks to break down the distinction between the novel and history as institutions. See, for example, Jason Weiss's "An Interview with Carlos Fuentes," *Kenyon Review* 5/4 (1983): 105–18. Fuentes remarks that "after all, history is only what we remember about history. What is fact in history? The novel asks this question" (p. 106).

32. See Roberto González Echevarría's "The Case of the Speaking Statue: Ariel and the Magisterial Rhetoric of the Latin American Essay" in his *The Voice of the Masters: Writing and Authority in Modern Latin American Literature* (Austin: University of Texas Press, 1985): esp. 12–14.

33. See Fernández Retamar's "Caliban: apuntos sobre la cultura en nuestra América," in *Para El Perfil Definitivo Del Hombre*, pp. 219–90. For an English translation by Roberto Márquez, see "Caliban: Notes Toward a Discussion of Culture in Our America," *Massachusetts Review* 15/1 and 2 (1974): 7–72.

34. Ibid., 24. As Fernández Retamar tells us, "Our Symbol then is not Ariel, as Rodó thought, but rather Caliban. . . . I know no other metaphor more expressive of our cultural situations, of our reality."

35. Steve Hellman, "The Cuban Pulitzer," *San Francisco Chronicle Review*, July 20, 1986, pp. 2, 10. A journalist from San Pablo, California, Hellman is the first U.S. judge to participate in the Casa Prize since Rolando Hinojosa in 1980 and Allen Ginsberg in 1962.

36. Only two years after Rolando Hinojosa's new narrative *Klail City y sus alrededores* (Havana: Casa de las Américas, 1976) was published, Hinojosa's text from south Texas found its way into the Eastern bloc, via the German Democratic Republic in a German version entitled *Klail City und Umgebund*, trans. and epilogue by Yolanda Julia Broyles (East Berlin: Volk und Welt, 1980). In recognition of the Chicano novel's merits, the Federal Republic of Germany's premier "canonical" publisher, Suhrkamp Verlag, adopted the East German edition for publication in the West as *Klail City und Umgebund* (Frankfurt, 1981).

37. Werner Sollors, *Beyond Ethnicity: Consent and Descent in American Culture* (New York: Oxford University Press, 1986): 14. Subsequent references are cited in the text.

38. See my comments on Doctorow's "False Documents" in n. 31 above.

39. Ntozake Shange, "Diario Nicaragüense," in *See No Evil: Prefaces, Essays & Accounts 1976–1983* (San Francisco: Momo's Press, 1984): 62.

40. Ntozake Shange, interview with author, University of Houston, May 5, 1985.

41. Ntozake Shange, "Bocas: A Daughter's Geography," in *A Daughter's Geography* (New York: St. Martin's Press, 1983): 19–21.

42. See Russell A. Berman's *The Rise of the German Novel: Crisis and Charisma* (Cambridge, Mass.: Harvard University Press, 1986): 3.

43. Some recent exceptions to this rule are Marta Ester Sánchez's "Three Latin American Novelists in Search of 'Lo Americano': A Productive Failure," diss., University of California, San Diego, 1977; and *Process of Unity in Caribbean Society: Ideology and Literature*, eds. Ileana Rodríguez and Marc Zimmerman (Minneapolis: Institute for the Study of Ideologies and Literature, 1983). See also Sandra E. Drake's "The Uses of History in the Caribbean Novel," diss., Stanford University, 1977; and *Voices from Under: Black Narrative in Latin America and the Caribbean*, ed. William Luis (Westport, Conn.: Greenwood Press, 1984).

44. See *The Borzoi Anthology of Latin American Literature: The Twentieth Century from Borges and Paz to Guimarraes Rosa and Donoso*, ed. Emir Rodríguez Monegal (New York: Alfred A. Knopf, 1977), esp. 687–89. Also relevant here are two politically distinct views of the boom: Monegal's *El boom de la novela latinoamericana* (Caracas: Editorial Tiempo Nuevo, 1972) and José

Donoso's *The Boom in Spanish American Literature,* trans. Gregory Kolovakos (New York: Columbia University Press, 1977).

45. For an analysis of Borges's influence on North American metafictionalists, see Tony Tanner's *City of Words: American Fiction, 1950–1970* (New York: Harper & Row, 1971). According to Tanner, "a part of the appeal that Borges has for American writers is his sense that 'reality' is an infinitely plural affair, that there are many different worlds and that the intersection points might not be so fixed as some people think, that the established ways in which we classify and order reality are as much 'fictions' as his stories" (p. 42). Also see John Barth's "The Literature of Exhaustion," *Atlantic Monthly* 222 (August 1967): 29–34. For an alternative analysis of Borges's impact on postmodernism in general, see Jean Franco's "The Utopia of a Tired Man: Jorge Luis Borges," *Social Text* 4 (Fall 1981): 52–78. According to Franco, "the graph of Borges' reputation" began to rise rapidly after 1961, "precisely the time when Gerard Genette, Foucault, Barthes, Derrida, the *Tel Quel* group, and others had begun to challenge the procedures of discourse and the assumption on which traditional narrative, history, metaphysics, and science based their authority. . . . Everyone surely wanted to join [Borges's] revolution which involved no bloodshed" (p. 52).

46. Steven Mailloux, "Rhetorical Hermeneutics," *Critical Inquiry* 11 (June 1985): 630. All further references will be paginated in the text. See also Stanley Fish's "Demonstration vs. Persuasion: Two Models of Critical Acts," in *Is There a Text in This Class?: The Authority of Interpretive Communities* (Cambridge, Mass.: Harvard University Press, 1980): 356–73.

47. Robert Coover, "The Writer as God and Saboteur," review of *The Real Life of Alejandro Mayta,* by Mario Vargas Llosa, *New York Times Book Review,* February 2, 1986, p. 1.

48. Marlise Simmons, "A Talk with Gabriel García Márquez," *New York Times Book Review,* December 5, 1982, pp. 7, 60.

49. Gabriel García Márquez, "La soledad de Latina América," *Proceso* 319 (December 13, 1982). I cite Marina Castañeda's translation, "The Solitude of Latin America," *New York Times,* February 6, 1982, sec. 4: 17. All subsequent references will be paginated in the text.

50. Gabriel García Márquez, *One Hundred Years of Solitude,* trans. Gregory Rabassa (New York: Avon, 1970): 383.

2 "Squeezed by the Banana Company"

1. For García Márquez's influence on contemporary African American writers, see Vera M. Kutzinski's "The Logic of Wings: Gabriel García Márquez and Afro-American Literature," *Latin American Literary Review* 13/25 (January–June 1985): 133–46. García Márquez's influence on Chicano and Chicana writers has been much commented on. A representative Chicano position is the following by Raymund A. Paredes, who suggests that contemporary Chicano writers "often rejected the Anglo-American literary

models and instead did what writers of Mexican heritage in the Southwest had done traditionally: they turned southward and did their literary apprenticeships in the works of authors such as Rulfo, Borges, and García Márquez." See Paredes, "The Evolution of Chicano Literature," in *Three American Literatures: Essays in Chicano, Native American, and Asian-American Literature*, ed. Houston A. Baker, Jr. (New York: MLA Publications, 1982): 60–61. More recently, in a lecture delivered at the University of California, Santa Cruz, on November 10, 1989, Maxine Hong Kingston discussed García Márquez's influence on her notions of "speculative history" in *The Woman Warrior: Memoirs of a Girlhood Among Ghosts* and in *China Men*.

2. See Lewis P. Simpson, "Southern Fiction," *Harvard Guide to Contemporary American Writing*, ed. Daniel Hoffman (Cambridge, Mass.: Harvard University Press, 1979): 153–91; also relevant here is Lois Parkinson Zamora's *Writing the Apocalypse* (New York: Cambridge University Press, 1989).

3. According to Raymond Williams, "García Márquez's reading of Kafka during the 1940s allowed the discovery that literature . . . can not only present moral problems in social contexts, but also place into question the matter of reality itself." See Williams, *Gabriel García Márquez* (Boston: Twayne, 1984): 14. For García Márquez's evaluation of Jorge Luis Borges, the following comments by the author are telling: "I carry [Borges's *Collected Works*] in my suitcase; I am going to read them every day, and he is a writer I detest. . . . But, on the other hand, I am fascinated by the violin he uses to express things. . . . I think that Borges's writings are a literature of evasion. Something strange happens to me with Borges: he is one of the authors I read most and have read most and perhaps the one I like least. I read Borges because of his extraordinary capacity for verbal artifice. I mean he teaches you how to tune up your instrument for saying things." See *La novela en América Latina: Diálogo* (1976), pp. 36, 40.

4. See Fernando Alegría, *Nueva historia de la novela hispanoamericano* (Hanover, N.H.: Ediciones Norte, 1986): 311.

5. See Larry Rohter, "García Márquez: Words into Film," *New York Times*, August 13, 1989, sec. 2: 28.

6. See Aijaz Ahmad's "Jameson's Rhetoric of Otherness and the National Allegory," *Social Text* 17 (Fall 1987): 17.

7. See, for example, *The Fragrance of Guava: Plinio A. Mendoza in Conversation with Gabriel García Márquez*, trans. Ann Wright (London: Verso, 1983). In a section devoted to a discussion of his politics and his political education in Colombia's secondary schools, García Márquez tells us, "The algebra teacher would give us classes on historical materialism during break, the chemistry teacher would lend us books by Lenin and the history teacher would tell us about the class struggle. When I left that icy prison [in Zipaquirá] I'd no idea where north and south were but I did have two very strong convictions. One was that good novels must be a poetic transposition of reality, and the other was that mankind's immediate future lay in socialism" (p. 96).

8. For a good overview of dependency theory, see André Gunder

Frank's *Capitalism and Underdevelopment in Latin America* (New York: Monthly Review Press, 1969). See also Fernando Henrique Cardoso and Enzo Faletto, *Dependency and Development in Latin America,* trans. Marjory Mattingly Urquidi (Berkeley: University of California Press, 1979).

9. Gabriel García Márquez, *One Hundred Years of Solitude,* trans. Gregory Rabassa (New York: Avon, 1971): 20–21. All further references to the novel will be paginated in the text.

10. See Claudia Dreifus's "Playboy Interview: Gabriel García Márquez," *Playboy* 30/2 (February 1983): 74.

11. According to Regina Janes, "*LeafStorm,* Gabriel García Márquez's first novel, is one of false starts: a technical dead end, important as the first attempt to deal with the materials of *One Hundred Years of Solitude* and, as is usually said on these occasions, instructive in its failures." See Janes, *Gabriel García Márquez: Revolutions in Wonderland* (Columbia: University of Missouri Press, 1981): 26. For an alternative reading, see Frank Dauster's "Ambiguity and Indeterminacy in *La hojarasca,*" *Latin American Literary Review* 13/25 (January–June 1985): 24–29.

12. John Updike, "Living Death," review of *Collected Stories,* by Gabriel García Márquez, *New Yorker,* May 20, 1985, p. 122.

13. Ibid.

14. In *Go Down, Moses* (1942), William Faulkner uses two very different narrative modes, the mythic and the notorial ledger, to show us the different ways of experiencing history in the Old and New South. For a superb analysis of Faulkner's formal innovations, see Susan Willis, "Aesthetics of the Rural Slum: Contradictions and Dependency in 'The Bear,' " *Social Text* 2 (Summer 1979): 82–103.

15. Gabriel García Márquez, "Big Mama's Funeral," *Collected Stories* (New York: Harper & Row, 1984): 186. All future references to this tale will be paginated in the text.

16. See Mikhail M. Bakhtin's *Rabelais and His World,* trans. Helene Iswolsky (Cambridge, Mass.: MIT Press, 1965).

17. Roberto González Echevarría, "Doña Bárbara Writes the Plain," *The Voice of the Masters: Writing and Authority in Modern Latin American Literature* (Austin: University of Texas Press, 1985): 59.

18. Ibid., pp. 56–60.

19. For an interesting analysis of García Márquez's "Big Mama's Funeral" from a structuralist perspective, see David William Foster's "The Double Inscription of the *Narrataire* in 'Los funerales de la Mamá Grande,' " in his *Studies in the Contemporary Spanish-American Short Story* (Columbia: University of Missouri Press, 1979): 51–63.

20. The best article on García Márquez's *One Hundred Years of Solitude* and its kinship to legalistic and anthropological discourses is Roberto González Echevarría's "*Cien años de soledad:* The Novel as Myth and Archive," *Modern Language Notes* 99/2 (March 1984): 358–80. I have learned a good deal from this article, in which the author spells out three major moments in the evolution of the Latin American narrative: the chronicles of discovery and conquest; the nineteenth-century "scientific" descriptions of the Amer-

icas; and the parodying of anthropological discourses in the new narrative, especially *One Hundred Years of Solitude*.

21. Gabriel García Márquez quoted in Williams, *Gabriel García Márquez*, p. 79.

22. Miguel Fernández-Braso and Gabriel García Márquez, *Gabriel García Márquez: Una conversación infinita* (Madrid: Azur, 1969), p. 59.

23. García Márquez's use of Colombian and Caribbean history in his new narratives has been much commented on. See, for example, Lucila Inés Menes's exhaustive study, *La función de la historia en Cien años de soledad* (Barcelona: Plaza & Janes, 1979). See also Mario Vargas Llosa's remarkable book, *García Márquez: historia de un deicidio* (Barcelona: Barral Ediciones, 1971). Finally, see Stephen Minta's *García Márquez: Writer of Colombia* (New York: Harper & Row, 1987) and Gene H. Bell-Villada's *García Márquez: The Man and His Work* (Chapel Hill: University of North Carolina Press, 1990). Although I am much indebted to Menes's, Vargas Llosa's, and Bell-Villada's historical scholarship, my own approach to history, ideology, and historiography differs from theirs.

24. *La violencia* arose out of the superimposition of Colombia's crisis of modernization. See Robert H. Dix's *Colombia: The Political Dimension of Change* (New Haven, Conn.: Yale University Press, 1967).

25. For a more complete account of ideology, see Louis Althusser's "Ideology and Ideological State Apparatuses," in *Lenin and Philosophy*, trans. Ben Brewster (New York: Monthly Review Press, 1971).

26. Dreifus, "Playboy Interview," p. 76. Also relevant here is Susanne Kappeler's feminist reading of *One Hundred Years of Solitude*. According to Kappeler, Úrsula Buendia is "the first historian" in García Márquez's novel. "History," for Úrsula, "is also the history of patriarchy, and as such necessarily the critique of patriarchal order. . . . As the successive failures of the bearer of patriarchy are recorded, the values of the [male Buendías's] motivations are exposed." See Kappeler, "Voices of Patriarchy: Gabriel García Márquez's *One Hundred Years of Solitude*," in *Teaching the Text*, ed. Kappeler and Norman Bryson (London: Routledge, 1983): 160.

27. Theodor Adorno and Max Horkheimer, "The Culture Industry: Enlightenment as Mass Deception," in *Dialectic of Enlightenment*, trans. John Cumming (New York: Continuum, 1972): 120–67.

28. Fredric Jameson, *The Political Unconscious: Narrative as a Socially Symbolic Act* (Ithaca, N.Y.: Cornell University Press, 1981). Also relevant here is Jameson's "Metacommentary," in *PMLA* 86 (1971): 9–18.

29. See, for example, the remarks on "symbols" in Graciela Maturo's *Claves Simbólicos de García Márquez* (Buenos Aires: F. García Cumbeiro, 1972): 113–71.

30. See Emir Rodríguez Monegal's representative comments in *The Borzoi Anthology of Latin American Literature*, vol. 2 (New York: Alfred A. Knopf, 1977): 886–87.

31. According to numerous critics, the incest taboo in *One Hundred Years of Solitude* is a metaphor for "original sin." See, for example, the Freudian readings by Suzanne Jill Levine, "La maldición del incesto en *Cien años de*

soledad," Revista Iberoamericana (July 1971): 711–24, and George R. McMurray, *Gabriel García Márquez* (New York: Fredrick Ungar, 1977).

32. See Jean Franco's comparative study, "The Limits of the Liberal Imagination: *One Hundred Years of Solitude* and *Nostromo*," *Punto de Contacto* 1/2 (December 1975): 4–16.

33. See Mario J. Valdés, *Shadows in the Cave: A Phenomenological Approach to Literary Criticism Based on Hispanic Texts* (Toronto: University of Toronto Press, 1982): 64–76.

34. Alfred J. MacAdam, *Modern Latin American Narratives: The Dreams of Reason* (Chicago: University of Chicago Press, 1977): 78–88.

35. Regina Janes, *Gabriel García Márquez* (Columbia: University of Missouri Press, 1981): 48–69.

36. Joan Didion, *Salvador* (New York: Simon & Schuster, 1983): 59.

37. See, for instance, the following studies and interviews: Guillermo Ochoa, "Primero soy un hombre político," *Excelsior* 15/2 (April 15, 1971): 1 and 14–22, and Mario Vargas Llosa, "Diálogo entre Gabriel García Márquez y Mario Vargas Llosa," *Universitaria* (May 8, 1968).

38. Gabriel García Márquez, "The Solitude of Latin America," *New York Times*, February 6, 1982, sec. 4, p. 1.

39. Gabriel García Márquez and Vargas Llosa, *La novela en América Latina* (1976), p. 8.

40. Ibid., p. 9.

41. Marx's "Okonomisch-philosophische Manuskripte" (1844), quoted in Herbert Marcuse's *Reason and Revolution: Hegel and the Rise of Social Theory* (Boston: Beacon, 1960): 274.

42. For a penetrating reading of *One Hundred Years of Solitude* as a Marxist text, see Gregory Lawrence's "Marx in Macondo," *Latin American Literary Review* 2/4 (1974): 49–57. See also Victor Farías's dialectical treatment in his *Los manuscritos de Melquíades: Cien años de soledad: burguesía latinoamericana y dialéctica de la reproducción ampliada de negación* (Frankfurt/Main: Verlag Klaus Dieter Vervuert, 1981). It seems to me that any effort to read *One Hundred Years of Solitude* as a Marxist text needs to be accompanied by a reminder of what is essentially "biblical" about it, as so much of literature unquestionably is, for as Fernanda tells us in García Márquez's novel, "If they believe it in the Bible . . . I don't see why they shouldn't believe it from me," García Márquez, *One Hundred Years of Solitude*, p. 277.

43. Dreifus, "Playboy Interview," p. 65.

44. The phrase "alienation from meaning," of course, comes from Herbert N. Schneidau's *Sacred Discontent: The Bible and Western Tradition* (Berkeley: University of California Press, 1977).

45. The term "world-historical" event is Marx's and is defined in sections 1 and 2 of *The German Ideology* (1888) as the process by which local individuals, facts, or events become empirically significant on a wider scale: "world-historical existence of individuals, i.e., existence of individuals which is directly linked up with world history." I use the text edited by Robert C. Tucker in *The Marx-Engels Reader*, 2nd ed. (New York: W. W. Norton, 1978): 161, 163, 172.

46. Alejo Carpentier, *The Kingdom of this World,* trans. Harriet de Onís (New York: Alfred A. Knopf, 1957).

47. Fernández-Braso and García Márquez, *Gabriel García Márquez,* p. 59.

48. See Enrico Mario Santí's *Pablo Neruda: The Poetics of Prophecy* (Ithaca, N.Y.: Cornell University Press, 1982): 182.

49. Vargas Llosa, *Historia de un deicidio,* p. 36.

50. See Kumkum Sangari's "The Politics of the Possible," *Cultural Critique* 7 (Fall 1987): 157–86.

51. See Michael Ryan's *Marxism and Deconstruction: A Critical Articulation* (Baltimore: Johns Hopkins University Press, 1982): 24.

52. For an interesting reading of the Banana Company episode, see Robert Lewis Sims's "The Banana Massacre: A Microstructural Example of *Bricolage* and Myth," in *The Evolution of Myth in Gabriel García Márquez: From* La Hojarasca *to* Cien años de soledad (Miami: Ediciones Universal, 1981): 53–66.

53. The best historical study of the Banana Company massacre is Lucila Inés Menes's "La Huelga De La Companía Bananera Como Expresión De Lo Real Maravilloso Americano en *Cien años de soledad,*" *Bulletin Hispanique* 74/3–4 (1972): 379–405.

54. See Jorge Elicer Gaítan, *Los mejores discursos: 1919–1948,* ed. Jorge Villaveces (Bogotá: Editorial Jorvi, 1968): 56.

55. Menes, "La Huelga De La Companía Bananera," p. 400.

56. See Emir Rodríguez Monegal's classic essay, "The Last Three Pages of *One Hundred Years of Solitude,*" *Books Abroad* 47 (1973): 485–89. My own reading of the novel's ending owes much to this essay.

57. Jorge Luis Borges, "Las ruinas circulares," *Ficciones* (Buenos Aires: Emecé Editores, 1956): 61–79.

3 Chicano Border Narratives as Cultural Critique

1. Mary Louise Pratt argues in "Comparative Literature as a Cultural Practice" that García Márquez is read today in the West not as a representative of Our America but as a "genuis" of the South American continent. See *Profession 86* (New York, 1986): 33.

2. Kenneth Burke, *The Philosophy of Literary Form* (Baton Rouge: Louisiana State University Press, 1941): 110–11.

3. See Steven Mailloux, "Reading *Huckleberry Finn:* The Rhetoric of Performed Ideology," in *New Essays on Adventures of Huckleberry Finn,* ed. Louis J. Budd (New York: Cambridge University Press, 1985): 108. All subsequent references will be paginated in the text.

4. In his *Prison Notebooks,* Antonio Gramsci divides intellectuals into organic intellectuals, which any new class needs in order to organize a new social order, and traditional intellectuals, who have a tradition going back to an earlier historical period. See *Selections from the Prison Notebooks of Antonio Gramsci,* ed. and trans. Quintin Hoare and Geoffrey Nowell Smith (New York: International Publishers, 1971): 3–23.

5. See Friedrich Nietzsche, *The Use and Abuse of History,* trans. Adrian Collins (Indianapolis: Bobbs-Merrill, 1957).

6. See Necah S. Furman's "Walter Prescott Webb: Pioneer of The Texas Literary Tradition," in *The Texas Literary Tradition: Fiction, Folklore, History,* ed. Don Graham et al. (Austin, Tex.: Division of the Humanities, 1983): 35, n. 16.

7. Walter Prescott Webb, *The Texas Rangers: A Century of Frontier Defense* (Cambridge, Mass.: Houghton Mifflin, 1935): 14.

8. Furman, "Walter Prescott Webb," p. 33.

9. On January 31, 1919, Mr. Canales presented eighteen charges against the Texas Rangers, claiming that during 1915, 1916, 1917, and 1918 the Rangers had committed, in Canales own words, "outrageous acts." According to Canales, the Rangers "would arrest persons and after the persons were arrested they would be shot by the Rangers unceremoniously." See Webb's *The Texas Rangers,* p. 514. Of relevance is Rolando Hinojosa's essay on the Rangers, "River of Blood," *Texas Monthly* (January 1986; sesquicentennial collector's issue): 196.

10. See Américo Paredes's *"With His Pistol in His Hand": A Border Ballad and Its Hero* (Austin: University of Texas Press, 1958): 136. According to Paredes, "Catarino Garza, native of the Brownsville-Matamoros area [at the mouth of the Rio Grande] led what was probably the first rebellion against Díaz . . ."; he "organized his force in Texas and crossed into Mexico from Zapata County" (Paredes, p. 136). Also relevant here is José E. Limón, "Mexican Ballads, Chicano Epic: History, Social Dramas and Poetic Persuasion" (1986), Stanford Center for Chicano Research [hereinafter SCCR] Working Paper No. 14: 1–35.

11. José E. Limón, "Américo Paredes: A Man from the Border," *Revista Chicano-Riqueña* 8/3 (Verano, 1980): 4. Also of relevance are these incisive essays on Paredes: José E. Limón, "The Return of the Mexican Ballad: Américo Paredes and His Anthropological Text as Persuasive Political Performance" (SCCR Working Paper No. 16): 1–50, and Renato Rosaldo, "Politics, Patriarchy, and Laughter" (SCCR Working Paper No. 18): 1–31.

12. Teresa McKenna, "Immigrants in Our Own Land: A Chicano Literature Review," *ADE Bulletin* (forthcoming): 2–3.

13. Paredes, *"With His Pistol in His Hand,"* p. 15. All subsequent references will be paginated in the text.

14. For an incisive commentary on the corrido, see John Holmes McDowell, "The Corrido of Greater Mexico as Discourse, Music, and Event," in *"And Other Neighborly Names"; Social Process and Cultural Image in Texas Folklore,* ed. Richard Bauman and Roger D. Abrahams (Austin: University of Texas Press, 1981): 44–75.

15. See Américo Paredes, *A Texas-Mexican Cancionero: Folksongs of the Lower Border* (Urbana: University of Illinois Press, 1976): 64–67, for a complete transcription of "El Corrido de Gregorio Cortez."

16. Renato Rosaldo, "Politics, Patriarchies, and Laughter," SCCR Working Paper No. 18: 6.

17. See Ramón Saldívar's "The Form of Texas Mexican Fiction," in *The Texas Literary Tradition*, ed. Graham et al., p. 139.

18. See Tomás Rivera's and Rolando Hinojosa's comments on Américo Paredes in Juan Bruce-Novoa's *Chicano Authors: Inquiry by Interview* (Austin: University of Texas Press, 1980): 49–65, 139–61.

19. See Juan Rodríguez, "The Problematic in Tomás Rivera's . . . *And the Earth Did Not Part*, in *Revista Chicano-Riqueña* (Año 6): 42–50, for a summary of the most blatant misreadings of *Tierra.*

20. See Fredric Jameson's *The Political Unconscious: Narrative as a Socially Symbolic Act* (Ithaca, N.Y.: Cornell University Press, 1981): especially his chapter, "The Dialectic of Utopia and Ideology." Here Jameson argues that "all class consciousness . . . all ideology in the strongest sense, including the most exclusive forms of ruling-class consciousness, is in its very nature Utopian." Such collectivities are allegorical insofar as they are "figures for the ultimate concrete collective life" (p. 289).

21. Bruce-Novoa, *Chicano Authors*, p. 150. All subsequent references will be paginated in the text.

22. Ricardo Romo, "Afterword—East Los Angeles since 1930," in *East Los Angeles: History of a Barrio* (Austin: University of Texas Press, 1983): 163–73.

23. Rodolfo Acuña, *Occupied America: The Chicano's Struggle for Liberation* (New York: Harper & Row, 1972): 233–37, details this ascendancy.

24. Tomás Rivera, *Y no se lo tragó la tierra* (Berkeley: Quinto Sol Publications, 1971). I cite the Editorial Justa bilingual edition (Berkeley: Editorial Justa, 1977), p. 1. All subsequent references will be paginated in the text.

25. Rivera's concept of identity in *Tierra,* I believe, is essentially an existential concept. Rivera sees identity as the sum of his characters' choices, of their projections of themselves into the world. Identity, then, is a process of becoming. Also relevant here is Juan Rodríguez's "La búsqueda de identidad y sus motivos en la literatura chicana," in *The Identification and Analysis of Chicano Literature,* ed. Francisco Jiménez (New York: Bilingual Review Press, 1979): 170–78.

26. See Fredric Jameson's *Marxism and Form: Twentieth-Century Dialectical Theories of Literature* (Princeton, N.J.: Princeton University Press, 1971): 53. Of relevance here is Ramón Saldívar's "The Dialectics of Difference: Towards a Theory of the Chicano Novel," *MELUS* 6/3 (1979): 73–92. In formulating my reading of Rivera's narrative, I have also been influenced by Héctor Calderón's "To Read Chicano Narratives: Commentary and Metacommentary," *MESTER* 11/2 (1983): 3–14.

27. See Rodríguez, "La búsqueda de identidad," pp. 170–78.

28. See Yolanda Julia Broyles, "Hinojosa's *Klail City y sus alrededores,*" in *The Rolando Hinojosa Reader: Essays Historical and Critical,* ed. José David Saldívar (Houston: Arte Público Press, 1985): 109. All subsequent references to this essay will be paginated in the text.

29. Rolando Hinojosa, interview with author, March 22, 1985.

30. Karl Marx and Frederick Engels, *Selected Works* 2 vols. (Moscow: Foreign Languages Publishing House, 1962), 1: 247.

31. George L. Robertson, quoted in Arnoldo De León's *They Called Them Greasers: Anglo Attitudes toward Mexicans in Texas, 1821–1900* (Austin: University of Texas Press, 1983).

32. See De León's *They Called Them Greasers,* p. 1. All subsequent references will be paginated in the text.

33. Stephen F. Austin to Mrs. Mary Austin Holley, August 21, 1835, Austin Papers 3: 100–103.

34. *Klail City Death Trip* series, the project title of Rolando Hinojosa's Chicano historical novel, comprises *Estampas del Valle y Otras Obras* (Berkeley: Quinto Sol Publications, 1973); *Klail City y sus alrededores* (Havana: Casa de las Américas, 1976), subsequently published in a bilingual edition in the United States under the new title, *Generaciones y semblanzas,* trans. Rosaura Sánchez (Berkeley: Editorial Justa, 1977); *Korean Love Songs* (Berkeley: Editorial Justa, 1978); *Mi querido Rafa* (Houston, 1981); *Rites and Witnesses* (Houston: Arte Público Press, 1982); *The Valley* (Ypsilanti, Mich.: Bilingual Review Press, 1983); *Partners in Crime: A Rafe Buenrostro Mystery* (Houston: Arte Público Press, 1985); *Claros Varones de Belken/Fair Gentlemen of Belken* (Tempe, Ariz.: Bilingual Review Press, 1986); and *Klail City: A Novel* (Houston: Arte Público Press, 1987).

35. David Montejano, *Anglos and Mexicans in the Making of Texas, 1836–1986* (Austin: University of Texas Press, 1987). Montejano's extraordinary study, I believe, furnishes the socioeconomic and historical setting for all of Hinojosa's fiction whose scene is Mexican Texas. All subsequent references will be paginated in the text.

36. Rolando Hinojosa, "The Sense of Place," *The Rolando Hinojosa Reader,* p. 19.

37. In classical Marxism, reification is the act of transforming human beings, relations, and actions into properties. See Georg Lukác's *History and Class Consciousness,* trans. Rodney Livingston (Cambridge, Mass.: MIT Press, 1971).

38. See Mikhail M. Bakhtin's *The Dialogic Imagination: Four Essays,* ed. Michael Holmquist, trans. Caryl Emerson and Michael Holmquist (Austin: University of Texas Press, 1981): 301–31.

39. See Tom Zigal and Pat Jaspers, "Viewpoint: A Conversation with Rolando Hinojosa-Smith," *Texas Arts* (Summer 1983): 9.

40. The useful phrase "the political unconscious" is, of course, Fredric Jameson's. What Jameson means by it is the collective denial or suppression of society's underlying contradictions.

41. For a reading of Hinojosa's *Korean Love Songs* as a Chicano Border ballad or *corrido* of resistance, see Ramón Saldívar, "*Korean Love Songs:* A Border Ballad and Its Heroes," in *The Rolando Hinojosa Reader:* 143–56.

42. J. D. Saldívar, "Our Southwest: An Interview with Rolando Hinojosa," *The Rolando Hinojosa Reader,* p. 182.

43. Hayden White, *The Content of the Form: Narrative Discourse and Historical Representation* (Baltimore: Johns Hopkins University Press, 1987): 16. All further references to this work will be paginated in the text.

44. For a reevaluation of contemporary ethnographic practice, see *Writ-*

ing Culture: The Poetics and Politics of Ethnography, ed. James Clifford and George E. Marcus (Berkeley: University of California Press, 1986). See esp. Clifford's "Introduction: Partial Truths," pp. 1–26.

45. See Zigal and Jasper, "Viewpoint," p. 8.

46. My reading of *Partners in Crime* is influenced by Max Horkheimer's essay, "The End of Reason," in *The Essential Frankfurt School Reader*, eds. Andrew Arato and Eike Gebhardt (New York: Continuum, 1982): 26–49.

47. In his essay "Chronotope of the Novel," Bakhtin says of the historical novel, "for a long time the central and almost sole theme of the purely historical novel was the theme of war. This fundamentally historical theme—which has other motifs to it, such as conquest, political crimes . . . dynastic revolutions, the fall of kingdoms, the founding of new kingdoms and so forth—is interwoven with personal life narrative of historical figures. . . . The major task of the modern historical novel has been to overcome this duality: attempts have been made to find an historical aspect of private life, and also to represent history in its domestic light." See Bakhtin's *The Dialogic Imagination*, p. 217. This is precisely what Hinojosa achieves in his *Klail City Death Trip* series.

48. See Arnoldo De León, *The Tejano Community, 1836–1900* (Albuquerque: University of New Mexico Press, 1982); David Montejano, *Anglos and Mexicans in the Making of Texas, 1836–1986* (Austin: University of Texas Press, 1987); Manuel Peña, *The Texas Mexican Conjunto: History of a Working-Class Music* (Austin: University of Texas Press, 1985); Evangelina Vigil, *Thirty AN' Seen a Lot* (Houston: Arte Público Press, 1983); and Pat Mora, *Borders* (Houston: Arte Público Press, 1986).

49. Gloria Anzaldúa, *Borderlands/La Frontera: The New Mestiza* (San Francisco: Spinsters/Aunt Lute, 1987). All subsequent references to this work will be paginated in the text.

50. Fredric Jameson, "Third World Literature in the Era of Multinational Capitalism," *Social Text* 15 (1986): 84.

4 The Real and the Marvelous in Charleston

1. For a Fanonian reading of Shange's "combat-breathing" in *For Colored Girls*, see Sandra R. Richards's "Conflicting Impulses in the Plays of Ntozake Shange," in *Black American Literature Forum* 17/2 (Summer 1983): 73–78. For a reading of Shange's "lyricism" in *Sassafrass, Cypress & Indigo*, see Hortense J. Spillers's review in *American Book Review* 5 (Summer 1983): 13. Although Spillers notes that Shange's narrative style is very similar to Jean Toomer's *Cane*, she fails to mention the cultural conversations among Toomer, Claude McKay, Langston Hughes, and Countee Cullen with African and Caribbean writers living in Paris. Perhaps these dialogues may explain Toomer's lyricism in *Cane* and its subsequent influence on Shange's poetics. Finally, see Michael Awkward, *Inspiriting Influences: Tradition, Revision, and Afro-American Women's Novels*, (New York: Columbia University

Press, 1989), and Houston Baker, Jr., *Working of the Spirit: Afro-American Women's Writing* (Chicago: University of Chicago Press, 1991).

2. See Henry Louis Gates, Jr., *The Signifying Monkey: A Theory of Afro-American Literary Criticism* (New York: Oxford University Press, 1988): xxii. Throughout this chapter I rely on Gates's notion of the "Signifyin[g]" vernacular tradition in African American literature and culture. Like Gates, I have elected to write the black term with a bracketed final g to connote that this word is spoken by black people without the final g as "signifyin." To signify, for Gates, is "to engage in certain rhetorical games" (p. 48). More precisely, "Signifyin[g]" is always "black double-voicedness; because it always entails formal revision and an intertextual relation . . ." (p. 51).

3. W. Lawrence Hogue, *Discourse and the Other: The Production of the Afro-American Text* (Durham, N.C.: Duke University Press, 1986): 7. All future references will be paginated in the text.

4. Gates's notion of the double-voiced African American text, of course, relies on Bakhtin's theory of the double-voiced word. For Bakhtin, a double-voiced word is a sort of palimpsest in which the uppermost inscription is a commentary on the one beneath it. For Gates, however, the African American vernacular tradition of "Signifyin[g]" decolonizes the Western inscriptions beneath it.

5. See *Perspectives,* University of Houston System 6/7 (March 1984): 2.

6. Fredric Jameson, "On Magic Realism in Film," *Critical Inquiry* 12 (Winter 1986): 301.

7. For its new interpretations of García Márquez, Carpentier, and magic realism, see Fernando Alegría *Nueva Historia De La Novela Hispanoamericana* (Hanover, N.H.: Ediciones Norte, 1986): 186–297; see also Roberto González Echevarría, "Carpentier y el realismo mágico," in *Otros Mundos, Otros Fuegos,* ed. Donald Yates, Congreso Internacional de Literatura Iberoamericana 16 (East Lansing: Michigan State University, Latin American Studies Center, 1975): 221–31; and Amaryll Beatrice Chanady, *Magical Realism and the Fantastic: Resolved Versus Unresolved Antimony* (New York: Garland, 1985).

8. Roberto González Echevarría, *Alejo Carpentier: The Pilgrim at Home* (Ithaca, N.Y.: Cornell University Press, 1977): 107–29. All subsequent references will be paginated in the text.

9. Arturo Uslar Pietri used the term "realismo mágico" in his book *Letra y hombres de Venezuela* (Mexico: Fondo de Cultura Económica, 1948); Carpentier used the term "lo real maravilloso" in his "Prólogo" to *El reino de este mundo* in 1949.

10. Angel Flores, "Magical Realism in Spanish American Fiction," *Hispania* 38/2 (May 1955): 190.

11. Luis Leal, "El realismo mágico en la literatura hispanoamericana," *Cuadernos Americanos* 153/4 (July–August 1967): 234.

12. Echevarría argues in *The Pilgrim at Home,* for instance, that in Asturias's and Carpentier's fiction, there is "a primitivistic orientation," p. 112.

13. See Tristan Tzara's "Dada Manifesto," in Robert Motherwell's *Dada Painters and Poets* (New York: George Wittenborn Publishers, 1951): 78–79.

14. See André Breton's "What Is Surrealism?" in *The Modern Tradition,* ed. Richard Ellman and Charles Feidelson, Jr. (New York: Oxford University Press, 1965): 601–16.

15. Breton, "What Is Surrealism?," pp. 601–16.

16. Quoted in Gerald J. Langowski, *El surrealismo en la ficción hispanoamericana* (Madrid: Gredos, 1982): 89.

17. Emir Rodríguez Monegal, "Alejo Carpentier: lo real y lo maravilloso en *El reino de este mundo,*" *Revista Iberoamericana* 37 (1971): 619–49.

18. Alejo Carpentier, "Prólogo," *El reino de este mundo* (Santiago: Editorial Universitaria, 1967): xiv–xv. The translation is mine. All subsequent references to the "Prólogo" will be paginated in the text.

19. Gabriel García Márquez and Plinio Apuleyo Mendoza, *El olor de la guayaba* (Barcelona: Brugera), trans. T. Nairn as *The Fragrance of Guava: Plinio Apuleyo Mendoza in Conversation with Gabriel García Márquez* (London: Verso, 1983): 54–55.

20. Fernando Alegría, "Latin America: Fantasy and Reality," *Americas Review* 14/3–4 (Fall–Winter 1986): 117. All subsequent references will be paginated in the text.

21. Gabriel García Márquez, "The Solitude of Latin America," *New York Times,* February 6, 1982, sec. iv, p. 17.

22. Jameson, "On Magic Realism in Film," p. 311.

23. For a reactionary reading of Shange's ethnopoetics, see John Simon's review of *For Colored Girls,* where he states: "What accounts for the . . . inordinate praise of too many black plays is not so much black talent as white guilt." *New Leader* 7/5 (1976): 21–22.

24. Claudia Tate, *Black Women Writers at Work* (New York: Continuum, 1983): 163.

25. Ibid.

26. Barbara Christian, "Trajectories of Self-Definition: Placing Contemporary Afro-American Women's Fiction," *Conjuring: Black Women, Fiction, and Literary Tradition,* ed. Marjorie Pryse and Hortense J. Spillers (Bloomington: Indiana University Press, 1985): 242.

27. Spillers, review of *Sassafrass, Cypress & Indigo,* p. 13.

28. Ntozake Shange, interview with author, May 5, 1985.

29. Ntozake Shange, *Sassafrass, Cypress & Indigo* (New York: St. Martin's Press, 1982): 3. All subsequent references will be paginated in the text.

30. Quoted in Michael G. Cooke, *Afro-American Literature in the Twentieth Century: The Achievement of Intimacy* (New Haven, Conn.: Yale University Press, 1984): 22.

31. See, for example, the feminist essays by Carol Delaney and Emily Martin in *Blood Magic: The Anthropology of Menstruation,* ed. Thomas Buckley and Alma Gottlieb (Berkeley: University of California Press, 1988).

32. Barbara Christian, "No More Buried Lives: The Theme of Lesbianism in Audre Lorde's *Zami,* Gloria Naylor's *The Women of Brewster Street,* Ntozake Shange's *Sassafrass, Cypress & Indigo,* and Alice Walker's *The Color Purple,*" in *Black Feminist Criticism: Perspectives on Black Women Writers* (New York: Pergamon Press, 1985): 192.

33. Spillers, review of *Sassafrass, Cypress & Indigo*, p. 13.

34. See *Foreign Broadcast Information Service, Daily Report* 6/77 (1976): Q-1: 8.

35. See Immanuel Wallerstein, *The Modern World System*, II: *Mercantilism and the Consolidation of the European World-Economy, 1600–1750* (New York: Academic Press, 1980): 103.

36. See Stuart Hall's "Cultural Identity and Diaspora," in *Identity: Community, Culture, Difference*, ed. Jonathan Rutherford (London: Lawrence and Wishart, 1990), 222–37.

5 The Hybridity of Culture in *The Rain God*

1. See, for example, *The Invention of Ethnicity*, ed. Werner Sollors (New York: Oxford University Press, 1989); Fredric Jameson, "Third World Literature in the Era of Multinational Capitalism," *Social Text* 15 (1986): 65–88; Gilles Deleuze and Félix Guattari, *Kafka: Toward a Minor Literature*, trans. Dana Polan (Minneapolis: University of Minnesota Press, 1986); and David Lloyd, *Nationalism and Minor Literature: James Clarence Mangan and the Emergence of Irish Cultural Nationalism* (Berkeley: University of California Press, 1987).

2. Charles Newman, *The Post-Modern Aura: The Act of Fiction in an Age of Inflation* (Evanston, Ill.: Northwestern University Press, 1985): 185.

3. William Boelhower, *Through a Glass Darkly: Ethnic Semiosis in American Literature* (New York: Oxford University Press, 1987): 33.

4. See *The Invention of Ethnicity*, ed. Sollors.

5. Arnold Krupat, *The Voice in the Margin: Native American Literature and the Canon* (Berkeley: University of California Press, 1989). Subsequent references will be cited in the text.

6. Editors at mainline New York publishers, of course, represent the Professional Managerial Class and are by no means neutral cultural workers. Of relevance here is Pierre Bourdieu's *Distinction: A Social Critique of Taste*, trans. Richard Nice (Cambridge, Mass.: Harvard University Press, 1984).

7. See Richard Ohmann, "The Shaping of a Canon: U.S. Fiction, 1860–1975," *Critical Inquiry* 10 (September 1983): 202; and Janice Radway, "The Book of the Month Club and the General Reader: On the Uses of Serious Fiction," *Critical Inquiry* 14 (Spring 1988): 521.

8. Arturo Islas Papers, Folder 1—Correspondence, 1974–1975, Special Collections, Green Library, Stanford University.

9. Raymond Mungo, "Strange Murder in the Desert," review of *The Rain God, San Francisco Chronicle*, November 4, 1984, p. 5.

10. Carol Fowler, "Death and Family Dominate Novel," review of *The Rain God, Contra Costa Times*, January 26, 1985.

11. See Henry Louis Gates Jr., "Introduction: Writing 'Race' and the Difference It Makes," in *"Race," Writing, and Difference*, ed. Gates (Chicago: University of Chicago Press, 1986): 1–20.

12. Islas Papers, Folder 1—Correspondence, 1974–75.

13. Computer Curriculum Corporation of Palo Alto was the first northern California corporation to lend support to literature. Alexandrian Press was established as its division to publish a few novels of "genuine merit" each year.

14. Eileen Walsh, "The Book Report," *Campus Report*, Stanford University, January 16, 1985.

15. Ibid.

16. Howard J. Taylor, "Chicano Writers Can't Crack Prejudice of New York Publishers," *San Francisco Sunday Examiner & Chronicle*, August 5, 1984, p. 2.

17. Walsh, "The Book Report."

18. Taylor, "Chicano Writers Can't Crack Prejudice."

19. Ibid.

20. Ibid.

21. See José Antonio Villareal's *Pocho* (New York: Doubleday, 1959) and Edmundo Villaseñor's *Macho!* (New York: Bantam Books, 1973). All subsequent references to these books will be paginated in the text.

22. See *La Chicana: The Mexican-American Woman*, ed. Evangelina Enríquez and Alfredo Mirandé (Chicago: University of Chicago Press, 1979): 160–61.

23. Charles Tatum, *Chicano Literature* (Boston: Twayne, 1982): 135.

24. For a historical analysis of the consensus ideology in classic American literature, see Sacvan Bercovitch's "The Rites of Assent: Rhetoric, Ritual, and the Ideology of American Consensus," in *The American Self: Myth, Ideology, and Popular Culture* (Albuquerque: University of New Mexico Press, 1981): 5–42.

25. Islas Papers, Folder 1—Correspondence, 1974–75.

26. Ibid.

27. W. J. Cash, *The Mind of the South* (New York: Alfred A. Knopf, 1941): 386–87.

28. Friedrich Nietzsche, *The Genealogy of Morals*, trans. Walter Kaufmann and R. J. Hollingdale (New York: Vintage, 1969). I would have been technically indebted to a few points in Rosaura Sánchez's reading of Islas's novel had her fine talk "Ideological Discourses in Islas's *The Rain God*," delivered at Stanford University on May 30, 1986, not been given after my own work was drafted.

29. Arturo Islas, *The Rain God: A Desert Tale* (Palo Alto: Alexandrian Press, 1984). Subsequent references will be paginated in the text.

30. Quoted in Stephen Donadio, *Nietzsche, Henry James and the Artistic Will* (New York: Oxford University Press, 1978): 122.

31. Ibid.

32. Mungo, "Strange Murder in the Desert," p. 5.

33. Terry Comito, *In Defense of Winters: The Poetry and Prose of Yvor Winters* (Madison: University of Wisconsin Press, 1986).

34. Yvor Winters, "Poetic Styles, Old and New," in *Four Poets on Poetry,*

ed. Don Cameron Allen (Baltimore: Johns Hopkins University Press, 1958): 71.

35. See Daniel Hoffman, "Poetry: After Modernism," in *Harvard Guide to Contemporary American Writing* (Cambridge, Mass.: Harvard University Press, 1979): 442.

36. Stevens quoted in ibid.

37. See Frank Lentricchia's brilliantly audacious reading of Wallace Stevens's male utopian visions in "Writing after Hours," in *Ariel and the Police: Michel Foucault, William James, Wallace Stevens* (Madison: University of Wisconsin Press, 1988): 156.

38. Wallace Stegner, "The New Literary Frontier," *San Francisco Examiner,* August 5, 1990, p. E 3.

39. Wallace Stegner, "Willa Cather, *My Ántonia,*" in *The American Novel: From James Fenimore Cooper to William Faulkner,* ed. Wallace Stegner (New York: Basic Books, 1965): 145.

40. Mikhail M. Bakhtin, *The Dialogic Imagination: Four Essays,* ed. Michael Holquist, trans. Caryl Emerson and Michael Holquist (Austin: University of Texas Press, 1981). Hybridization, for Bakhtin, is the mixing within a single concrete utterance of two or more different linguistic consciousnesses, often widely separated in time and space.

6 The School of Caliban

1. For a collection that brings together examples of the New Historicism and Cultural Materialism, see *Political Shakespeare: New Essays in Cultural Materialism,* ed. Jonathan Dollimore and Alan Sinfield (Ithaca, N.Y.: Cornell University Press, 1985). Also relevant is *The New Historicism,* ed. H. Aram Veeser (New York: Routledge, 1989).

2. Rob Nixon, "Caribbean and African Appropriations of *The Tempest,*" *Critical Inquiry* 13 (Spring 1987): 560.

3. See Marjorie B. Garber, *Dream in Shakespeare: From Metaphor to Metamorphosis* (New Haven, Conn.: Yale University Press, 1974). In looking through my undergraduate Yale University notebooks, I came across the following statement by Professor Garber: "Caliban is, like Ariel, a denizen of the dream world of the irrational, but his is the dark side of the dream."

4. Steven Mullaney, *The Place of the Stage: License, Play and Power in Renaissance England* (Chicago: University of Chicago Press, 1987): vi–vii. All further citations will be paginated in the text.

5. See Stephen Greenblatt's "Introduction," *The Forms of Power and the Power of Forms in the Renaissance,* ed. Greenblatt (Norman: University of Oklahoma Press, 1982): 3–6.

6. See Walter Cohen, "Political Criticism of Shakespeare," in *Shakespeare Reproduced: The Text in History and Ideology,* ed. Jean E. Howard and Marion F. O'Connor (New York: Methuen, 1987): 34.

7. Stephen Greenblatt, *Shakespearean Negotiations: The Circulation of So-*

cial Energy in Renaissance England (Berkeley: University of California Press, 1988): 142. All further references will be paginated in the text.

8. For a brief discussion of the history of book burning, see Leo Lowenthal, "Caliban's Legacy," in *Cultural Critique* (Winter 1987–88): 5–17.

9. Raymond Williams, "Afterword," in *Political Shakespeare.*

10. See Francis Barker and Peter Hulme, "Nymphs and Reapers Heavily Vanish: The Discursive Con-texts of *The Tempest,*" in *Alternative Shakespeare,* ed. John Drakakis (London: Methuen, 1985): 191–205; and Terence Hawkes, *That Shakespeherian Rag: Essays in a Critical Process* (London: Methuen, 1986): 51–72. All further references to these texts will be paginated in the text.

11. George Lamming, *The Pleasures of Exile* (London: Allison & Busby, 1960). All further references will be paginated in the text.

12. For an English translation of Fernández Retamar's *Caliban,* see Roberto Márquez, "Caliban: Notes Toward a Discussion of Culture in Our America," in *Massachusetts Review* 15/1–2 (1974): 7–72.

13. See Nixon, "Caribbean and African Appropriations of *The Tempest,*" p. 561.

14. See Ian Munro and Reinhard Sander, eds. *Kas-Kas: Interviews with Three Caribbean Writers in Texas: George Lamming, C. L. R. James, Wilson Harris* (Austin: Occasional Publication of the African and Afro-American Research Institute, University of Texas, 1972): 6.

15. Aimé Césaire quoted in S. Belhassen, "Aimé Césaire's *A Tempest,*" in *Radical Perspective in the Arts,* ed. Lee Baxandall (Harmondsworth: Penguin, 1972): 176.

16. Aimé Césaire, *A Tempest,* trans. Richard Miller (New York: UBU, 1986): 71. All further references will be paginated in the text.

17. See Fernández Retamar, *Caliban,* pp. 219–90.

18. Richard Rodriguez, *Hunger of Memory: The Education of Richard Rodriguez* (New York: Bantam Books, 1983); Ernesto Galarza, *Barrio Boy: The Story of a Boy's Acculturation* (Notre Dame, Ind.: University of Notre Dame Press, 1977); Cherríe Moraga, *Loving in the War Years: lo que nunca pasó por sus labios* (Boston: South End Press, 1983); Houston Baker, Jr., *Modernism and the Harlem Renaissance* (Chicago: University of Chicago Press, 1987). All further references will be paginated in the text.

19. It seems self-evident that American readers are more likely to be familiar with those Ariel writer-intellectuals who lean toward Prospero's aesthetics than with those who practice Caliban's deformation of mastery. In Rodriguez's case, he has become a favorite with American professors of composition and rhetoric. Selections from *Hunger of Memory* are now anthologized in virtually all new freshman "readers" in the country.

20. See Ramón Saldívar, "Ideologies of the Self: Chicano Autobiography," *Diacritics* (Fall 1985): 26.

21. The term "normalization" is Michel Foucault's. In *Discipline and Punish: The Birth of the Prison,* trans. Alan Sheridan (New York: Vintage, 1979), Foucault writes: "In a sense, the power of normalization imposes

homogeneity; but it individualizes by making it possible to measure gaps, etc.," p. 184.

22. Frank Lentricchia, *Criticism and Social Change* (Chicago: University of Chicago Press, 1983): 7.

23. Renato Rosaldo, "Others of Invention: Ethnicity and Its Discontents," *Village Voice Literary Supplement* 82 (February 12, 1990): 28.

24. Mihail M. Bakhtin, *The Dialogic Imagination: Four Essays*, ed. Michael Holquist, trans. Caryl Emerson and Holquist (Austin: University of Texas Press, 1981): 116.

25. Alfred Kazin, *An American Procession: The Major American Writers from 1830 to 1930—The Crucial Century* (New York: Alfred A. Knopf, 1983): 280–81.

26. See Ernesto Galarza, *Merchants of Labor* (Santa Barbara: McNally and Lofton, 1978), *Spiders in the House and Workers in the Fields* (Notre Dame, Ind.: University of Notre Dame Press, 1970), and *Farm Workers and Agribusiness in California, 1947–1960* (Notre Dame, Ind.: University of Notre Dame Press, 1977). These books are penetrating critiques of the bracero program.

27. Fredric Jameson, *The Political Unconscious: Narrative as a Socially Symbolic Act* (Ithaca, N.Y.: Cornell University Press, 1981): 102.

28. Ernesto Galarza, quoted in Carlos Muñoz's "Galarza: Scholar on the Ramparts," lecture, SCCR (1987):2.

29. Ramón Saldívar, "Ideologies of the Self," p. 30.

30. See Hayden White, *Metahistory: The Historical Imagination in Nineteenth-Century Europe* (Baltimore: Johns Hopkins University Press, 1973): 37–38.

31. According to Werner Sollors, ethnic American autobiographies adopt a conversion paradigm that moves from "shallow assimilationist to reborn ethnic." See Sollors, *Beyond Ethnicity: Consent and Descent in American Culture* (New York: Oxford University Press, 1986): 31–32. Moraga adopts this model in *Loving in the War Years* by writing that her autobiography is the story of "a white girl gone brown" (p. 60).

32. Herbert Marcuse, *Eros and Civilization: A Philosophical Inquiry into Freud* (New York: Random House, 1955): 29.

33. Houston Baker, Jr., "Caliban's Triple Play," in *"Race," Writing, and Difference*, ed. Henry Louis Gates, Jr. (Chicago: University of Chicago Press, 1986): 389.

Afterword

1. Of the recent writings that articulate and analyze postcolonial cultural theory and identity, three have been particularly helpful: Kumkum Sangari's "The Politics of the Possible," *Cultural Critique* 7 (Fall 1987): 157–86; Norma Alarcón's "The Theoretical Subject(s) of *This Bridge Called My Back* and Anglo-American Feminism"; and Barbara Harlow's "Sites of Struggle: Immigration, Deportation, Prison, and Exile," both in *Criticism in the Borderlands: Studies in Chicano Literature, Culture, and Ideology*, ed. Héctor

Calderón and José David Saldívar (Durham, N.C.: Duke University Press, 1991).

2. James Clifford, "Notes On Travel and Theory," *Inscriptions* 5 (1989): 179.

3. Guillermo Gómez-Peña, "Border Culture: A Process of Negotiation Toward Utopia," *La Linea Quebrada* 1 (1986): 1. Subsequent references will be cited in the text.

4. Renato Rosaldo, "Ideology, Place, and People Without Culture," *Cultural Anthropology* 3 (1988): 78. Subsequent references will be cited in the text.

5. George Lipsitz, *Time Passages: Collective Memory and American Popular Culture* (Minneapolis: University of Minnesota Press, 1990): 5.

6. See Fredric Jameson's "Reification and Utopia in Mass Culture," *Social Text* 1 (1979): 131–48.

7. For an account of the Nueva Canción movement, see Fernando Reyes Mata's "The New Song and Its Confrontation in Latin America," in *Marxism and the Interpretation of Culture*, ed. Cary Nelson and Lawrence Grossberg (Urbana: University of Illinois Press, 1988): 447–60.

8. See William Carlos Williams, *In the American Grain* (New York: New Directions, 1956).

9. For a comparative reading of hybridity in García Márquez's and Salman Rushdie's magical narratives, see Sangari's "The Politics of the Possible." Also of relevance here is *Nation and Narration*, ed. Homi K. Bhabha (New York: Routledge, 1990).

10. Rubén Blades, "Agua de Luna" (Electra Records, DDD 60721-2, 1987).

References

Acuña, Rodolfo. 1972. *Occupied America: A History of Chicanos*. New York: Harper & Row.

Adorno, Theodor W., and Max Horkheimer. 1972. *Dialectic of Enlightenment*, trans. John Cumming. New York: Continuum.

Ahmad, Aijaz. 1987. "Jameson's Rhetoric of Otherness and the 'National Allegory.'" *Social Text* 17 (Fall): 3–25.

Alarcón, Norma. 1991. "The Theoretical Subject(s) of *This Bridge Called My Back*," in *Criticism in the Borderlands: Studies in Chicano Literature, Culture, and Ideology*, ed. Héctor Calderón and José David Saldívar. Durham, N.C.: Duke University Press: 28–39.

Alegría, Fernando. 1970. *Literatura y revolución*. México: Fondo de Cultura Económica.

———. 1986. *Nueva historia de la novela hispanoamericana*. Hanover, N.H.: Ediciones del norte.

———. 1986. "Latin America: Fantasy and Reality." *Americas Review* 14/3: 115–18.

Allen, Don Cameron, ed. 1958. *Four Poets on Poetry*. Baltimore: Johns Hopkins University Press.

Althusser, Louis. 1971. *Lenin and Philosophy*, trans. Ben Brewster. New York: Monthly Review Press.

Anaya, Rudolfo. 1972. *Bless Me, Ultima*. Berkeley: Quinto Sol Publications.

Anderson, Benedict. 1983. *Imagined Communities: Reflections on the Origins and Spread of Nationalism*. London: Verso.

Anzaldúa, Gloria. 1987. *Borderlands/La Frontera: The New Mestiza*. San Francisco: Spinsters/Aunt Lute.

Arato, Andrew, and Eike Gebhardt, eds. 1982. *The Essential Frankfurt School Reader*. New York: Continuum.

Arnold, A. James. 1981. *Modernism and Negritude: The Poetry and Poetics of Aimé Césaire*. Cambridge, Mass.: Harvard University Press.

Asturias, Miguel Angel. 1950. *Viento fuerte*. Buenos Aires: Editorial Losada.

———. 1954. *El Papa verde*. Buenos Aires: Editorial Losada.

———. 1960. *Los ojos de los enterrados*. Buenos Aires: Editorial Losada.

Awkward, Michael. 1989. *Inspiriting Influences: Tradition, Revision, and Afro-American Women's Novels*. New York: Columbia University Press.

Baker, Houston A., Jr. 1984. *Blues, Ideology, and Afro-American Literature: A Vernacular Theory*. Chicago: University of Chicago Press.

———. 1985. "Caliban's Triple Play," in *"Race," Writing, and Difference*, ed. Henry Louis Gates, Jr. Chicago: University of Chicago Press: 381–95.

———. 1987. *Modernism and the Harlem Renaissance*. Chicago: University of Chicago Press.

———. 1991. *Workings of the Spirit: Afro-American Women's Writing*. Chicago: University of Chicago Press.

Bakhtin, Mikhail. 1965. *Rabelais and His World,* trans. Helene Iswolsky. Cambridge, Mass.: MIT Press.

———. 1981. *The Dialogic Imagination: Four Essays,* ed. Michael Holquist, trans. Caryl Emerson and Michael Holquist. Austin: University of Texas Press.

Barker, Francis, and Peter Hulme. 1985. "Nymphs and Reapers Heavily Vanish: The Discursive Con-texts of *The Tempest,*" in *Alternative Shakespeare;* ed. John Drakakis. London: Metheun: 191–205.

Barth, John. 1967. "The Literature of Exhaustion." *Atlantic Monthly* 222 (August): 29–34.

Baxandall, Lee, ed. 1972. *Radical Perspectives in the Arts.* Harmondsworth: Penguin.

Bell-Villada, Gene H. 1990. *García Márquez: The Man and His Work.* Chapel Hill: University of North Carolina Press.

Benedetti, Mario. 1982. *Panorama Histórico-Literario de Nuestra América.* Havana: Casa de las Américas.

Bercovitch, Sacvan. 1981. "The Rites of Assent: Rhetoric, Ritual, and the Ideology of the American Consensus," in *The American Self: Myth, Ideology, and Popular Culture,* ed. Sam Girgus. Albuquerque: University of New Mexico Press: 5–42.

———. 1986. *Reconstructing American Literary History.* Cambridge, Mass.: Harvard University Press.

———. 1986. "America as Canon and Context: Literary History in a Time of Dissensus." *American Literature* 58/1: 99–107.

———. 1986. "The Problem of Ideology in American Literary History." *Critical Inquiry* 12: 631–53.

Bercovitch, Sacvan, and Myra Jehlen, eds. 1986. *Ideology and Classic American Literature.* New York: Cambridge University Press.

Berman, Russell. 1986. *The Rise of the German Novel: Crisis and Charisma.* Cambridge, Mass.: Harvard University Press.

Bhabha, Homi K., ed. 1990. *Nation and Narration.* New York: Routledge.

Blades, Rubén. 1987. "Agua de Luna." Electra Records, DDD 60721-2.

Boelhower, William. 1987. *Through a Glass Darkly: Ethnic Semiosis in American Literature.* New York: Oxford University Press.

Borges, Jorge Luis. 1956. *Ficciones.* Buenos Aires: Emecé Editores.

———. 1964. "El arte y la magia," in *Discusión.* Buenos Aires: Emecé Editores, S.A.: 71–79.

———. 1981. *Borges: A Reader,* ed. Emir Rodríguez Monegal and Alastair Reid. New York: E. P. Dutton.

Bourdieu, Pierre. 1984. *Distinction: A Social Critique of Taste,* trans. Richard Nice. Cambridge, Mass.: Harvard University Press.

Breton, André. 1969. *Les Manifestes du surrealisme.* Paris: Gallimard.

Bruce-Novoa, Juan. 1980. *Chicano Authors: Inquiry by Interview.* Austin: University of Texas Press.

———. 1982. *Chicano Poetry: A Response to Chaos*. Austin: University of Texas Press.

Buckley, Thomas, and Alma Gottlieb, eds. 1988. *Blood Magic: The Anthropology of Menstruation*. Berkeley: University of California Press.

Burke, Kenneth. 1941. *The Philosophy of Literary Form*. Baton Rouge: Louisiana State University Press.

Calderón, Héctor. 1983. "To Read Chicano Narratives: Commentary and Metacommentary." *Mester* 13/2: 3–14.

———. 1985. "On the Uses of Chronicle, Biography and Sketch in Rolando Hinojosa's *Generaciones y semblanzas*," in *The Rolando Hinojosa Reader: Essays Historical and Critical*, ed. José David Saldívar. Houston: Arte Público Press: 133–42.

Cardoso, Henrique, and Enzo Faletto. 1979. *Dependency and Development in Latin America*, trans. Marjory Urquidi. Berkeley: University of California Press.

Carpentier, Alejo. 1967. *El reino de este mundo*. Santiago: Editorial Universitaria.

———. 1966. *Tientos y diferencias*. Havana: Union Nacional de Escritores y Artistas.

Cash, W. J. 1941. *The Mind of the South*. New York: Alfred A. Knopf.

Césaire, Aimé. 1983. *Aimé Césaire: The Collected Poetry*, trans. Clayton Eshleman and Annette Smith. Berkeley: University of California Press.

———. 1986. *A Tempest*, trans. Richard Miller. New York: Ubu Repertory Publications.

Chevigny, Bell, and Gari Laguardia, eds. 1986. *Reinventing the Americas: Comparative Studies of Literature in the United States and Spanish America*. New York: Cambridge University Press.

Christian, Barbara. 1985. *Black Feminist Criticism: Perspectives on Black Women Writers*. New York: Pergamon Press.

Clifford, James, and George E. Marcus, eds. 1986. *Writing Culture: The Poetics and Politics of Ethnography*. Berkeley: University of California Press.

———. 1988. *The Predicament of Culture: Twentieth-Century Ethnography, Literature, and Art*. Cambridge, Mass.: Harvard University Press.

———. 1989. "Notes on Travel and Theory." *Inscriptions* 5: 177–88.

Comito, Terry. 1986. *In Defense of Winters*. Madison: University of Wisconsin Press.

Cooke, Michael G. 1984. *Afro-American Literature in the Twentieth Century: The Achievement of Intimacy*. New Haven, Conn.: Yale University Press.

Coover, Robert. 1986. "The Writer as God and Saboteur." *New York Times Book Review*, February 2, pp. 1 and 10.

Cortes-Vargas, Carlos. 1929. *Los sucesos de los bananeros*. Bogotá: La Lúa.

Dearborn, Mary V. 1986. *Pocahontas's Daughters: Gender and Ethnicity in American Culture*. New York: Oxford University Press.

De León, Arnoldo. 1983. *They Called Them Greasers: Anglo Attitudes towards Mexicans in Texas, 1821–1900*. Austin: University of Texas Press.

Degler, Carl. 1984. *Out of Our Past: The Forces That Shaped Modern America.* 3rd ed. New York: Harper & Row.

Deleuze, Gilles, and Félix Guattari. 1986. *Kafka: Toward a Minor Literature,* trans. Dana Polan. Minneapolis: University of Minnesota Press.

Derrida, Jacques. 1976. *Of Grammatology,* trans. Gayatri Chakravorty Spivak. Baltimore: Johns Hopkins University Press.

Didion, Joan. 1983. *Salvador.* New York: Simon & Schuster.

Dix, Robert H. 1967. *Colombia: The Political Dimension of Change.* New Haven, Conn.: Yale University Press.

Doctorow, E. L. 1983. "False Documents" in *E. L. Doctorow: Essays and Conversations,* ed. Richard Trenner. Princeton, N.J.: Ontario Review Publications, 16–27.

Dollimore, Jonathan, and Alan Sinfield, eds. 1985. *Political Shakespeare: New Essays in Cultural Materialism.* Ithaca, N.Y.: Cornell University Press.

Donadio, Stephen. 1978. *Nietzsche, Henry James and the Artistic Will.* New York: Oxford University Press.

Donoso, José. 1977. *Historia personal del "boom",* trans. Gregory Kolovakos as *The Boom in Spanish American Literature.* New York: Columbia University Press.

Drake, Sandra. 1977. "The Uses of History in the Caribbean Novel." Diss. Stanford University.

———. 1986. *Wilson Harris and the Modern Tradition.* Westport, Conn.: Greenwood Press.

Dreifus, Claudia. 1983. "Playboy Interview: Gabriel García Márquez." *Playboy* 30/2: 235–55.

Emerson, Ralph Waldo. 1971. "The American Scholar" in *The Collected Works of Ralph Waldo Emerson.* I: *Nature, Addresses, and Lectures,* intro. and notes Robert E. Spiller. Cambridge, Mass.: Belknap Press.

Enríquez, Evangelina, and Alfredo Mirandé. 1977. *La Chicana: The Mexican-American Woman.* Chicago: University of Chicago Press.

Fallas, Carlos Luis. 1972. *Mamita Yanqi.* Santiago de Chile: Editora Quimontu.

Fanon, Frantz. 1966. *The Wretched of the Earth,* trans. Constance Farrington. New York: Grove Press.

———. 1967. *Black Skin, White Masks,* trans. Charles Markmann. New York: Grove Press.

Farías, Victor. 1981. *Los manuscritos de Melquíades: Cien años de soledad, burguesía latinoamericana y dialética de la reproducción de negación.* Frankfurt: Klaus Dieter Vervuert.

Fernández-Braso, Miguel. 1969. *Gabriel García Márquez (una conversación infinita).* Madrid: Azur.

Fernández Moreno, Cesar. 1980. *Latin America in Its Literature.* New York: Holmes & Meier.

Fernández Retamar, Roberto. 1975. *Para una teoría de la literatura hispanoamericana y otras aproximaciones.* Havana: Casa de las Américas.

———. 1976. "Nuestra América y Occidente," *Casa de las Américas* 98: 36–57.

———. 1979. *José Martí: Ensayos sobre arte y literatura.* Havana: Editorial Letras Cubanas.

———. 1981. "Caliban: Apuntos sobre la cultura en nuestra América," in *Para El Perfil Definitivo Del Hombre.* Havana: Editorial Letras Cubanas, 219–90.

———. 1986. "The Modernity of Martí," in *José Martí, Revolutionary Democrat,* ed. Christopher Abel and Nissa Torrents. Durham, N.C.: Duke University Press, 1–15.

———. 1986. "Caliban Revisitado," *Casa de las Américas* 157/27: 152–59.

———. 1989. *Caliban and Other Essays,* trans. Edward Baker. Minneapolis: University of Minnesota Press.

Fish, Stanley. 1980. *Is There a Text in This Classroom?: The Authority of Interpretive Communities.* Cambridge, Mass.: Harvard University Press.

Flores, Angel. 1955. "Magical Realism in Spanish American Fiction." *Hispania* 38/2: 187–92.

Foner, Philip S., ed. 1977. *Inside the Monster by José Martí: Writings on the United States and American Imperialism,* trans. Elinor Randall, Juan de Onís, and Roslyn Foner. New York: Monthly Review Press.

———, ed. 1977. *Our America by José Martí: Writings on Latin America and the Struggle for Cuban Independence,* trans. Elinor Randall. New York: Monthly Review Press.

Foster, David William. 1979. *Studies in the Contemporary Spanish-American Short Story.* Columbia: University of Missouri Press.

Foucault, Michel. 1972. *The Archaeology of Knowledge,* trans. A. M. Sheridan Smith. London: Harper Colophon.

———. 1979. *Discipline and Punish,* trans. Alan Sheridan. New York: Vintage.

———. 1984. "Nietzsche, Genealogy, History," in *The Foucault Reader,* ed. Paul Rabinow. New York: Pantheon Books, 76–100.

Franco, Jean. 1969. *An Introduction to Spanish American Literature.* Cambridge: Cambridge University Press.

———. 1975. "The Limits of the Liberal Imagination: *One Hundred Years of Solitude* and *Nostromo,*" *Punto de Contacto* 11/1: 4–16.

———. 1981. "The Utopia of a Tired Man: Jorge Luis Borges." *Social Text* 4 (Fall): 52–78.

———. 1989. *Plotting Women.* New York: Columbia University Press.

Frank, André Gunder. 1967. *Capitalism and Underdevelopment in Latin America.* New York: Monthly Review Press.

Fredrickson, George M. 1981. *White Supremacy: A Comparative Study in American and South African History.* New York: Oxford University Press.

Furman, Necah S. 1983. "Walter Prescott Webb: Pioneer of the Texas Literary Frontier," in *The Texas Literary Tradition: Fiction, Folklore, History,* ed. Don Grahm et al. Austin: Division of the Humanities, University of Texas.

Galarza, Ernesto. 1970. *Spiders in the House and Workers in the Fields.* Notre Dame, Ind.: University of Notre Dame Press.

———. 1977. *Barrio Boy: The Story of a Boy's Acculturation*. Notre Dame, Ind.: University of Notre Dame Press.

———. 1978. *Merchants of Labor*. Santa Barbara: McNally and Lofton.

———. *Collected Papers*, Special Collections, Green Library, Stanford University.

Garber, Marjorie B. 1974. *Dreams in Shakespeare: From Metaphor to Metamorphosis*. New Haven, Conn.: Yale University Press.

García, Mario T. 1981. *Desert Immigrants: The Mexicans of El Paso, 1880–1920*. New Haven, Conn.: Yale University Press.

García Márquez, Gabriel. 1955. *La hojarasca*, trans. G. Rabassa as *Leafstorm and Other Stories*. New York: Avon, 1970.

———. 1962. *Los funerales de la Mamá Grande*, trans. J. S. Bernstein as *No One Writes to the Colonel and Other Stories*. New York: Avon, 1968.

———. 1967. *Cien años de soledad*, trans. G. Rabassa as *One Hundred Years of Solitude*. New York: Avon, 1970.

———. 1982. "La soledad de Latina América," *Proceso* 319, December 13, trans. Marina Castañeda as "The Solitude of Latin America." *New York Times*, February 6, 1983, sec. 4: 17.

———. 1984. *Collected Stories*. New York: Harper & Row.

———, and Mario Vargas Llosa. 1968. *La Novela en América Latina: Diálogo*. Lima: Carlos Milla Batres/Ediciones Universidad Nacional de Ingeniería.

Gates, Henry Louis, Jr., ed. 1986. *"Race," Writing, and Difference*. Chicago: University of Chicago Press.

———. 1988. *The Signifying Monkey: A Theory of Afro-American Literary Criticism*. New York: Oxford University Press.

Gómez-Peña, Guillermo. 1986. "Border Culture: A Process of Negotiation Toward Utopia." *La Linea Quebrada*. 1: 1–6.

González Echevarría, Roberto. 1977. *Alejo Carpentier: The Pilgrim at Home*. Ithaca, N.Y.: Cornell University Press.

———. 1978. "Roberto Fernández Retamar: An Introduction." *Diacritics* (Winter): 70–75.

———. 1981. "Criticism and Literature in Revolutionary Cuba." *Cuban Studies/Estudios Cubanos* 11/1: 1–18.

———. 1984. "*Cien años de soledad:* The Novel as Myth and Archive." *Modern Language Notes* 99/2: 358–80.

———. 1985. *The Voice of the Masters: Writing and Authority in Modern Latin American Literature*. Austin: University of Texas Press.

Gramsci, Antonio. 1971. *Selections from the Prison Notebooks of Antonio Gramsci*, trans. Quintin Hoare and Geoffrey Smith. New York: International Publishers.

Greenblatt, Stephen, ed. 1982. *The Forms of Power and the Power of Forms in the Renaissance*. Norman: University of Oklahoma Press.

———. 1988. *Shakespearean Negotiations: The Circulation of Social Energy in Renaissance England*. Berkeley: University of California Press.

Guevara, Che. 1970. "The Most Dangerous Enemies and Other Stupidities," trans. Rolando E. Bonachea and Nelson P. Valdés., eds. *Che: Selected Works of Ernesto Guevara.* Cambridge, Mass.: MIT Press.

Hall, Stuart. 1990. "Cultural Identity and Diaspora," in *Identity: Community, Culture, Difference,* ed. Jonathan Rutherford. London: Lawrence and Wishart.

Haraway, Donna. 1989. *Primate Visions: Gender, Race, and Nature in the World of Modern Science.* New York: Routledge.

Harlow, Barbara. 1987. *Resistance Literature.* New York: Methuen.

———. 1991. "Sites of Struggle: Immigration, Deportation, Prison, and Exile," in *Criticism in the Borderlands: Studies in Chicano Literature, Culture, and Ideology,* ed. Héctor Calderón and José David Saldívar. Durham, N.C.: Duke University Press: 149–63.

Hawkes, Terrence. 1986. *That Shakespeherian Rag: Essays on a Critical Process.* London: Methuen.

Hellman, Stephen. 1986. "The Cuban Pulitzer," in *San Francisco Chronicle Review,* July 20, pp. 2, 10.

Hinojosa, Rolando. 1973. *Estampas del Valle y Otras Obras.* Berkeley: Quinto Sol Publications.

———. 1976. *Klail City y sus alrededores.* Havana: Casa de las Américas.

———. 1977. *Generaciones y semblanzas.* Berkeley: Editorial Justa Press.

———. 1978. *Korean Love Songs.* Berkeley: Editorial Justa Press.

———. 1981. *Mi querido Rafa.* Houston: Arte Público Press.

———. 1982. *Rites and Witnesses.* Houston: Arte Público Press.

———. 1983. *The Valley.* Ypsilanti, Mich.: Bilingual Press.

———. 1985. *Partners in Crime: A Rafe Buenrostro Mystery.* Houston: Arte Público Press.

———. 1986. *Claros Varones de Belken/Fair Gentlmen of Belken County.* Tempe, Ariz.: Bilingual Press.

———. 1987. *Klail City: A Novel.* Houston: Arte Público Press.

Hoffman, Daniel. 1979. *Harvard Guide to Contemporary American Writing.* Cambridge, Mass.: Harvard University Press.

Hogue, W. Lawrence. 1986. *Discourse and the Other: The Production of the Afro-American Text.* Durham, N.C.: Duke University Press.

Howard, Jean E., and Mariam F. O'Connor, eds. 1987. *Shakespeare Reproduced: The Text in History and Ideology.* New York: Methuen.

Hunt, Lynn, ed. 1989. *The New Cultural History.* Berkeley: University of California Press.

Iduarte, Andrés. 1982. *Martí, escritor,* 3rd. México: J. Mortiz.

Islas, Arturo. 1984. *The Rain God: A Desert Tale.* Palo Alto: Alexandrian Press.

———. 1974–85. *Collected Papers.* Special Collections, Green Library, Stanford University.

James, C. L. R. 1963. *The Black Jacobins: Toussaint l'Ouverture and the San Domingo Revolution.* New York: Random House.

Jameson, Fredric. 1971. *Marxism and Form: Twentieth-Century Dialectical Theories of Literature.* Princeton, N.J.: Princeton University Press.

———. 1979. "Reification and Utopia in Mass Culture." *Social Text* 1: 130–48.

———. 1981. *The Political Unconscious: Narrative as a Socially Symbolic Act.* Ithaca, N.Y.: Cornell University Press.

———. 1984. "Postmodernism, or the Cultural Logic of Late Capitalism." *New Left Review* 146 (July–August): 53–93.

———. 1986. "On Magic Realism in Film." *Critical Inquiry* 12/2: 301–25.

———. 1986. "Third World Literature in the Era of Multinational Capitalism." *Social Text* 15: 65–88.

———. 1990. *Late Marxism: Adorno, or, the Persistence of the Dialectic.* London: Verso.

Janes, Regina. 1981. *Gabriel García Márquez: Revolutions in Wonderland.* Columbia: University of Missouri Press.

JanMohamed, Abdul. 1983. *Manichean Aesthetics: The Politics of Literature in Colonial Africa.* Amherst: University of Massachusetts Press.

Jehlen, Myra. 1990. "The Ties That Bind: Race and Sex in *Pudd'nhead Wilson*," *American Literary History* 2/1 (Spring): 39–55.

Jiménez, Francisco, ed. 1979. *The Identification and Analysis of Chicano Literature.* New York: Bilingual Press.

Johnson, Lemuel A. 1971. *The Devil, the Gargoyle, and the Buffoon: The Negro as Metaphor in Western Literature.* Port Washington, N.Y.: Kennikat Press.

Kappeler, Susanne. 1983. "Voices of Patriarchy: Gabriel García Márquez's *One Hundred Years of Solitude*," in *Teaching the Text*, ed. S. Kappeler and N. Bryson. London: Routledge: 148–63.

Kazin, Alfred. 1983. *An American Procession: The Major American Writers from 1830–1930—The Crucial Century.* New York: Alfred A. Knopf.

Kirk, John. 1983. *José Martí: Mentor of the Cuban Nation.* Tampa: University Presses of Florida.

Kolodny, Annette. 1984. *The Land Lay Before Her: Fantasy and Experience of the American Frontiers, 1630–1680.* Chapel Hill: University of North Carolina Press.

———. 1985. "The Integrity of Memory: Creating a New Literary History in the United States." *American Literature* 57/2: 291–307.

Krupat, Arnold. 1989. *The Voice in the Margin: Native American Literature and the Canon.* Berkeley: University of California Press.

Kutzinski, Vera, M. 1985. "The Logic of Wings: Gabriel García Márquez and Afro-American Literature." *Latin American Literary Review* 13/25: 133–46.

———. 1987. *Against the American Grain: Myth and History in William Carlos Williams, Jay Wright, and Nicolás Guillén.* Baltimore: Johns Hopkins University Press.

Lamming, George. 1960. *The Pleasures of Exile.* London: Allison & Busby.

Lauter, Paul. 1984. "Reconstructing American Literature: A Synopsis of an Educational Project of the Feminist Press," in *MELUS* 11 (Spring): 33–45.

———. 1984. "Society and the Profession, 1958–1983." *PMLA* (centennial issue, May): 414–26.

———. 1985. "History and the Canon." *Social Text* 12: 94–101.

Lawrence, Gregory. 1974. "Marx in Macondo." *Latin American Literary Review* 2/4: 49–57.

Leal, Luis. 1967. "El realismo mágico en la literatura hispanoamericana." *Cuadernos Americanos* 25/4: 230–35.

———. 1971. *Breve historia de la literatura hispanoamericana.* New York: Alfred A. Knopf.

Lentricchia, Frank. 1983. *Criticism and Social Change.* Chicago: University of Chicago Press.

———. 1988. *Ariel and the Police: Michel Foucault, William James, Wallace Stevens.* Madison: University of Wisconsin Press.

Levine, Susanne Jill. 1971. "La maldición del incesto en *Cien años de soledad.*" *Revista Hispanoamericana* 37: 711–24.

Lindenberger, Herbert. 1984. "Toward a New History in Literary Study." *Profession 84* (MLA): 16–24.

Limón, José E. 1980. "Américo Paredes: A Man from the Border." *Revista Chicano Riqueña* 8/3: 1–5.

———. 1983. "Folklore, Social Conflict, and the United States-Mexico Border," in *Handbook of American Folklore,* ed. Richard Dorson. Bloomington: Indiana University Press, 216–26.

———. 1986. "Mexican Ballads, Chicano Epic: History, Social Dramas, and Poetic Persuasion." Stanford Center for Chicano Research Working Paper 14: 1–35.

———. 1989. " 'A Southern Renaissance' for Texas Letters," in *Range Wars: Heated Debates, Sober Reflections, and Other Assessments of Texas Writing,* ed. by Craig Clifford and Tom Pilkington. Dallas: Southern Methodist University Press, 59–68.

Lipsitz, George. 1990. *Time Passages: Collective Memory and American Popular Culture.* Minneapolis: University of Minnesota Press.

Lloyd, David. 1987. *Nationalism and Minor Literature: James Clarence Mangan and the Emergence of Irish Cultural Nationalism.* Berkeley: University of California Press.

Lukács, Georg. 1971. *History and Class Consciousness: Studies in Marxist Dialectics,* trans. Rodney Livingston. Cambridge, Mass.: MIT Press.

Ludmer, Josefina. 1972. Cien años de soledad: *Una interpretación.* Buenos Aires: Editorial Tiempo Contemporáneo.

Lyotard, Jean François. 1984. *The Postmodern Condition: A Report on Knowledge,* trans. Geoff Bennington and Brian Massumi. Minneapolis: University of Minnesota Press.

MacAdam, Alfred J. 1977. *Modern Latin American Narratives: The Dreams of Reason.* Chicago: University of Chicago Press.

McDowell, John Holmes. 1981. "The Corrido of Greater Mexico as Discourse, Music, and Event," in *"And Other Neighborly Names": Social Process and Cultural Image in Texas Folklore,* ed. Richard Bauman and Roger D. Abrahams. Austin: University of Texas Press, 44–75.

McMurray, George R. 1977. *Gabriel García Márquez.* New York: Frederick Ungar.

Mailloux, Steven. 1985. "Rhetorical Hermeneutics." *Critical Inquiry* 11/4: 620–41.

———. 1985. "Reading *Huckleberry Finn:* The Rhetoric of Performed Ideology," in *New Essays on Adventures of Huckleberry Finn*, ed. Louis J. Budd. New York: Cambridge University Press, 107–33.

Mandel, Ernest. 1975. *Late Capitalism*. London: NLB.

Marcuse, Herbert. 1955. *Eros and Civilization: A Philosophical Inquiry into Freud*. New York: Random House.

———. 1960. *Reason and Revolution: Hegel and the Rise of Social Theory*. Boston: Beacon Press.

Marinello, Juan. 1975. *Once ensayos martianos*. Havana: Comisión Nacional Cubana de la Unesco.

Martí, José. 1963–65. *Obras Completas*. Segunda edición. Havana: Editorial de Cienias Sociales.

———. 1966. "A Glance at the North American's Soul Today," in *Martí on the U.S.A.*, trans. Luis A. Baralt. Carbondale: Southern Illinois University Press.

———. 1975. "The Washington Pan-American Congress." *La Nación*, December 19–20, 1889, in *Inside the Monster by José Martí: Writings on the United States and American Imperialism*, trans. Elinor Randall, with additional trans. Juan de Onís and Roslyn Held Foner, ed. Philip S. Foner. New York, 1975: 355–56.

Marx, Karl. 1906. *Capital. Vol. 1*, trans. S. Moore and E. Aveling. New York: Charles Kerr.

———, and Friedrich Engels. 1978. *The Communist Manifesto*, in Robert C. Tucker, *The Marx-Engels Reader*. New York: W. W. Norton.

Mattelart, Armand. 1979. *Multinational Corporations and the Control of Culture*, trans. Michael Urquidi. New York: Humanities Press/Brighton, Harvester Press.

———. 1983. *Transnationals and the Third World: The Struggle for Culture*, trans. David Buxton. South Hadley, Mass.: Bergin & Garvey.

Maturo, Graciela. 1971. *Claves simbólicos de Gabriel García Márquez*. Buenos Aires: F. García Cambeiro.

Menes, Lucila Inés. 1972. "La huelga de la companía bananera como expresión de lo "Real Maravilloso" americano en *Cien años de soledad*." *Bulletin Hispanique* 74: 379–405.

———. 1979. *La función de la historia en Cien años de soledad*. Barcelona: Plaza & Janes, S.A.

Mendoza, Plinio Apuleyo. 1982. *El olor de la guayaba*. Barcelona: Bruguera, trans. T. Nairn as *The Fragrance of Guava; Plinio Apuleyo Mendoza in Conversation with Gabriel García Márquez*. London: Verso, 1983.

Minta, Stephen. 1987. *García Márquez: Writer of Colombia*. New York: Harper & Row.

Monteforte, Mario Toledo. 1957. *Una Manera de Morir*. México: Tezontle.

Montejano, David. 1987. *Anglos and Mexicans in the Making of Texas, 1836–1986*. Austin: University of Texas Press.

Mora, Pat. 1986. *Borders*. Houston: Arte Público Press.

Moraga, Cherríe. 1983. *Loving in the War Years: lo que nunca pasó por sus labios.* Boston: South End Press.

Mullaney, Steven. 1987. *The Place of the Stage: License, Play, and Power in Renaissance England.* Chicago: University of Chicago Press.

Mungo, Raymond. 1984. "Strange Murder in the Desert." Review of *The Rain God,* by Arturo Islas, *San Francisco Chronicle,* November 4: 5.

Munro, Ian, and Reinhard Sander, eds. 1972. *Kas-Kas: Interviews with Three Caribbean Writers in Texas: George Lamming, C. L. R. James, Wilson Harris.* Austin: Occasional Publications of the African and Afro-American Research Institute, University of Texas.

Nelson, Cary, and Lawrence Grossberg, eds. 1988. *Marxism and the Interpretation of Culture.* Urbana: University of Illinois Press.

Neruda, Pablo. 1967. *Obras Completas.* 3rd ed, 2 vols. Buenos Aires: Losada.

Newman, Charles. 1985. *The Post-Modern Aura: The Act of Fiction in an Age of Inflation.* Evanston, Ill.: Northwestern University Press.

Nietzsche, Friedrich. 1957. *The Use and Abuse of History,* trans. Adrian Collins. Indianapolis: Bobbs-Merrill.

———. 1969. *The Genealogy of Morals,* trans. Walter Kaufmann and R. J. Hollingdale. New York: Vintage.

Ohmann, Richard. 1983. "The Shaping of a Canon: U.S. Fiction, 1960–1975." *Critical Inquiry* 10: 199–223.

Nixon, Rob. 1987. "Caribbean and African Appropriations of *The Tempest.*" *Critical Inquiry* 13: 557–78.

Oberhelman, Harley Dean. 1980. *The Presence of Faulkner in the Writings of García Márquez.* Lubbock: Texas Tech University.

Osorio, Nelson. 1982. *La Formación de la vanguardia literaria en América Latina.* Caracas: Centro de Estudios Latinoamericanos Romulo Gallegos.

Paredes, Américo. 1958. *"With His Pistol in His Hand": A Border Ballad and Its Hero.* Austin: University of Texas Press.

———. 1964. "El folklore de los grupos de origen mexicano en Estados Unidos." *Folklore Americano* 14/14: 146–63.

———. 1970. *Folktales of Mexico.* Chicago: University of Chicago Press.

———. 1976. *A Texas-Mexican "Cancionero": Folksongs of the Lower Border.* Urbana: University of Illinois Press.

———. 1979. "The Folk Base of Chicano Literature," in *Modern Chicano Writers: A Collection of Critical Essays,* ed. Joseph Sommers and Tomás Ybarra Frausto. Englewood Cliffs, N.J.: Prentice-Hall: 4–17.

Paredes, Raymund A. 1982. "The Evolution of Chicano Literature," in *Three American Literatures: Essays in Chicano, Native American, and Asian-American Literature,* ed. Houston Baker, Jr. New York: MLA Publications: 33–79.

Paz, Octavio. 1979. "Mexico and the United States." *New Yorker,* September 17, pp. 136–53.

Peña, Manuel. 1985. *The Texas-Mexican Conjunto: History of a Working-Class Music.* Austin: University of Texas Press.

Pérez Firmat, Gustavo. 1986. *Literature and Liminality: Festive Readings in the Hispanic Tradition.* Durham, N.C.: Duke University Press.

———, ed. 1990. *Do the Americas Have a Common Literature?* Durham, N.C.: Duke University Press.

Pratt, Mary Louise. 1986. "Comparative Literature as a Cultural Practice." *Profession 86* (MLA): 33–35.

———. 1988. "Humboldt y la reinvención de América." *Nuevo Texto Critico* 1/1: 35–53.

Pryse, Marjorie, and Hortense J. Spillers, eds. 1985. *Conjuring: Black Women, Fiction, and Literary Tradition.* Bloomington: Indiana University Press.

Radway, Janice. 1988. "The Book of the Month Club and the General Reader: On the Uses of Serious Fiction." *Critical Inquiry* 14: 516–38.

Rama, Angel. 1981. "El boom en perspectiva," in *Más allá del boom: Literatura y mercado,* ed. Angel Rama. México: Marcha Editores, S.A.: 51–110.

———. 1982. *Transculturación, narrativa y la novela latinoamericana.* México: Siglo XXI.

Reyes, Mata Fernando. 1988. "The New Song and Its Confrontation in Latin America," in *Marxism and the Interpretation of Culture,* ed. Cary Nelson and Lawrence Grossberg. Urbana: University of Illinois Press, 447–60.

Richards, Sandra. 1983. "Conflicting Images in the Plays of Ntozake Shange." *Black American Literature Forum* 17/2: 73–78.

Rivera, Tomás. 1971. *Y no se lo tragó la tierra.* Berkeley: Quinto Sol Publications.

Robinson, Cecil. 1977. *Mexico and the Hispanic Southwest in American Literature.* Tucson: University of Arizona Press.

Rodríguez, Juan. 1979. "La búsqueda de identidad y sus motivos en la literatura chicana," in *The Identification and Analysis of Chicano Literature,* ed. Francisco Jiménez. New York: Bilingual Press.

Rodriguez, Richard. 1983. *Hunger of Memory: The Education of Richard Rodriguez.* New York: Bantam Books.

Rodríguez Monegal, Emir. 1972. *El boom de la novela latinoamericana.* Caracas: Editorial Tiempo Nuevo, S.A.

———. 1973. "*One Hundred Years of Solitude:* The Last Three Pages." *Books Abroad* 47/3: 485–89.

———, ed. 1977. *The Borzoi Anthology of Latin American Literature.* New York: Alfred A. Knopf.

Rohter, Larry. 1989. "García Márquez: Words into Film." *New York Times,* August 13, sec. 2: 1 and 28.

Romo, Ricardo. 1983. *East Los Angeles: History of a Barrio.* Austin: University of Texas Press.

Rosaldo, Renato. 1985. "Chicano Studies, 1970–1984." *Annual Review of Anthropology* 14: 405–27.

———. 1986. "Politics, Patriarchy, and Laughter." Stanford Center for Chicano Research, Stanford University, Working Paper 18/6.

———. 1988. "Ideology, Place, and People Without Culture." *Cultural Anthropology* 3/1: 77–87.

———. 1989. *Culture and Truth: The Remaking of Social Analysis.* Boston: Beacon Press.

———. 1990. "Others of Invention: Ethnicity and Its Discontents," *Village Voice Literary Supplement* 82 (February 12): 27–29.

Ruíz, Ramon E. 1970. *Cuba: The Making of a Revolution.* New York: W. W. Norton.

Ryan, Michael. 1982. *Marxism and Deconstruction: A Critical Articulation.* Baltimore: Johns Hopkins University Press.

Sábato, Ernesto. 1979 *El escritor y sus fantasmas.* Barcelona: Seix Barral.

Said, Edward W. *Orientalism.* 1978. New York: Pantheon Books.

———. 1983. *The World, The Text, and The Critic.* Cambridge, Mass.: Harvard University Press.

Saldívar, José David. 1982. "The Real and the Marvelous in Nogales, Arizona." *Denver Quarterly* 17: 141–44.

———, ed. 1985. *The Rolando Hinojosa Reader: Essays Historical and Critical.* Houston: Arte Público Press.

———. 1990. "The Limits of Cultural Studies." *American Literary History* 2/2: 251–66.

Saldívar, Ramón. 1979. "A Dialectics of Difference: Toward a Theory of the Chicano Novel." *MELUS* 6/3: 73–92.

———. 1983. "The Form of Texas-Mexican Fiction," in *The Texas Literary Tradition: Fiction, Folklore, History.* Austin: College of Liberal Arts, University of Texas at Austin, Texas State Historical Association, 139–44.

———. 1985. "Ideologies of Self: Chicano Autobiography." *Diacritics* (Fall): 25–34.

———. 1990. *Chicano Narrative: The Dialectics of Difference.* Madison: University of Wisconsin Press.

Saldívar-Hull, Sonia. 1991. "Feminism on the Border: From Gender Politics to Geopolitics," in *Criticism in the Borderlands: Studies in Chicano Literature, Culture, and Ideology,* ed. Héctor Calderón and José David Saldívar. Durham, N.C.: Duke University Press: 203–20.

Sánchez, Marta E. 1976. "Caliban: The New Latin American Protagonist of *The Tempest.*" *Diacritics* 6/1: 54–61.

Sánchez, Rosaura. 1983. *Chicano Discourse: Socio-historic Perspectives.* London: Newbury House.

Sangari, Kumkum. 1987. "The Politics of the Possible." *Cultural Critique* 7: 157–86.

Santí, Enrico, M. 1982. *Pablo Neruda: The Poetics of Prophecy.* Ithaca, N.Y.: Cornell University Press.

———. 1986. "José Martí and the Cuban Revolution." *Cuban Studies* 16: 139–45.

Sarmiento, Domingo Faustino. 1979. *Facundo: Civilización y barbarie.* Buenos Aires: Centro Editor de América Latina.

Schneidau, Herbert. 1977. *Sacred Discontent: The Bible and Western Tradition.* Berkeley: University of California Press.

Shakespeare, William. 1987. *The Tempest,* ed. Northrop Frye. New York: Penguin.

Shange, Ntozake. 1977. *For Colored Girls Who Have Considered Suicide, When the Rainbow Is Enuf.* New York: Macmillan.

———. 1982. *Sassafrass, Cypress & Indigo.* New York: St. Martin's Press.
———. 1983. *A Daughter's Geography.* New York: St. Martin's Press.
———. 1984. "Diario Nicaragüense," in *See No Evil: Prefaces, Essays & Accounts, 1976–1983.* San Francisco: Momo's Press.
Sims, Robert L. 1981. *The Evolution of Myth in García Márquez from* Lo hojarasca *to* Cien años de soledad. Miami: Universal.
Simmons, Marlise. 1982. "A Talk with Gabriel García Márquez," *New York Times Book Review,* December 5.
Sollors, Werner. 1986. *Beyond Ethnicity: Consent and Descent in American Culture.* New York: Oxford University Press.
———, ed. 1989. *The Invention of Ethnicity.* New York: Oxford University Press.
Spillers, Hortense. 1983. Review of *Sassafrass, Cypress & Indigo,* by Ntozake Shange. *American Book Review* (Summer): 13.
Stegner, Wallace E., ed. 1965. *The American Novel from James Fenimore Cooper to William Faulkner.* New York: Basic Books.
———. 1990. "The New Literary Frontier." *San Francisco Examiner,* August 5, 1990, pp. E 1 and 3.
Tate, Claudia, ed. 1983. *Black Women Writers at Work.* New York: Continuum.
Tatum, Charles. 1982. *Chicano Literature.* Boston: Twayne.
Taylor, Howard J. 1984. "Chicano Writers Can't Crack Prejudice of New York Publishers." *San Francisco Examiner,* August 5, p. E 2.
Tompkins, Jane. 1985. *Sensational Designs: The Cultural Work of American Fiction, 1790–1860.* New York: Oxford University Press.
Turner, Victor. 1974. *Dramas, Fields, and Metaphors.* Ithaca, N.Y.: Cornell University Press.
Valdés, Mario J. 1982. *Shadows in the Cave: A Phenomenological Approach to Literary Criticism Based on Hispanic Texts.* Toronto: University of Toronto Press.
Vargas Llosa, Mario. 1971. *García Márquez: historia de un deicidio.* Barcelona: Barral Editores.
———. 1975. *La orgia perpetua: Flaubert y Madame Bovary.* Madrid: Taurus.
Verani, Hugo. 1986. *Las Vanguardias Literarias en Hispanoamerica.* Roma: Bulzonia Editore.
Vigil, Evangelina. 1983. *Thirty AN' Seen A Lot.* Houston: Arte Público Press.
Villareal, José Antonio. 1959. *Pocho.* New York: Doubleday.
Villaseñor, Edmundo. 1973. *Macho!* New York: Bantam Books.
Vinas, David. 1981. *Más Allá del Boom.* México: Marcha Editores.
———. 1985. *Dorrego: Tupac-Amaru.* Buenos Aires: Editorial Galerna.
Wallerstein, Immanuel. 1974. *The Modern World System.* I: *Capitalist Agriculture and the Origin of the European World-Economy in the Sixteenth-Century.* New York: Academic Press.
———. 1980. *The Modern World System.* II: *Mercantilism and the Consolidation of the European World-Economy, 1600–1750.* New York: Academic Press.
———. 1989. *The Modern World System.* III: *The Second Era of Great Expansion of the Capitalist World-Economy, 1730–1840s.* New York: Academic Press.

Walsh, Eileen. 1985. "The Book Report." *Campus Report*, Stanford University, January 16, 1985, n.p.

Webb, Walter Prescott. 1935. *The Texas Rangers: A Century of Frontier Defense.* Boston: Houghton Mifflin.

Weiss, Judith. 1977. *Casa De Las Américas: An Intellectual Review in the Cuban Revolution.* Chapel Hill, N.C.: Estudios Hispanofila.

West, Cornel. 1989. *The American Evasion of Philosophy.* Madison: University of Wisconsin Press.

White, Hayden V. 1973. *Metahistory: The Historical Imagination in Nineteenth-Century Europe.* Baltimore: Johns Hopkins University Press.

———. 1978. *Tropics of Discourse: Essays in Cultural Criticism.* Baltimore: Johns Hopkins University Press.

———. 1987. *The Content of the Form: Narrative Discourse and Historical Representation.* Baltimore: Johns Hopkins University Press.

Williams, Raymund. 1977. *Marxism and Literature.* Oxford: Oxford University Press.

Williams, Raymond L. 1984. *Gabriel García Márquez.* Boston: Twayne.

Williams, William Carlos. 1956. *In the American Grain.* New York: New Directions.

Willis, Susan. 1979. "Aesthetics of the Rural Slum: Contradiction and Dependency in 'The Bear.'" *Social Text* 2 (Summer): 82–103.

Zamora, Lois P. 1989. *Writing the Apocalypse: Historical Vision in Contemporary U.S. and Latin American Fiction.* New York: Cambridge University Press.

Index

About the Author

José David Saldívar is Associate Professor of Literature and Cultural Studies at the University of California, Santa Cruz, where he specializes in pan-American literatures. He is the author of numerous articles on Chicana/o and Latin American literature, editor of *The Rolando Hinojosa Reader: Essays Historical and Critical* (1985), and editor, with Héctor Calderón, of *Criticism in the Borderlands: Studies in Chicano Literature, Culture, and Ideology* (1991).

Library of Congress Cataloging-in-Publication Data

Saldívar, José David.
The dialectics of our America : genealogy, cultural critique, and literary history / by José David Saldívar.
p. cm. — (Post-contemporary interventions)
Includes bibliographical references and index.
ISBN 0-8223-1161-5 (cloth). — ISBN 0-8223-1169-0 (pbk.)
1. America—Literatures—History and criticism. I. Title.
II. Series.
PN843.S24 1991
809'8973—dc20 91-3114
CIP